Deleuze and Architecture

Deleuze Connections

'It is not the elements or the sets which define the multiplicity. What defines it is the AND, as something which has its place between the elements or between the sets. AND, AND, AND – stammering.'

Gilles Deleuze and Claire Parnet, *Dialogues*

General Editor
Ian Buchanan

Editorial Advisory Board

Keith Ansell-Pearson
Rosi Braidotti
Claire Colebrook
Tom Conley

Gregg Lambert
Adrian Parr
Paul Patton
Patricia Pisters

Visit the Deleuze Connections website at
www.euppublishing.com/series/delco

Deleuze and Architecture

Edited by Hélène Frichot and
Stephen Loo

EDINBURGH
University Press

© editorial matter and organisation Hélène Frichot and Stephen Loo, 2013
© the chapters their several authors

Edinburgh University Press Ltd
22 George Square, Edinburgh EH8 9LF

www.euppublishing.com

Typeset in 10.5/13 Adobe Sabon
by Servis Filmsetting Ltd, Stockport, Cheshire,
and printed and bound in Great Britain by
CPI Group (UK) Ltd, Croydon CR0 4YY

A CIP record for this book is available from the British Library

ISBN 978 0 7486 7464 0 (hardback)
ISBN 978 0 7486 7465 7 (paperback)
ISBN 978 0 7486 7466 4 (webready PDF)
ISBN 978 0 7486 7467 1 (epub)

The right of the contributors
to be identified as author of this work
has been asserted in accordance with
the Copyright, Designs and Patents Act 1988.

Contents

Acknowledgements

The editors would like to thank all the contributors to *Deleuze and Architecture*, our copy-editor David Kelly and Carol Macdonald at Edinburgh University Press. We would also like to thank Katja Grillner and Architecture in Effect, Strong Research Environment, Swedish Schools of Architecture, and the Faculty of Science Engineering and Technology, University of Tasmania for research funding support. We are also indebted to our patient families.

List of Illustrations

Introduction

The Exhaustive and the Exhausted – Deleuze AND Architecture

Hélène Frichot and Stephen Loo

> The combinatorial exhausts its object, but only because its subject is himself exhausted. The exhaustive *and* the exhausted [*l'exhaustif et l'exhausté*]. (Deleuze 1998: 154)

How is it that the legacy of the French philosopher Gilles Deleuze has lasted so long and impacted so greatly on both the practice and thinking of architecture? Is this because of a certain fundamental friendship that exists between philosophy and architecture? In their last work *What Is Philosophy?*, Deleuze and his long-time collaborator Félix Guattari define friendship as 'a type of competent intimacy, a sort of material taste and potentiality, like that of a joiner with wood' (Deleuze and Guattari 1994: 3). The philosophers' answer to 'what is philosophy?' is always already architectural when they say it is 'the art of forming, inventing and fabricating concepts' (1994: 2).

The uptake of the philosophy of Deleuze, and Guattari, in design practice and critical thinking in architecture since the 1980s has been fast, furious and multifarious. From an analysis of the differences between 'smooth' and 'striated' space, to ubiquitous formal translations of the process of 'folding', to appropriations of concepts such as 'immanence' and the 'virtual' in digital architecture, the consumption of Deleuze's philosophical concepts has fuelled more than a generation of architectural thinking, and is manifest in the design of a global range of contemporary built environments. Deleuzian philosophy also suggests critical approaches to crucial ecological, political and social problems with which architecture must continue to grapple, contributing significantly to the relations between aesthetics and ethics. We can say that Deleuze's concepts have provided architecture with lines of flight or the conditions of possibility of thinking otherwise, at the same time reinforcing architecture's relevance to the discipline of philosophy, whether metaphorical or ontological.

Deleuze AND Architecture: In light of this friendship we present the legacy and ongoing influence of Deleuze in the discipline and practice of architecture, in the context of the open-ended conjunctive series fostered by Edinburgh University Press under the rubric 'Deleuze Connections'. We take seriously the conjunction AND fostered by the series, to present writings that maintain exhaustive relations between philosophy and architecture, resonating between disciplinary constancy and variation, following what Deleuze and Guattari themselves demonstrate in *A Thousand Plateaus* as the productive struggle between the constancy of *être* (to be) and variations promoted by the conjunction *et* (and) (1987: 98). Each contribution has its own speeds and intervals, placing concepts and practices in constant variation, drawing and redrawing lines at/as the limits of disciplines: 'creative stammering', 'a new form of redundancy, AND . . . AND . . . AND . . .' (1987: 98).

It is important to remember that this volume is but one selection from a proliferating range of work conjoining Deleuze and architecture. Concepts that have been borrowed from Deleuze and Guattari's *oeuvre* over the last thirty or so years, with a peak in interest through the closing years of the last millennium, have provided many in the discipline of architecture with a compelling critical and creative apparatus. Philosophical work is by nature unending: infinitesimal, rhizomic and therefore perpetual, driven by a self-organising internal force. There are different speeds and slownesses by which philosophy and then architecture as disciplines consume their concepts and thinkers. Philosophy, with great love and care, lingers with its thinkers, works back over problems, forwards new applications, and continues the intricate and scholarly work of commentary as well as concept construction and reconstruction. Architecture moves rather more swiftly through its theoretical fascinations, so that in rapid succession architects appeared at one point to be 'doing' Derrida, and then, quite abruptly, 'doing' Deleuze. Deleuze was fervently consumed and endlessly cited in architectural discourse primarily from the 1980s through to the 1990s, but now Deleuze's name is cited less frequently.

Exhaustion

Has architecture *exhausted* its friendship with Deleuze? Is philosophy resigned to exhaustion by the constant variations architecture places on the spatialities and temporalities that are central to its disciplinary possibilities? Architectural thinkers and practitioners have indeed been *exhaustive* in finding ways to appropriate the works of the philosopher

Deleuze, and there persists a concern that architectural thinking has *exhausted* Deleuzian philosophy on account of the seemingly circular refrain of philosophical concepts arranged across the plane of organisation that is architecture.

Against the rumours of exhaustion we will argue for the ongoing relevance and persisting legacy of Deleuze's philosophical, ethical and aesthetic work for the thinking-doing of architecture. Deleuze's presence, even where he is not directly named, is truly rhizomatic in its insistence: facilitating the formation of new relations between ideas and practices; impacting upon the ethical and aesthetic issues raised in architecture; informing attitudes to the uptake of new technologies; allowing for the imagining of new ethologies and ecologies that recombine buildings, peoples and things. That is, Deleuze's influence in architecture is *exhausted* in Deleuze's own sense of the concept.

To Deleuze, 'being exhausted is much more than being tired' (1998: 152). As he famously differentiates, to be tired is to be tired of, or by, a certain possibility already voiced or enunciated in language. Being exhausted, however, arrives when we renounce preference, goals or choices regardless of the possibilities that lie in front of us. The realm of possibilities then remains an open-ended interconnected web not limited by predetermination – in potential. We can say with Deleuze that being exhausted in this way is productive as it provides access to the realm of the virtual.[1] Exhaustion is a comportment, or posture, in the world that the authors in *Deleuze and Architecture* demonstrate as their investigations and experimentations into architectural relations with Deleuze refrain from turning the exhaustiveness of their research into tiredness. The creative potential of an unlimited number of combinations from the available material is here presented and embraced, and the works cause further permutations and novel combinations of Deleuzian concepts to emerge in which architecture can creatively and critically invest in the potentiality of spaces yet to come.

Strata

The intrigue and uncertainty that often surround the possible conjunctions between philosophy and architecture – what is philosophy *and* architecture? – may stem from the assumption that what constitutes architecture belongs solely in the domain of built projects. There is also the assumption that the architect, most usually gendered male, stands as the creative source behind the designed architectural object. Architecture is a discipline that provides an exemplary site where the relay between theory and practice is crucial, leading to a curious blend of cultural and material production and discursive frameworks of architecture. That is to say, architecture invests in words, or all the things that can be said and written about a built (or unbuilt and speculative) form, as much as it engages in its seemingly central task, which is to design, form and construct indisputably material edifices, spaces and objects. Architecture not only pertains to the built environment and signature buildings but includes a spectacular history of unbuilt and unbuildable as well as utopian projects. From eighteenth-century utopian projects such as Étienne-Louis Boullée's Newton cenotaph to the optimistic technological expressions of Archigram and Superstudio in the 1960s, architecture has also consistently exercised an imaginary of new possible worlds, inhabited by all manner of hybrid quasi-subjects and quasi-objects.

It is valuable to frame the activities of architecture as a 'thinking-doing', because when it is practised, when architectural environments are constructed, immanent to all this activity the productive role of critical and creative thinking exhaustively continues. What the philosophy of Deleuze and also Guattari provides are the critical and creative skills by which we can further expand the field of architecture, question authorship and creativity, reconsider architectural ethics and politics, and rethink what architecture can do and what it can become. It follows that an architect, with her required spatial, temporal, corporeal and affectual abilities, participates in 'forming, inventing and fabricating concepts' (Deleuze and Guattari 1994: 2) thus becoming-philosopher.

In this light, it is possible to map the Deleuzian 'strata' as they have unevenly gathered in architecture, providing a diagram of serial evocations and appropriations of Deleuzian philosophy by a discipline that is itself very rarely mentioned specifically in the philosopher's work, but whose fundamental concepts and empirical materialism organise much of Deleuzian thought. The 'strata' are both an exteriority, in the sense of an archaeology of actual and material sedimentations of concepts that make up the conceptual schema of architecture, and a genealogy, where these conceptual series towards infinity, or towards exhaustion, are the very events that orchestrate the multiplicity and emergence, that is the very interiority or conditions of possibility, of what is architectural.

Although Deleuze remains our primary conceptual persona in this book, Deleuze-and-Guattari, the double signature of an indissociable pair, marked the early readings and borrowings by the architectural discipline, specifically in response to the two volumes that make up *Capitalism and Schizophrenia*, that is *Anti-Oedipus* and *A Thousand Plateaus*. Concepts such as machinic assemblages, smooth and striated space, becoming- . . ., the Body without Organs (BwO), were recognised as philosophically relevant to the new thinking of a discipline that in general revolves around concrete material practices. Later, in the early 1990s when Deleuze became more fully popularised through such publications as *AD: Folding in Architecture* (guest edited by Greg Lynn in 1993 and republished in 2004), as well as in the influential ANY (Architecture New York) series of conferences, conference journals and magazines edited by Cynthia Davidson at the close of that decade, concepts such as the fold, the distinction between the virtual and the actual, and the diagram also entered into circulation.

By the turn of the millennium, Deleuze had seemingly become yet another dead white philosopher and architectural theory itself fallen into crisis, but the subterranean rumble of a Deleuzian influence could still be felt. At this juncture architectural commentators and practitioner-theorists such as Michael Speaks (2000, 2002), Sarah Whiting and R. E. Somol (2002, 2005) were calling for a novel, post-critical or projective approach to architecture that celebrated newly emerging digital techniques and technologies, or 'design intelligence' (Speaks 2002), and sought new ways of celebrating design practice-based research. Although critical theory appeared to be falling into disrepute, for all of these commentators Deleuzian concepts were still proving indispensable, promising active ways of engaging with new agendas for architectural research, with an emphasis on practice. Contemporaneous to these theory troubles, following Antonio Negri and Michael Hardt's unfolding trilogy, *Empire*, *Multitude* and *Commonwealth* (2000, 2004, 2009), an architectural project engaging the legacy of Deleuze has become one that is concerned with global issues such as security, governance, new compositions of the multitude and biopolitics. At much the same time, following the increasing uptake of Actor Network Theory and its aftermath, and through the influence of such writers as Bruno Latour, Nigel Thrift and Albena Yaneva, new ways of understanding the social and technological contexts in which architecture is being produced also emerged. Actor Network Theory admits to a close allegiance with the rhizomatics of Deleuze and Guattari specifically in its study of the human and non-human actors that gather into its complex and dynamic assemblages. In this way, Actor Network Theory redefines ecology through a new materialism.

As its reflexive consciousness grows, we suggest that architecture has renewed its investments in social concerns and a politics of space, becoming increasingly open to new and vibrant material understandings of a fragile world that is intricately and globally interconnected.

Although these are quite crude temporalisations, it should be stressed that over nearly three decades a constellation of Deleuzian concepts came to populate the disciplinary terrain that is architecture. These key concepts and others will be addressed in the following chapters. Although it may seem at times that the discipline has surely exhausted these concepts, or applied the tools until they have become clumsy and their edges blunt, what persists is an ethos which perhaps no longer even needs to be signed by Deleuze, so fully has it been incorporated into what it is to pursue an ethico-aesthetic architecture.

Structure

Our aim with *Deleuze and Architecture* is to provide critical genealogies of Deleuze's influence in architecture, as well as critical commentaries on, and evidence for, the ongoing relevance of this philosopher to the discipline, and also new creative conceptual work that arrives out of this conjunction. A selection of fifteen essays by a current generation of key transdisciplinary scholars – influenced not only by Deleuze, but by his major secondary commentators operating at the threshold of the architectural discipline, including John Rajchman, Elizabeth Grosz, Anthony Vidler, Sanford Kwinter, Brian Massumi and Manuel DeLanda – reflect on the following questions: What is a critical history of Deleuze's influence in architecture? How has Deleuze's work challenged architecture's disciplinary construction, and how, through novel readings of Deleuze, has the discipline of architecture contributed to philosophical thinking? How does an engagement in the philosophy of Deleuze contribute to an architectural understanding of the complex politics of space of our increasingly networked world? How can it enable new ethical, ecological and participatory approaches to architecture? The range of responses to this is multifarious, and some of the work undertaken in this book will track the global impact of Deleuze on architectural practitioners and theorists. We have made the greatest efforts to achieve an international representation, and to this end we have included contributors from Australia, the United Kingdom, France, the Netherlands and Sweden, as well as the United States.

We have divided the book into four sections: siting, constructing, gathering, caring. We use these rather ordinary and mundane categories to draw attention to the daily activities that are pertinent to the very conditions of possibility for architectural thinking and disciplinary formation in architecture. The more 'complex' lexicon of Deleuzian philosophy is then introduced and discussed in the chapters. We are interested in what happens when these mundane yet central categories meet Deleuze's practical philosophy.

In the first part of this book, 'Siting', we aim to locate and collect the strata of the historical Deleuzian archive as it has incrementally gathered in architecture. We map the legacy of Deleuze's influence on the discipline of architecture from the point of view of a number of different contexts that accept both minor and major voices. Notable early references to Deleuze include those made by the Dutch architect Rem Koolhaas, who used Deleuzian concepts such as the smooth and the striated to discuss his work, and the description of the growing influence of Deleuzian criticism from the late 1980s by the influential Italian architectural theorist Manfredo Tafuri, who resisted it, insisting it is necessary *not* to make rhizomes. At the same time, Deleuze was taken up by a number of feminist architectural theorists such as Jennifer Bloomer and Meaghan Morris, showing the way to an alternative minoritarian history. We open the book with Karen Burns's survey chapter, which presents the influence of Deleuze conjoined with the work of feminist theorists from the political point of view of the minor architectural voices, with their long-standing commitment to difference, mobility, change. The concept of becoming in Burns's chapter refuses the discipline's normative values, working instead to produce a post-object architecture. She traverses geopolitical territories to track the powerful if sometimes worrying 'agencies' produced through the philosophy of Deleuze where it meets architecture. Deborah Hauptmann and Andrej Radman treat the collective archive of contemporary Dutch architects OMA, UN Studio and NOX as a series of conceptual personae. They plunge us into the difficult conceptual territory of Deleuze and Guattari's first collaborative book, *Anti-Oedipus*, in order to account for the 'northern line' in architectural thought and production as it has emerged in the Dutch context. We conclude the first section with Marko Jobst's critique of the ways in which Deleuze has been introduced to architecture through popular architectural theory readers, as well as of the persistent deferral to the comforts of phenomenological thought in architecture, despite the promises of a Deleuzian post-phenomenological trajectory.

The second part, 'Constructing', offers an account of the aesthetic and affective strategies that have been employed by architectural practitioners and theorists in their production of architecture. 'Constructing' presents the strategic zone of Deleuze's influence on the search for novel forms, materials and spatial organisations in architecture. Since the early 1990s, emerging techniques and technologies of computation in architecture populate their conceptual artillery with useful tactical concepts appropriated from Deleuze's aesthetics. The opening chapter by Hélène Frichot tells the story of the superfold in architecture. The dominant story of the fold in architecture, authorised through Deleuze's voice, produces architectures that succumb to troubling power relations even while aiming to produce techno-liberatory effects, risking the exhaustion of Deleuze's political and ethical project through an emphasis on formal experimentation and aesthetics. The task is to turn this exhaustion around, from a dissipative energy to a productive one, while accepting, though with critical care, some of the innovations procured through novel digital architectures. Then Bernard Cache reframes his concept of the objectile, an important influence on Deleuze's writing of *The Fold: Leibniz and the Baroque*.[2] We open Cache's chapter with an introductory conversation between Cache and his compatriot Christian Girard, an architect and theorist. Mike Hale looks closely at the potential for following material flows as expressions that constitute affects towards innovation in architectural construction, through examining the metallurgical trope that Deleuze and Guattari introduce in *A Thousand Plateaus*. This section concludes with a political contribution from Kim Dovey which reminds us that the strategies of assemblage in architectural construction in the context of the institution, in this case the school, can both open us up to new relations and close us down into habitual segmentary modes of occupation.

In the third part, 'Gathering', we consider how Deleuze has been used as a means of resisting the oppressive forces of the present, how – through his radical empiricism – he has offered new ways forward out of stultifying problems, and how his concepts can be mobilised when we encounter the 'line of the outside' as it throws contingent events in our way. This section also frames the influence of Deleuze at an urban scale and with respect to the issues that can be associated with how contemporary cities co-perform, with their constituent communities, as assemblages, arrangements and gatherings.

We open with a chapter by Simone Brott, who intelligently rethinks the vexed relationship between subject and object. Through Deleuze she extends the transformative array of effects that produce subjects across human and non-human arrangements. Gathering here manifests in the architectural encounter, producing effects that compose different subjectivities and other logics of agency. Brott suggests that it is exactly through encounters in the world that subjects come to be formulated – architectural, human and other – and that the event of the encounter necessarily precedes the emergence of the subject, displacing the habitual architectural privileging of the phenomenological subject.

Catharina Gabrielsson then takes us on a holey walk through Istanbul, a city that gathers the forces of Western and Eastern worlds. Holey space, as both smooth and striated, enacts absences and intervals in human interpretation of the environment, its meaning, identities and boundaries. It is the embedded practice of walking that shifts dependencies and codes in architecture and urban space, inverting space-time and producing uncontainable psychogeographies. The subject as traditionally understood disappears, replaced instead by compositions of variable relations and effects between concepts, behaviour and environment. Andrew Ballantyne's chapter reminds us that the role of the vernacular and everyday architectures, such as the Tudor style in the United Kingdom, can also be analysed through a Deleuzian lens. By following the global drift of the Tudor style, Ballantyne suggests new ways of understanding the processes of social fabrication in urban contexts. In the final chapter in Part III, Adrian Parr offers a tough critique of some of the habitual responses architects make in a contemporary milieu, including the valorisation of abstract form production over the affective and messy struggles of community and the environment. This is a rallying call for architecture as a mode of political activism.

In the fourth part, 'Caring', we follow the singularities and live subjectivations, or new and potential molecular ethologies, that are hooked up with radical and responsible engagements within small and large architectural ecologies. We associate care with performance of the architectural that allows novel diagrams of movement to emerge, towards the generation of new political and aesthetic collectivities. It opens with a chapter by Cameron Duff, who argues for an expanded definition of what constitutes a body and what a body can do, so that relations between live human subjects and material architectural contexts can be foregrounded. In his words, 'bodies are forever becoming elsewise in an ethological city built from relational capacities'. Chris Smith's chapter sees architecture as symptomatology: a reading of the health of the world, an indulgence in effect, and a concern with what constitutes, constructs and accompanies a particular condition of a life event. He does this through a compelling rethinking of Carlo Scarpa's Brion-Vega cemetery. Through a mathematisation of the Deleuzian plane of immanence, Stephen Loo discusses the performativity required in the care for abstraction, which requires a different economy of attention at the moment when geometry as the exteriority of architecture folds into the interiority of individuation. We conclude the section, and our book, with a conversation between Anne Querrien, Doina Petrescu and Constantin Petcou. Petrescu and Petcou, who have often collaborated with Querrien, are well known for their successful participatory practice *atelier d'architecture autogérée (aaa)*. Together they discuss the possibilities of enabling civic actors to stage their own forces of deterritorialisation in order to compose architecture. They argue for the continuously varying line of partial knowledge that enables the thinking and doing of architecture, which expands the definition of who might practise architecture. It is in this final part, dedicated to caring, that we hope to re-conjoin an aesthetics with an ethics, as Guattari has described in *Chaosmosis* (1995), an ethico-aesthetics that is also very much an ethics of immanence.

Vincent Descombes has described, after Maurice Blanchot, the role that rumour has in influencing readers to approach one philosopher or another (Descombes 1980: 4). Once upon a time, as architecture students, we heard the names Deleuze and Guattari being murmured as a shibboleth by a privileged few. It seemed, at that early stage in our education in the late 1980s, that no easy access would be allowed to the difficult material that made up their work. Now, some thirty years later, that is to say since the names Deleuze and Guattari first began to circulate as a kind of currency in the discipline of architecture, we hope to present a book that delivers a crucial cross-section through the indisputable influence of Deleuze, including the influence of Guattari. We want to make this book accessible not only to researchers and practitioners who are currently engaged in the field between Deleuze and Architecture, and beyond, but also to students of architecture, design and art who are still wondering what all the fuss is about and still wondering what is the worth of reading Deleuze.

Architectural thinking and doing, ignited then exhausted by a panoply of Deleuzian concepts, contributes to the formation of other kinds of subjectivities and groupuscules of subjectivity. Through exhaustion we see an ethology of care that articulates new mobile and material assemblages of human and non-human actors. If we exhaust space, we also make any encounter possible, Deleuze observes.

Notes

1. Deleuze also puts this in another way. The tired (*le fatigué*) is someone who can no longer actualise the possibilities that still exist for them. The exhausted (*l'épuisé*), however, is someone who can no longer provide the conditions for possibilities.
2. Bernard Cache is the exception to the rule in this collection, as his influence spans a period that started with the part he played in the early reception of Deleuze in

architecture and extends through to the architectural work he continues to practise today.

References

Deleuze, G. (1998), *Essays Critical and Clinical*, London: Verso.

Deleuze, G. and F. Guattari (1984), *A Thousand Plateaus: Capitalism and Schizophrenia*, Minneapolis, MN: University of Minnesota Press.

Deleuze, G. and F. Guattari (1994), *What Is Philosophy?*, New York: Columbia University Press.

Descombes, V. (1980), *Modern French Philosophy*, Cambridge: Cambridge University Press.

Foucault, M. and G. Deleuze (1977), 'Intellectuals and Power', in M. Foucault, *Language, Counter-Memory, Practice*, New York: Cornell University Press, pp. 205–17.

Guattari, F. (1995), *Chaosmosis: An Ethico-Aesthetic Paradigm*, Bloomington, IN: Indiana University Press.

Hardt, M. and A. Negri (2000), *Empire*, Cambridge, MA: Harvard University Press.

Hardt, M. and A. Negri (2004), *Multitude: War and Democracy in the Age of Empire*, London: Penguin.

Hardt, M. and A. Negri (2009), *Commonwealth*, Cambridge, MA: Belknap Press of Harvard University Press

Speaks, M. (2000), 'Which Way Avant Garde?', *Assemblage*, 41 (April), 78.

Speaks, M. (2002), 'Design Intelligence and the New Economy', *Architectural Record*, 190: 1, 72–5.

Whiting, S. and R. E. Somol (2002), 'Notes Around the Doppler Effect and Other Moods of Modernism', *Perspecta*, 33, 72–7.

Whiting, S. and R. E. Somol (guest eds) (2005), 'Okay, Here's the Plan', in *Log 5: Observations on Architecture and the Contemporary City*, New York: Anyone Corp., pp. 5–58.

PART I

SITING

Chapter 1

Becomings: Architecture, Feminism, Deleuze – Before and After the Fold

Karen Burns

> Architecture has traditionally relied on an immunological system (consisting of Platonic, Cartesian, and Euclidean conceptions of space) to keep the problem of difference and especially sexual difference from contaminating its practice and theory – as if, one could say from a different vantage point, sexuality possessed nothing of the technical, the geometric, the spatial. (Ingraham 1998: 111)

> Folding in Architecture is most often acknowledged for the formative role that it played in the 'digital' revolution. [. . .] For almost two decades, architecture had been the subject of what Lynn describes in his original introduction as 'formal conflicts' [. . .]. Deconstruction was the ultimate conclusion of all these musings [. . .]. Rather than identifying and highlighting the differences between formal systems, Lynn's 'architectural curvilinearity' aspired to an intensive integration of differences in an architecture of 'the folded, the pliant and the supple'. (Castle 2004: 9)

The past is always heterogeneous. Historians shape and trim the ragged edges of archives to craft coherent stories. But in pursuit of clarity writing reduces difference, uncertainty and ambiguity (Fox-Genovese 1982: 29). The history of Deleuze's architectural reception has been briefly told but this sparse story can be supplemented with divergent texts and voices from the archive, and this chapter introduces greater plurality by tracing a history of encounters between architecture, Deleuze and sexual difference.

To date, writings and projects on Deleuze and gender have been largely marginalised or excised from reviews of Deleuzian architectural thought (Ballantyne 2007; Buchanan and Lambert 2005; Brott 2010). I offer here a counter-history, retrieving a more diverse, architectural Deleuzianism from the archives as well as offering an account of how the plurality of the period has been gradually expunged. From 1989 to 2006 Deleuze's texts provided a basis for investigations of gender and minor architecture, anthropomorphism, capital, geometry, performativity and materiality. Many of these topics overlapped with a broader Deleuzian reception, a reception which was diverse and divergent. The subsequent simplifying of Deleuze's architectural interpretation took two forms. Firstly sexual difference theory was gradually erased from the circulation of Deleuze's work. Secondly, the period's widespread engagement with poststructuralism was increasingly elided and superseded by an unambiguous explanation of historical change as the story of one architectural father figure replaced by another: the fall of Derrida and the rise of Deleuze.[1] As Catherine Ingraham points out, tidying up the messy chaos of differences is part of architecture's immunological work.

My history of Deleuze reinstates the two other histories noted above: sexual difference projects and a diverse poststructuralism. This chapter reprises three moments in the reception of Deleuzian sexual difference. Firstly I examine poststructuralist explorations of Deleuze and gender undertaken in North America and Australia during the period 1989 to early 1993. Many poststructuralist authors were invoked in the feminist architectural discourse of this period and Deleuze was a sporadic but important source for inquiries into architecture's anthropomorphism, the gendered urban landscapes of late capital and a counter formation of 'minor architecture'. The second historical moment, from 1991 to 1993, is addressed in the middle part of the chapter, and the events of this period are refracted through a critical account of the ascent of Deleuze and the gradual erasure of other figures who had dominated the poststructuralist transformation of architecture. In parallel with his ascent, feminist theorists frequently expressed concerns about the mainstream architectural interpretation of Deleuze, one which aligned him with prevailing disciplinary norms. As I demonstrate, feminist apprehension was justified, for as Deleuze's work became mainstream, the sexual difference component of architectural Deleuzian work was erased. The final part of the chapter examines a third, later, moment – uncovering work that began in 1999 but circulated widely in 2004–6. In this instance Deleuzian commentaries and writings were consciously used to produce a new formation in British feminism.

In each of these moments writers and practitioners working with feminist material and Deleuze explored issues of sexual difference to question architecture's disciplinary definitions, knowledge systems and protocols. Questions of sexual difference have been used, over a long period, to think about and transform disciplinary paradigms. Feminist work crafts a different kind of architecture.

1989–92 Version 1: A Minor Architecture

The architectural reception of Deleuze occurred within a longer engagement with poststructuralism. Our story about feminism and sexual difference begins in North America towards the end of the 1980s, when a critical mass of 'new' writers and strong institutional support led to an identifiable alliance of emerging architectural theorists working on poststructuralist material.[2] There were, of course, differences in position and political intent among this group, but their works were connected by a common interest in interrogating the discipline, its knowledge systems and protocols. I focus on the use of Deleuze by two of these writers – Jennifer Bloomer and Catherine Ingraham. Both worked on material traditionally considered peripheral to architecture, in order to displace conventional definitions of architecture, including its forms of authority and cultural work.

Architectural scholarship often aligns the poststructuralist architectural work developed from 1986 to 1993 with Jacques Derrida; however, many writers on sexual difference worked with an expanded range of references. For example, Bloomer's writings and projects ranged across the work of Julia Kristeva, Hélène Cixous, Catherine Clément, James Joyce, Alice Jardine, Luce Irigaray, Adolf Loos, Martin Heidegger and Manfredo Tafuri among others, with references to Deleuze and Guattari scattered through as well. A lack of affiliation to one primary author powered work on sexual difference. Feminism's heterogeneous sources may have ensured its obscuration in accounts of architectural work that have drawn upon Derrida and then Deleuze. It was always difficult to identify feminist writers as dutiful daughters or sons.

Bloomer was the most prominent poststructuralist feminist thinker of this period. Her interest in Deleuze was most apparent and pronounced in her 'Big Jugs' project, developed between 1987 and 1992. As with all Bloomer's projects, the themes of 'Big Jugs' were various. Her 1992 essay on the project centred on architectural aesthetics, and the link between narrow definitions of architecture and the inherent phallocentrism of architecture's aesthetic paradigms. 'Big Jugs' offered a critique of dominant aesthetics and alternatives in the evidence of a found, vernacular building and 'Six Milles Femmes', a project designed by Bloomer and a team of collaborators. Deleuze and Guattari's concept of 'minor literature' was appropriated to name these new practices.

In 'Big Jugs' Bloomer uncovered the gendered nature of architectural aesthetics, observing: 'Western architecture is, by its very nature, a phallocentric discourse: containing, ordering, and representing through firmness, commodity and beauty . . .' (Bloomer 1992b: 72). Instead of crudely equating architecture's aesthetic values with the phallus, Bloomer demonstrated that a commitment to aesthetic norms regulated the potential form and subject matter of architectural work. She identified architecture's privileging of visuality as part of its disciplinary project (1992b: 83).

Feminist interrogations of visuality were central to art history and cinema studies in this period. At its simplest, the feminist critique engaged the problem of 'woman as spectacle, object of the gaze', by noting woman's constant place in a regime of sight (Bloomer 1992b: 80). Bloomer's feminist critique exposed a larger architectural problem: the discipline's continuing investment in architecture's appearance circumscribed experimentation and supported an aesthetic regime dominated by sight.

Bloomer's project mobilised matter normally considered abject – bodily waste, dirt, animal enclosures, animal tracks/animal habitats – to construct a different architectural practice. Writing was also used to contest architecture's visual regime. Disrupting architecture's text/object distinction, she sought to 'begin to delineate a line of scrimmage between making architectural objects and writing architectonic texts' (Bloomer 1992b: 86, note 9). Deleuze's 'minor literature' was appropriated to name this collection of different architectural practices gathered together in the new term 'minor architecture'.

'Minor architecture' had no singular definition. It could distinguish itself from 'major architecture' or the canon: 'Minor literature is writing that takes on the conventions of a major language and subverts it from the inside' (1992b: 86, note 9). In another definition, 'minor architecture' is analogous to Deleuze's literary example of a practice that 'a minority constructs within a major language, involving a deterritorialisation of that language' (ibid.). She identified two further elements: the intensely political nature of minor languages and their collective character (collective assemblages). For Bloomer a minor architecture could be explored through two Deleuze and Guattari tactics: a Joycean artificial enrichment of the language, swelling it up 'through all the resources of symbolism', and a Kafkaesque approach that takes the poverty of the language further, to the point of sobriety (ibid.). The transfer of literary tactics into architecture revealed the complexity of the relationship between writing and making architecture/space. Writing interrupts conventional ideals of visual form. Writing, particularly metaphor, fosters links between material considered to be dissonant or dissimilar.

The canon, or majority architecture, was undone by Bloomer's introduction of buildings both excluded from the canon and unrecognisable within the category 'architecture' – in this case, a southern US rural chicken hatchery. Furthermore, she used the hatchery to pry open assumptions about architecture and writing, observing 'It is a house, but not architecture . . . a writing machine', 'The biddies, the chicks, scratch marks in the dirt.' So a different kind of architecture emerged from a vernacular rural building form. Moreover, this architectural form offered a way of conceptualising human beings as animals. Generally species distinctions and species hierarchy foster humans' dissociation from the animal world. But in Bloomer's hands the body became a multi-constituted hatchery 'collective, anonymous, authorless' (1992b: 75).

This work radically decentred architecture's anthropomorphic interest in habitats designed by Man. From the vantage point of 2012 the strategy seems particularly prescient given the recent architectural interest in nature and biomimetic architectural form. Bloomer's exploration of a minor architecture working through animal habitations as 'non-architectural' material was then radically extended in a subsequent essay/project, 'Abodes of Theory and Flesh: Tabbles of Bower', published in the same year as 'Big Jugs'. Abodes, a large-scale installation and text, worked to deconstruct the ornament/structure binary by crafting a project from other 'architectural' genealogies: barnacle-like structures, cow hide, tabby (a regional building technique of concrete aggregate made from oyster shells), bone and ready-made ornaments such as fake fingernails. Through a rereading of the work of Chicago architect Louis Sullivan, the project located architecture and animals by remembering Chicago's historical role as a meat-processing centre. In 'Abodes' Bloomer worked with traditional architectural aesthetic norms (bi-axial symmetry, structure, columnation, ornament) in radically different ways but displaced the primacy of the human body as a model for architecture, replacing it with beasts and barnacles. Architecture was becoming Animal (Marks 1998: 24). This radical use of animal matter as a building material, and of human-built animal habitations as architectural forms, distinguished her from the later widespread uptake of 'biologically inspired' architectural designs.

In the same period, Bloomer's colleague at Iowa University, Catherine Ingraham, also mobilised animal tropes, and examined relationships between animals and environments through investigations of disciplinary paradigms. A literary theorist by training, Ingraham came to prominence working on architecture and Derridean texts, particularly rereading the figure of geometry in philosophy and architecture. Her work often touched on issues of sexual difference in architecture without being primarily concerned with this topic. She was able to rethink architecture's disciplinary paradigms by introducing insects and animals as examples of habitation and human/environment relations.

In her 1991 essay 'Animals 2: The Question of Distinction (Insects for Example)' Ingraham explored problems in accounts of the relationship between human subjects and architecture. She disrupted conventional readings of this relationship by studying the dynamics between insects and their environments. Arguing that insects and their camouflage patterns formed a distinctive relationship with their environments, Ingraham claimed that these examples offered a different model for body/environment relations. The insect's lack of distinction, its lack of morphological boundaries, provided a challenge to Foucauldian readings of architecture as a 'producer' of human subjects. She used certain anomalies in insect/environment relations – for example the failure of camouflage to always provide the insect with a refuge from predators – to argue against determinist accounts in favour of a looser fit between subject and environment (Ingraham 1991: 27). In another part of the essay she extended the implications of animal metaphors by describing architecture as an animal (dumb, speechless) whose most important quality is its materiality, not its presumed capacity for speech (ibid.: 28). This metaphor questioned the emphasis on architecture's ability to make and transmit meaning.

Insights drawn from studying insects challenged prescriptive accounts of architecture's cultural work. Ingraham claimed that architecture gives 'meaningful materiality' to the 'unsaid of culture'. That is, architecture does not instrumentally produce subjects; rather, its success at subject production depends on cultural habits. Architecture houses buildings, habits and spaces, and supports rather than enforces behaviour. She was not arguing that architecture was subordinate to culture or history. Ingraham borrowed Foucault's interest in a new mode of historiography understood through spatial tropes, in which space gives form to new formations. By this account architecture or space provides a methodology for historiography. This spatial turn in history shadowed Deleuze's reading of Foucault as a spatial historian. Like Bloomer Ingraham challenged the primacy of Man, questioning his status as the agent of historical change, instead locating transformation in new spatial configurations.

Ingraham continued to decentre architecture's hidden anthropomorphism in the 1996 essay 'Donkey Urbanism', a radical rereading of an essay by the famous modernist architect Le Corbusier. Corbusier's attempts to define architecture depend on binary distinctions – between nature and culture, primitivism and modernism, barbarism and civilisation – but Ingraham fastened on a detail in this account. Corbusier located the origins of the city in the trails worn by the hoofs of a pack donkey (Ingraham 1998: 67). This pack-donkey urbanism undid Corbusier's immutable categories and the imprint of a lowly beast, the hoof trail, threatened 'the triumph of geometry' (ibid.: 68).

The use of animal tropes, animal habitations and the material of animal bodies by Ingraham and Bloomer was unusual at this time. Later, Ingraham described these borrowings as ways of rewriting architecture's interior: to find what 'is difficult if not impossible to absorb into architecture and architectural history/theory' (Ingraham 2006: 14). Both Bloomer and Ingraham animalised architecture. The turn to animal matter and tropes suggested a general influence of Deleuzian metaphors – the 'animal' is quite outside the terrain of language, writing, the feminine, geometry and the other figures that inform the poststructuralist writers they worked on.

1990–93 Version 2: (Sub)Urban Australia

City/difference

I now want to turn to two Australian urban essays by Meaghan Morris and Rosemary Burne from the early 1990s, because these works mark the 1992/3 shift of architectural interest from the middle period of Deleuze and Guattari's work to the role of the aesthetic in the third period of Deleuze's work. Both essays were produced in Australia, but each had connections to the American scene. 'Great Moments in Social Climbing: King Kong and the Human Fly', by Sydney-based film writer, translator and then independent cultural studies scholar Meaghan Morris, was published in the influential 1992 collection *Sexuality and Space*. Architect Rosemary Burne's project 'Domesticating Space: A Baroque Interpretation and Anamorphic Representation' was reviewed as part of her Master's examination by Beatriz Colomina and Mark Wigley and then published in 1994 in *Transition*, an Australian architectural journal devoted to critical practice. The two essays used Deleuze to think about the urban environment and its transformation under late capitalism, as well as investigating issues of sexual difference.

Australian architectural theory is often left out of accounts of architectural postmodernity but European poststructuralist writing had first circulated in Australia from the mid-1970s. A group of Sydney-based writers, including Paul Foss and Paul Patton, read and sometimes translated European texts, including the work of Deleuze and Guattari. Meaghan Morris and, more peripherally, Elizabeth Grosz were involved in the Sydney reception of European poststructuralist thought and both were later invited to contribute to the poststructuralist push in North American architectural theory. From around 1987/8 Australian and European poststructuralist work was taken up by art and architecture critics and students linked with three Melbourne institutions: the Department of Architecture and *Transition* magazine at RMIT University, the George Paton Gallery and, later, the 200 Gertrude Street public art gallery. I too was a participant in this Melbourne scene.

Although sharing the territory of the city, the Morris and Burne projects related to two different moments in the architectural reception of Deleuze and Guattari. Morris's essay drew on the same Deleuze and Guattari projects as Bloomer and Ingraham – that is on the middle period of Deleuze and Guattari's work. Like Bloomer and Ingraham, Morris used the spatial tropes produced in *A Thousand Plateaus* (nomadism, holey space, smooth space, striated space) and she also deployed Deleuze and Guattari's reading of Kafka to name a process of change and the emergence of a minoritarian practice. Three years later, Burne's work reflected the shift of architectural interest to the third period of Deleuze's work and his investigation of aesthetic questions such as the Baroque and the fold.

Morris's multilayered essay investigated the development of a new corporate tower in downtown Sydney as part of the restructuring of urban space in late capitalism. Analysing the advertising campaigns, media footage and the representations of the tower allowed her to describe the tower as a symbolic good, aligned with other symbolic products (theory, architecture, services) that marked the late twentieth-century shift into a post-industrial economy.

In order to reconceptualise a tower's signifying function, Morris introduced Deleuze and Guattari's concept of faciality. She located her argument within psychoanalytic terms but she transformed conventional feminist readings of the tower as phallus. By her account the tower and city acquired meaning in the same way that Deleuze and Guattari's 'figure of the White Man' or 'the typical European', the figure of the majority, poured his drive for meaning into the world. The white man's faciality was a term for the White Man's identity (his face) and described signification as a quasi-architectural system –a white wall with black holes. Faciality is a system that insistently inscribes meanings onto blank surfaces, or 'white walls'. Faciality describes a process of subject formation for both the white man and the wall. Most importantly, Deleuze and Guattari displace subject and building formation away from the realm of rational production. Morris described these processes as 'paranoia and monomania, interpretation and passionality' (Morris 1992: 5).

The 'Great Moments' essay focused on 'becoming', a process by which the subject is withdrawn from the majority, from the mainstream, and a new medium or agent rises up from the minority (1992: 45). Like Bloomer Morris was interested in how Man might be dislodged from his position as a major identity and in the new practices entailed by minoritarian agents. Using Deleuze and Guattari's terms enabled Morris to avoid the traps of merely reversing established terms: man = phallus, tower = prosthesis, tower-as-empty-phallus = dildo. Rather she argued that these terms can be transformed and these changes produce an exterior place outside the phallic system. By focusing on the process of subject production (or subjectivation), Morris furthered the discussion established by Ingraham. Architecture and architects are touched by capital. In the act of producing a building architects are socially formed as subjects. Under late capital architects and architecture are symbolic goods and theory becomes a symbolic commodity in the architectural economy, augmenting and legitimising.

Morris's use of Deleuze and Guattari situated architecture in the broader context of the city, well beyond the boundary lot of the downtown tower. Her interest in the new spatial formations of the late capitalist city was an important reconnection back to Deleuze and Guattari's work in the first issue of *Zone* magazine (1986), briefly cited by Morris's text. Her essay mobilised the tower as a classic paradigm of the neoliberal city. In the next part of my story Rosemary Burne's urban project is a counterpoint to Morris's tower. She studied the suburb's haunting of the city, and the way the suburban refigures the city's masculine, downtown, finance identity.

City/suburbs

Burne, like Morris, identified the force of capital in restructuring the contemporary city. 'Domesticating Space: A Baroque Interpretation and Anamorphic Representation' concerned a project commissioned for a large-scale public art/architecture exhibition at a public gallery in Fitzroy, a rapidly gentrifying inner-city suburb. Reversing apparent oppositions between suburb and city, private and public, Burne read the spatial transformation of the city as the domesticating strategies of late capital, which privatise property, lifestyle and space.

Like Bloomer's projects, Burne's study was a creative, speculative artefact of text and drawings, analysing space through spatial means. She deployed Baroque representational devices, specifically anamorphic projection, as part of her technique of analysis. Following Deleuze, Burne argued that the Baroque is an 'operative function' and not 'an essence'. She augmented her understanding of anamorphic projection with Deleuze's definition of the fold as a central function of the Baroque: 'The characteristic of the Baroque is the fold that goes on to infinity' (Burne 1994: 83).

The project includes a set of anamorphic representations of the city and suburb – puzzling visual objects that only acquire coherency and legibility from a particular viewing position. These artefacts identify the domestic as the reference for metropolitan space. Burne joined these conventionally oppositional spatial formations, disrupting not only spatial figures but other binary values used to regulate the differences between these realms: urban/suburban, inner/outer, private/ public, female/male. She established the city as a compressed version of the suburbs rather than reinforcing the urban as the measure of difference between them. The shared condition of these two places was the monad, a particular spatial and subject-forming condition produced by capitalism. Following Deleuze's investigation of the monad as a cell – an autonomous interior, an interior without an exterior – Burne generalised the monad's condition. All space was now private, separate and interiorised. If the monad is the paradigm, the fold is its agent; the fold allows its operation across the different spatial realms, folding the condition of one into the other.

Burne's 1993 work on the Baroque and Deleuze was generated from her formal studies in the Cinema Department at the University of Melbourne. The fortuitous appearance of Mark Wigley and Beatriz Colomina as guest examiners of her work-in-progress connected her project to US East Coast architectural transformations of Deleuze's work, transformations that would soon be condensed into the figure of the fold.

1990–93 Version 3: The Mainstream

Having examined sporadic architectural uses of Deleuze in work on sexual difference from 1990 to 1993, I now turn to the mainstream architectural reception of Deleuze. In retrospect, 1992 can be seen as a crossover year for the architectural reception of Deleuze – from this point his writings and ideas increasingly entered mainstream architectural production and circulated with greater visibility. Greg Lynn's first *Assemblage* essay was published in 1992 – a paper infused with Deleuze among other poststructuralists, but critical in its biophysics focus on mathematical models and biological paradigms – and 1992 yielded the architecture issue of *Semiotext(e)* edited by Hraztan Zeitlian. *Semiotext(e)* gathered diverse writing and speculative architectural projects by academics such as Avital Ronell and Catherine Ingraham, and practitioners including Lebbeus Woods and Morphosis.

The *Semiotext(e)* issue is an important archival document. It is unclear why it failed to achieve prominence as a foundation text for architectural work on Deleuze (a prize claimed for itself by *Folding in Architecture*, the special issue of *Architectural Design* published in the following year). The *Semiotext(e)* journal played with the illicit – the cover image was dominated by pills, syringes and alphabet soup – and civil dissent in its sustained critique of the First Gulf War. Its contributors were diverse. A dark, high-contrast photocopy graphic design aesthetic provided a unifying look, but there was no singular architectural design aesthetic. Zeitlian's editorial established a Deleuzian focus. He continued the interest in the city as a strata of history and introduced the idea that would dominate architectural discourse in the coming years. He advocated the 'interaction of multiple organising systems' rather than 'singular, hierarchical ordering ideas' (Zeitlian 1992: 3). At this point, multiplicity was the master term in the architectural translation of Deleuze's ideas. 'The fold' was taken up in the following year.

Reading *Semiotext(e)* or other key essays from this moment such as John Rajchman's interpretation of Peter Eisenman's Rebstock Park published in *Unfolding Frankfurt* (1991), we see numerous Deleuzian terms in use rather than the predominance of a master term. Rajchman's essay was originally titled 'Perplications: On the Space and Time of Rebstockpark' and only later retitled 'Folding' when collected in his 1998 book *Constructions*. Perplication, multiplicity, complexity and the 'informal' were used as key terms, but the fold made constant appearances. The fold offered a means to interpret Eisenman's design strategy and Rajchman used the term to distinguish Eisenman's practice from Robert Venturi and Colin Rowe's work. Deleuze's name and ideas started to construct a genealogy of difference.

Even so, at this stage Deleuze was not *the* privileged name. Rajchman ranged across the writings of Derrida, Benjamin, Bataille, Levi-Strauss and Virilio. The same generalised poststructuralist roots characterised Greg Lynn's essay in the same *Unfolding Frankfurt* catalogue. For example, Lynn quoted Derrida's description of the fold. The term cannot be aligned with Deleuze exclusively.[3] Lynn gathered his critique of idealised geometry from both *A Thousand Plateaus* and Derrida's work on Husserl. The term 'multiplicity' was also sourced from both Derrida and Deleuze.[4] From 1991 to 1993, recognition of multiple authorship diminished and terms became increasingly identified with the singular figure of Deleuze.

Tracing minute shifts in words and authorship places the archival material in a shifting, unfolding milieu. For the participants the future was unknown and the present ambiguous and uncertain. Subsequent historical accounts have attributed more clarity and direction to the actors, texts and ideas. The archive provides multiple origins for the intersection of Deleuze and architecture. In the following section I excavate more material from the archive to demonstrate how another kind of difference – sexual difference – inhabited the foundations of mainstream architectural Deleuzianism.

Stranded

Greg Lynn's first 1992 *Assemblage* essay was a significant use of Deleuze and Deleuzian sources and the essay included a demonstration of alternative geometries' potential for design. In the section preceding his discussion of the Stranded Sears Towers project, designed for a Chicago competition, Lynn investigated the interior of the Statue of Liberty as part of a larger project contesting standard architectural geometries. The essay continued certain deconstructions of ideal geometry (as seen in Ingraham's work) and relied on a wide range of philosophic sources including Irigaray's 'Mechanics of Fluids' essay (Lynn 1992: 48, note 16). Lynn's analysis of the Statue countered the universalising logic of classical geometry with the local relationships of the interior, where different structural systems – the nine-bay grid and the folded surface – meet and negotiate their differences. From this preliminary work he generated the design of a horizontal tower based in an idea of non-identicality.

The 'Stranded' design was commensurate with key terms from sexual difference theory. Irigaray proposes that there might be an '"improper" language, a language that expresses multiplicity, and above all, fluidity' (Olkowski 2000: 94). The compatibility of Deleuze and Irigaray is evident in Lynn's essay and the Stranded Sears Tower project and, as I will argue below, it continues to inform architecture.

The choice of site work for Lynn's analysis – the Statue of Liberty – also linked the project to Bloomer's use of the Statue of Liberty in her group project Six Mille Femmes. The Six Mille Femmes work was included in 'Big Jugs', which was published in 1992 in a special journal issue co-edited by Greg Lynn. Co-designed by Bloomer, Robert Segrest and Derham Crout among others, Six Mille Femmes responded to a competition for the design of cultural artefacts commemorating the bicentenary of the French Revolution. Bloomer's project focused on the Statue of Liberty, a gift from the French to commemorate the American Revolution. Six Mille Femmes rewrote the Statue of Liberty as spectacle, as allegory, as medium of exchange and fetish by cutting nine sections through Liberty's body, through nine highly invested sites of desire.

Women's bodies and feminist work are sites of exchange for ideas. The intersecting Lynn and Bloomer examples contest the idea that feminist/sexual difference practice and 'mainstream' theory exist in separate spheres. However, when Stranded Sears was republished in the 1993 edition of *Folding in Architecture* (Lynn 1993c) there was no reference to the Statue of Liberty and no acknowledgement of the debt to Irigaray. Instead, other origins from the Sears project rose to prominence as generating points – Jean Baudrillard and the Twin Towers of New York (Lynn 1993b: 82). The earlier multiple account of the project's origins in the Statue of Liberty analysis and then the competition entry was erased and the body of Woman (the Statue of Liberty) and a woman theorist's writings (Irigaray) disappeared .

Folding in Architectural Design (AD) 1993

Lynn's 1993 'Architectural Curvilinearity' essay for *Folding in Architecture* positioned Deleuze's entry into architecture as a key moment of historical transformation. He revised Eisenman's role, now seeing Eisenman's work as Deleuzian. Transforming Eisenman from a general poststructuralist position to a Deleuzian one ensured that the new Eisenman inaugurated a discipline-wide rupture. First Lynn needed to establish the background context for Eisenman's revolt. Lynn sutured together authors from three different moments over two decades (Venturi, Rowe and Wigley/Johnson) into a shared project concerned with 'the production of heterogeneous, fragmented and conflicting formal systems' (Lynn 1993a: 8). Then he established a shift to the 'intensive integration of differences within a continuous yet heterogeneous system' (ibid.). He also resuscitated two projects from the 1988 Deconstructivist exhibition, arguing that they possess 'latent suggestions of smooth mixture and curvature'. Derrida, unfortunately, was not granted such a crossover. Lynn performed the role of architect as prophet of historical change, offering a selective diagnosis of historical patterns.

Lynn's new introduction for the 2004 reprint elided Derrida and Deconstructivist architecture more explicitly:

> At the moment of the book's publication there were two distinct tendencies among architectural theorists and designers. The first was a shift from the linguistic and representational focus of both Post-Modernism and Derridean Deconstruction towards the spatial, artistic and mathematical models of Deleuze, Foucault, Whitehead and even, to some degree, Lacan. Of these initial experiments it was the Deleuzian focus on spatial models, most of which were derived from Leibniz's monadology that took hold in the field. (Lynn 2004: 9)

The Deleuze-after-Derrida narrative constructed a straightforward story that preserved architecture's internal autonomy – historical change was driven by architecture's encounter with philosophy. An alternative account could argue that philosophy's new value in architecture was part of the intensification of post-Fordist systems of production: philosophy is cultural capital in the knowledge and culture economy. Moreover, the circulation, repetition and expansion of Deleuzian discourse were enabled by architecture's social organisation. Key institutions, particularly the conference and publication activities of the Any Corporation from 1991 to 2000, played a major role. Derrida appeared in the first 1991 ANY magazine but was notably absent thereafter. The rise of Deleuze was not a natural phenomenon, but an institutionally structured one.

Deleuze has observed that in the struggle between majoritarian and minoritarian tendencies, there is often an attempt to reduce chaotic difference to unity and sameness (Marks 1998: 4). This is a useful way to read *Folding in Architecture*. The 1993 edition did include an essay on the fold from the perspective of sexual difference: Claire Robinson's 'The Material Fold: Towards a Variable Narrative of Anomalous Topologies'. Her essay was also included in the 2004 reprint, but was not acknowledged in Lynn's new introduction or in Mario Carpo's historical overview 'Ten Years of Folding'. Moreover, in the 1993 issue only Jeffrey Kipnis acknowledged other work on Deleuze, and then in passing – he footnoted work by Jennifer Bloomer and Robert Somol (Kipnis [1993] 2004: 64).

Robinson's essay was unusual in the context of the 1993 collection. The essay can be read as an Irigarayan interpretation of the fold and catastrophe theory, although Robinson's engagement with René Thom's catastrophe theory and topology also links her work to Peter Eisenman and Greg Lynn's interests. Topological models produce artefacts with discontinuous surfaces but, in Robinson's interpretation, these discontinuities introduce a 'phenomenological otherness'. She was acutely aware that this alterity was at risk of being transformed into an image. She observed:

> This otherness has a materiality. To take the fold as solely formal gesture is the same as allowing its materiality to be evacuated.
>
> If one is content to uphold the extrapolated image of Thom's 'remarkable section' as an invitation to create a 'new form': the fold's spatial potential is suppressed in favour of a reiterated Platonism. (Robinson [1993] 2004: 80)

So, at the very time the fold was being consolidated by architecture, she worried that the fold's spatial potential was being suppressed in order to ground a 'reiterated Platonism'. Using Michel Serres's reading of Thom's work, Robinson observed that even though the theory may have been 'platonic in origin', it could be transformed. Following Serres, she noted the difference between the geometrical models produced in Plato's *Timaeus* and Thom's model of fluid and flow. Robinson retraced the Platonic origin in order to recover its own folds, its differences.

Taking the *Timaeus* as an origin and background for Thom's work Robinson reintroduced the key feminine spatial moment from the *Timaeus* – the emergence of Chora, 'a perpetually folding, constantly evolving, perpetually holding and loosing ephemeral place' ([1993] 2004: 80). In the *Timaeus*, Plato narrated the foundation story of the cosmos. The created cosmos is a visible, changing copy of a perfect, eternal model. If mimesis is the reproduction of an imperfect copy, the dynamic of originals and copies does not account for change. Plato solved certain problems in his logic and created others by offering a third term, chora, which is a process for all becoming and change, but one paradoxically figured through the simile of a receptacle. Chora stands between the intelligible and sensible, the mind and body, surface and interior, the image of a body and the possibility of a body, as change, becoming.

Chora had been ratified as an architectural term in the recent 1986 project *Choral Works*, produced by Eisenman and Derrida in collaboration. Derrida had traced the active work of Chora in all of the formed stable institutions (for example, the law) described in *Timaeus*. Robinson was strategic: chora might be an acceptable master term for becoming.

Robinson retained Thom's and Plato's reliance on becoming through her continual recourse to fluidity metaphors. She illustrated the implications of Thom's theory with the example of seaweed as a moving 'dancing turbulence', describing it as 'a continually folding entity'. Seaweed has weight and gravity but never forms into folds or borders and is always in 'spatial, temporal, material flux'. Following this model a building need not be autonomous and hermetically sealed without interstices or breaks ([1993] 2004: 80) Then, at the midpoint of the essay, Robinson returned the fold to the primary space of sexual difference production, noting, 'the architecture of the fold is one of becoming, one of a specific gestational process' (81). She introduced a more Irigarayan imagery, situating the fold within a maternal economy. Robinson introduced the figure of the 'graaf follicle'. Its continuity offered a different kind of structure. The fold was located in the uterus – a placental wall that was a receptacle within a receptacle. She described these as local conditions, in contrast to a universal space of 'orthogonal projective geometries and building systems' (81). We can see the similarity with Lynn's earlier observations on the Stranded Sears Towers: fluids over solids, local conditions over universal, becoming over orthogonal, projective geometry. But Robinson was careful to distinguish between the form of the fold and her interest in folding.

Robinson and Lynn worked with quite different models of history. Lynn identified the erroneous logic of Venturi and Rowe's fragmented, conflicted formal systems as a reduced model of complexity, which is then historically corrected by the introduction of multiplicity as difference. Robinson worked from a classic poststructuralist position: finding something else in the origin – an emergent possibility that has been ignored or suppressed. Thus she cast the Classical Architect as Herme Aphrodite, also a 'hermaphrodite architect'. Herme Aphrodite works on both sides of the fold: on one side losing the clear edges of plane geometry to find the feminine lurking somewhere in the centre; on the other embracing the 'grid' as overlay of order, where reason has triumphed over myth. She reminded the reader that authorship, reception and production are not decorporealised: 'You hold the book, the room you read in holds you; one pocket of thick contracting wall' ([1993] 2004: 81). Robinson returned the sexed body to the discussion.

Claire Robinson's essay stands at a pivot point in the mainstream architectural production of Deleuze. She argued for the materiality of the fold and the place of sexual difference and sexual production embedded in the fold's gestational process and imagery. These questions remain pertinent for discussions of folding and feminism. I want to turn now to 1996, to the next brief feminist intervention into the architectural discourse on the fold, to a project that also performs the double work apparent in Robinson's essay: tracing the question of sexual difference through a Deleuzian insight and offering a critique of mainstream readings of the fold in architecture.

Prisoners of Architecture

At the end of a 1996 essay Elizabeth Diller mused on the power of the 'fold' metaphor as a 'discourse for poststructuralist architecture' (Diller 1996: 92). Diller's remarks closed an account of her 'dissident ironing' project described in a text and black-and-white documentary photographs of folded, ironed men's shirts. Diller's folded shirts essay was published three years after *Folding in Architecture*. She noted that the crease was a more compelling metaphor 'because it presents a resistance to transformation'. Her elaboration of the crease's difference from the fold was partly an allegory of architecture as a disciplinary institution. By advocating the crease rather than the fold, Diller suggested that the discipline of architecture filtered Deleuze's architectural reception.

Architectural acts – pattern-making, organising, visualisation, structuring – were performed on the surface of garments that already possessed their own structure, hierarchy and coded symbolic language. In Diller's hands the shirts were white and crisp but their business-like aura was reordered. The shirt appeared identical to other business shirts but on closer investigation the viewer noticed that the shirt was not functional.

Her remarks on the differences between fold and crease situated the shirts and her text as a criticism of the mainstream reception of Deleuze formalised in the 1993 issue of *AD* (Diller 1996: 93). In her essay Diller uncovered a disciplinary context for the emergence of the crease/fold. She described the laundry work of prisoners in correctional facilities, observing that they develop a coded, communication language formed by ironing crease patterns into prison uniforms: 'Like the prison tattoo, another form of inscription on soft, pliable surfaces, the crease is a mark of resistance by the marginalised' (ibid.: 86). Unlike the tattoo, the crease 'acts directly on the institutional skin of the prison uniform' and, unlike the tattoo, its language is 'illegible to the uninitiated' (ibid.).

This section of Diller's essay established some of the problems in the mainstream architectural reception of Deleuze. Diller's argument for the crease concerned the operations performed by architecture on the fold, the necessity for resistance and the need for more durable records of the original Deleuzian proposition. The crease (and not the fold) possesses a resistance to transformation. A crease has a longer memory, it is harder to remove (smooth out or refold) and its resistance to erasure persists 'until a new order is inscribed with the illusion of permanence' (ibid.: 93). Like Robinson's warnings, Diller's remarks were minor points of resistance to the Deleuzian majority. Both provided other readings of Deleuze, but the sustained exploration of an alternative Deleuzian feminism emerged some years later on the other side of the Atlantic.[5]

Performing Altered Practices, 1999–2004

Throughout the 1990s architecture and sexual difference was discussed at a number of conferences: 'Sexuality & Space', 'Architecture and the Feminine', 'Desiring Practices' and 'Alterities: Interdisciplinarity and "Feminine" Practices of Space'. The final conference of the decade, 'Alterities' (1999 in Paris), was critical for self-consciously shaping new directions in British feminism, directions strongly influenced by Rosi Braidotti's confluence of Deleuzian and Irigarayan thought.

An edited collection of papers from the 'Alterities' conference was published in 2007 as *Altering Practices: Feminist Politics and Poetics of Space*. In her introduction, editor Doina Petrescu positioned alterities within a Deleuzian terminology of 'becomings': 'they are active, dynamic processes of thinking and transformation and an affirmation of "difference" as a positive quality' (Petrescu 2007: 3). Becomings would take on a new meaning. Like most architectural work on sexual difference, the projects collected in *Altering Practices* used an expanded range of practices that could be understood as micro-spatial interventions – installation, texts, images and drawing. These were actions and performances produced and improvised in specific spaces over time. They situated space and subjectivity as changing dynamics, altering and altering one another. Spatial practices are an architectural parallel to performance art and public art.

In their essay 'Taking Place and Altering It', Teresa Hoskyns and Doina Petrescu identified the 'Alterities' conference as a turning point when British architectural feminism, represented by the spatial practice collective Taking Place, turned from British feminism to French feminism. Hoskyns and Petrescu were part of The Taking Place collective and they distinguished their practice from the long-standing British feminist collective Matrix and its engagement with an Anglo-American school of thinking. They characterised the new alignment as a shift from politics to poetics, from identity to difference. I disagree with these binary definitions but understand the authors' attempt to stake out an alternative position to Matrix.

The binary of identity/difference dissolves a little when we consider the idea of strategic essentialism, an appeal to the unified concept of Women for the purposes of political activism. The politics/poetics opposition can be modified too. Sexual difference theory is inherently political but it is not the same as specifically politically organised struggles. If we consider feminism as a 'field of thought attempting to become other than itself', we can trace an ongoing feminist strategy of transformation rather than binaries (Colebrook 2000: 12).

Key concepts used to construct the Hoskyn/Petrescu position on 'difference' were strongly embedded in Braidotti's Deleuzian take on Irigaray, as articulated in her book *Nomadic Subjects*. Using her reliance on nomadology, Hoskyns and Petrescu defined their mobility across sites and disciplines. The work was more closely aligned to happenings and performances than straight architectural practice. Drawing on Judith Butler's notion of performativity, the act of making architecture was replaced with the act of making space (including telling stories) and with some collaborative and participatory practices. This is congruent with Braidotti's claim that a new materialism, a new sense of the embodied subject (sexually differentiated) is the starting point for a feminist redefinition of subjectivity (Braidotti 1994: 3) The trope of 'becomings' governs a practice engaged in spatial, subject and social transformation – an exploratory practice, distinguished from an instrumental approach.

Several of the essays in *Altering Practices* worked on matter – a long-standing feminist topic. In the years following, a new discourse on materiality emerged in architecture. Matter was a fertile site for British architectural work on sexual difference and Deleuze. This new materialism is the final topic of my survey.

A Material World, 2004/2006

Throughout the 1980s and 1990s feminism pursued an extensive and ongoing interest in questions of matter, and particularly corporeality. The interest was twofold. Firstly, feminists drew on the philosophical and cultural traditions constructing Woman as matter, as the ground for form-making and on a series of philosophical binaries – mind/body, reason/passion, subject/object, consciousness/non-consciousness, interiority/exteriority – and their correlation with masculine and feminine attributes (Grosz 1989: xiv–xv). Secondly, feminists were interested in corporeality as the primary category by which philosophy and culture constructed women and their experiences as different, but augmenting this by reading women's embodied subjectivity as a legitimate ground for a feminist politics and new theories of subjectivity (Grosz 1994: vii–xvi). My survey of the intersection of Deleuze, architecture and sexual difference ends by examining a new site for this intersection – 'materiality' – which also returns us to the beginning of the chapter and Bloomer's projects begun many years earlier.

By 2001, 'matter' and 'materiality' were becoming prominent terms in architectural discourse (Burns 2001; Hill 2001). It was a conversation that numerous feminists had already developed through the 1980s and 1990s (Grosz 1994). John Rajchman described the shift as the 'metaphysics of formed matter [being] replaced by a metaphysics of materials' (Rajchman 1998: 13). In her introduction to *Material Matters* (2007), Katie Lloyd Thomas, a member of The Taking Place collective, discussed the form/matter distinction in some detail, while cautioning that thinking about matter can often lead to a return to form (albeit working from the agency of matter). Indeed 'materiality' risked becoming a new transcendent category, abstract and strangely immunised from the mess of the material world.

Material Matters was a volume (arising from a 2004 conference) in which several contributors were attentive to gender. Helen Stratford's 'Unpleasant Matters' considered matter – how the matter permissible in buildings is constrained by building regulations. Following completion, other legislation regulates what matter is admitted to the building, so the arduous work of cleaning removes certain kinds of other/abject matter. Stratford used the cleaning schedule of the Imperial War Museum and her own experiences of constructing an installation from waste paper (the 'Paper Room' at a paper mill in Hemel Hempstead) to examine the ways in which physical, moral and governmental pollution is removed from buildings. Although the Paper Room used waste bales of paper, even this everyday debris needed regulation. It was sanitised and disinfected as 'contaminated bales of soft porn texts and hospital records were removed' (Stratford 2007: 218).

Architecture also performs an immunological work, maintaining borders as waste is identified and expelled. Drawing on feminist theory and performance work, Stratford used the constant work of maintenance (housework) to refigure the building as an environment. No longer an inert perfect form, it becomes a living part of its own circumstances. She argued that maintenance is a form of restoration and a creative act comparable to others in the building process (2007: 214). Housework has traditionally been undertaken by women or, in the new global economy, by immigrant workers. By focusing on an architect's role as maintainer and restorer, Stratford decentred the architect from a primary place as form-giver. Architecture was recast in Deleuzian terms as a series of processes and practices: an assemblage of physical, psychological and temporal dynamics – 'situations' continually in-the-making as opposed to pure creation. She drew on Deleuze's work on Spinoza to observe that a human being cannot be separated from its relations to the world (Stratford 2007: 222).

Women's everyday life and labour was the staging ground for another piece on Deleuze, architecture and sexual difference in the same volume. In 'Plenums: Re-Thinking Matter, Geometry and Subjectivity', Peg Rawes situated a woman's event or practice (the 'school run') as a scene for exploring questions of geometric, psychic and material embodiment through Leibniz's figure of the plenum. In Rawes's hands the school run and getting ready for it – finding bikes, coats, knee pads, getting down the steps, etc. – became an architectural event. She proposed the plenum as a way of rethinking the binary split between the qualitative and quantitative: the sense-based cultural, psychic, political, sensory experience of the world in opposition to the quantitative maths and sciences of building and engineering. In the plenum, 'both the formal and the sensory are simultaneously active' (Rawes 2007: 58).

Rawes advocated the plenum as a dynamic spatial figure akin to a continuum: 'Architectural practices and events are made up of continuously changing occurrences, spaces and relationships between people and the built environment' (2007: 56). Space was no longer defined in abstract definitions of 'geometric quantity or measurement'. Thus the school run becomes 'a plenum of daily life, in which bikes, porridge, steps, door handles, pavements, traffic and the schoolroom all come together in a topology of space-time, linked by the psychic and material expressions and feelings of three children and their mother' (ibid.: 60). The plenum was generated out of internal differences or limits. As Rawes noted, the plenum possesses the potential 'to undergo constant change'. She linked this to theories of 'difference' in metaphysical and poststructuralist philosophy (ibid.: 65). It is a science of magnitudes, not shapes. I also see this as a scalar difference, shrinking and expanding the relations of both built environment and subject in relation to each other.

Rawes's work, like other essays examined in this chapter, provided a base for critiquing dominant 'new' practices. She questioned the claims made for new, non-Euclidian geometric figures in contemporary architecture. She wondered if the practitioners of the 'new geometries' 'fail to register the extent to which their buildings uphold dominant interests in form-making, at the expense of other, more contingent, organic agents in architectural design and the building's use' (2007: 63). Leibniz's geometry offers the production of internal difference and of technical embodiment of qualitatively different relations (ibid.: 64).

Both contributions are sited in sexual difference work but do not foreground this question. Instead, they take women's traditional labour as sites where ideas and practice can be rethought. Both remain committed to the uncovering of differences within architecture's inhabitation, figuration and geometric modes of thought. Their engagement with everyday life is matched by an interest in places as spaces for minutely observed actions and shifting registers of occupation. These interests tie the work back to the performative turn announced at Alterities.

Conclusion

This chapter has examined work produced over a more than twenty-five-year period – from Bloomer's 1987 Six Mille Femmes to the matter essays published in 2007. Across these years we see striking continuities in the constellation of Deleuzian inflected topics, though they come in and out of focus at different periods. These texts and projects demonstrate architecture's continued engagement with poststructuralist philosophy over a long period, whatever the name of the favoured philosopher dominating a moment of discourse.

Can one write about the circulation of a philosopher like Deleuze in architecture without reproducing the discipline's economy of individual value, an economy that places a premium on the signature names of both philosophers and architects? In *What Is Philosophy?* Deleuze and Guattari observe the philosophical incarnation of this phenomenon – 'philosophical concepts work by being attached to figures or personalities' (Buchanan and Colebrook 2005: 6). In an architectural context, Catherine Ingraham points to 'the possession of space by marking' (Ingraham 1998: 99).

My chapter, in part, recovers other readings of Deleuze and, in some instances, resistances to the mainstream writing of Deleuze and his 'agency' in inaugurating historical transformation. This history contests the continuing project of architecture's 'emancipationist historicism' (Colebrook 2000: 16), the rhetoric of liberation that accompanies architectural design 'discoveries'.

The conscious, wilful declaration of a post-Derridean, Deleuzian period relied on certain operations – such as desexing, the removal of sexual difference – as part of a larger removal of the intertwined and parallel work of a number of poststructuralist philosophers. Mapping this history of sexual difference engagement with Deleuzian theory also reshapes our accounts of Deleuze's architectural reception. A new feminist account is not a separate, parallel history to the Deleuzian mainstream, nor is it a straightforward inclusion of gender material into an existing history. A feminist history reshapes the questions we ask of history. It returns a sense of uncertainty, conflict and ambiguity to the material. Restoring the heterogeneity of the archival material produces continuities in the poststructuralist architectural project. The archive returns to trouble us now: demonstrating the continuing difficulty of trying to think through and enact the insights of poststructuralist philosophy given the resistance of the discipline.

Notes

I sincerely thank Justine Clark for her superb editing of the chapter draft and for all her comradeship. Thanks too to Hélène Frichot for her patience and encouragement and to David Kelly for his meticulous copy-editing and tenacity.

1. In the words of Susannah Hagan, 'As Derrida dominated the 1980s, so Gilles Deleuze and Félix Guattari dominated the 1990s . . .' (Hagan 2001: 137).
2. *Assemblage* was founded in 1986, there was a theory session at the 1986 meeting of CAA in Florida, a 1990 Theory Conference at MOMA and the Chicago Institute for Architecture and Urbanism fellowships in part sponsored the theory revolution.
3. Lynn also attributes the fold to Derrida, writing, 'For a further discussion of the fold as a Passe-Partout between internal and external categories see Jacques Derrida . . .' (Lynn 1993b: 104, note 5).
4. Lynn also attributes the multiplicity concept to Derrida, writing, 'The "governed multiplicity" phrase in the text is cited from Derrida's *Edmund Husserl's Origin of Geometry*' (Lynn 1993b: 103, 105, note 22).
5. See Perella (1999: 6) for a critique of Lynn and Eisenman and an alternative architectural reading of Deleuze.

References

Ballantyne, A. (2007), *Deleuze and Guattari for Architects*, London: Routledge.
Bloomer, J. (1992a), 'Abodes of Theory and Flesh: Tabbles of Bower', *Assemblage*, 17 (April), 6–29.
Bloomer, J. (1992b), 'Big Jugs', *Fetish: The Princeton Architecture Journal*, eds S. Whiting, E. Mitchell and G. Lynn, 4, 72–87.
Braidotti, R. (1994), *Nomadic Subjects: Embodiment and Sexual Difference in Contemporary Feminist Theory*, New York: Columbia University Press.
Brott, S. (2010), 'Deleuze and the "Intercessors"', *Log*, 18, 135–51.
Buchanan, I. and C. Colebrook (eds) (2000), *Deleuze and Feminist Theory*, Edinburgh: Edinburgh University Press.
Buchanan, I. and G. Lambert (eds) (2005), *Deleuze and Space*, Edinburgh: Edinburgh University Press.

Burne, R. (1994), 'Domesticating Space: A Baroque Interpretation and Anamorphic Representation', *Transition: Discourse on Architecture*, 41, 76–89.

Burns, K. (2001), 'The Mutable Life of Architecture', *Assemblage*, 41, 16.

Carpo, M. (2004), 'Ten Years of Folding', in *AD: Folding in Architecture*, ed. G. Lynn, Chichester: Wiley-Academy, pp. 14–19.

Castle, H. (2004), 'Preface', in *AD: Folding in Architecture*, ed. G. Lynn, Chichester: Wiley-Academy, p. 7.

Colebrook, C. (2000), 'Introduction', in I. Buchanan and C. Colebrook (eds), *Deleuze and Feminist Theory*, Edinburgh: Edinburgh University Press, pp. 1–17.

Diller, E. (1996), 'Bad Press', in F. Hughes (ed.), *The Architect: Reconstructing Her Practice*, Cambridge MA: MIT Press, pp. 76–94.

Fox-Genovese, E. (1982), 'Placing Women's History in History', *New Left Review*, I: 133, 5–29.

Grosz, E. (1989), *Sexual Subversions: Three French Feminists*, Sydney: Allen & Unwin.

Grosz, E. (1994), *Volatile Bodies: Towards A Corporeal Feminism*, Sydney: Allen & Unwin.

Hagan, S. (2001), *Taking Shape: A New Contract Between Architecture and Nature*, Oxford: Architectural Press.

Hill, J. (2001), *Architecture – The Subject Is Matter*, London: Routledge.

Hoskyns, T., D. Petrescu and other mixed voices (2007), 'Taking Place and Altering It', in D. Petrescu (ed.), *Altering Practices: Feminist Politics and Poetics of Space*, London: Routledge, pp. 15–38.

Ingraham, C. (1991), 'Animals 2: The Question of Distinction (Insects for Example)', *Assemblage*, 14, 24–9.

Ingraham, C. (1998), *Architecture and the Burdens of Linearity*, New Haven, CT: Yale University Press.

Ingraham, C. (2006), *Architecture Animal Human: The Asymmetrical Condition*, New York: Routledge.

Kipnis, J. (1993), 'Towards A New Architecture', in *AD Folding in Architecture*, ed. G. Lynn, Chichester: Wiley-Academy, pp. 56–65.

Lloyd Thomas, K. (ed.), *Material Matters: Architecture and Material Practice*, London: Routledge.

Lynn, G. (1992), 'Multiplicitous and In-Organic Bodies', in *Assemblage*, 19, 32–49.

Lynn, G. (1993a), 'Architectural Curvilinearity: The Folded, the Pliant and the Supple', in *AD: Folding in Architecture*, Chichester: Wiley-Academy, pp. 8–15.

Lynn, G. (1993b), 'INeffective DESCRIPTions: SUPPLemental LINES', in P. Eisenman (ed.), *Re-working Eisenman*, London: Academy Editions, pp. 98–105.

Lynn, G. (1993c), 'Stranded Sears Tower', in *AD: Folding in Architecture*, Chichester: Wiley-Academy, pp. 82–5.

Lynn, G. (2004), 'Introduction', in *AD: Folding in Architecture*, ed. G. Lynn, Chichester: Wiley-Academy, pp. 8–13.

Marks, J. (1998), *Vitalism and Multiplicity*, London: Pluto Press.

Morris, M. (1992), 'Great Moments in Social Climbing: King Kong and the Human Fly', in B. Colomina (ed.), *Sexuality and Space*, Princeton, NJ: Princeton University Press, pp. 1–51.

Olkowski, D. (2000), 'Body, Knowledge and Becoming: Woman Morpho-logic in Deleuze and Irigaray', in I. Buchanan and C. Colebrook (eds), *Deleuze and Feminist Theory*, Edinburgh: Edinburgh University Press, pp. 86–109.

Perella, S. (1999), 'Hypersurface Theory > < Culture', *AD Hypersurface II*, 69: 9/10, 6–15.

Petrescu, D. (2007), 'Altering Practices', in D. Petrescu (ed.), *Altering Practices: Feminist Politics and Poetics of Space*, London: Routledge, pp. 1–14.

Rajchman, J. (1991), 'Perplications: On the Space and Time of Rebstockpark', in *Unfolding Frankfurt*, Berlin: Ernst, Wilhelm & Sohn, pp. 18–77.

Rajchman, J. (1998), 'Folding', in *Constructions*, Cambridge, MA: MIT Press, pp. 11–36.

Rawes, P. (2007), 'Plenums: Re-Thinking Matter, Geometry and Subjectivity', in K. Lloyd Thomas (ed.), *Material Matters: Architecture and Material Practice*, London: Routledge, pp. 56–66.

Robinson, C. (2004), 'The Material Fold: Towards a Variable Narrative of Anomalous Topologies', in *AD Folding in Architecture*, ed. G. Lynn, Chichester: Wiley-Academy, pp. 80–1.

Stratford, H. (2007), 'Unpleasant Matters', in K. Lloyd Thomas (ed.), *Material Matters: Architecture and Material Practice*, London: Routledge, pp. 209–24.

Zeitlian, H. (ed.) (1992), *Semiotext(e) Architecture*, New York: Columbia University Press.

Chapter 2

Northern Line

Deborah Hauptmann and Andrej Radman

Introduction

This chapter takes as a point of departure the Deleuzian concept of the 'Northern Line'. Scholarly accounts of the Dutch Baroque suggest that, in contrast to the organic force of their Italian counterparts, the Dutch painters set themselves apart with a genuinely new haptic painterly tradition, effectively creating an abstract machine with its power of repetition. It is with the seventeenth-century Dutch painter Johannes Vermeer that the unleashing of affect is first seen; to our mind this grants him the status of the bearer of the Deleuzian Northern Line (Deleuze 1997: 143). However, the most important 'Dutchman' in the eyes of Deleuze remains Spinoza, the prince of immanence. Thus our argument requires laying the pre-philosophical *plane of immanence*, creating a *Northern Line* concept and inventing the *conceptual personae*, or aesthetic figures, of the architects we see as the heirs of this tradition: UN Studio (UNS), NOX and OMA. This triad will be utilised to situate contemporary Dutch architecture within an aesthetic position that argues for a reciprocal determination of the abstract and concrete; or, with Deleuze, the virtual and the actual. We will draw on Deleuze and Guattari's reading of the Northern Line as a theoretical disposition towards the differential difference in contrast to the dialectical difference. The latter operates in terms of opposition, negation and, *ipso facto*, resistance correlative to a molar notion of power (*pouvoir*) and not, as with the former, the (molecular) level of 'desiring assemblages' (Deleuze and Guattari 2004: 496–7). Our argument will show that the Northern Line provides an aesthetic reading – neither distributed nor organised around the mind, nor oriented toward cognition – that is capable of escaping architecture's long-standing dependence on representationalism.

In *What Is Philosophy?* Deleuze and Guattari develop the *conceptual persona* (1994: 177); with this concept we will work through a process of decoding, of decomposing the architect and the work into a-personal and pre-subjective levels.[1] Put otherwise, we will engage Deleuze-Guattari where, working from desiring assemblages, they circumvent the phenomenon of ideology, treating it as an epiphenomenon; we similarly propose to treat architecture in terms of what they refer to as passive syntheses, which undermine the active synthesis of representation.[2] Of course, this extra-propositional and sub-representative level of thought-events requires a mode of analysis that cannot rely on the fully actual, for this would inevitably lead to conflating the material cause with the incorporeal effect. By this we mean to say that things themselves are bearers of ideal events, which do not coincide with their properties. Any (actual) incarnation may in fact be seen as a (provisional) 'solution' to the problem posed by the virtual, which is consequently not Ideal but problematic. The concept prevents regression into simple reductionism since there is no homology between the actual and virtual.

This chapter will present an analysis or, more in keeping with Deleuze-Guattari, a *schizoanalysis* of the working methods of the Dutch architects mentioned above. We will further suggest that it is not the architect who invents the conceptual persona, but rather the persona itself that provides the architectural body of work with a certain (endo)consistency formerly known as style. Finally, with this work we hope to develop a reading of several Deleuzian thought models which we believe have been somewhat overlooked in contemporary discourse on Deleuze and the impact of his philosophy on architecture. This will include the three syntheses of the connective, the disjunctive and the conjunctive in relation to the paranoiac, miraculating and celibate machines respectively.

Distribution of the Sensible

The idea of the 'idea behind architecture' is the Platonic idealism we wish to repudiate. With this, it is important to understand that Deleuze and Guattari see absolutely no distinction between a desiring-production and social production. As they argue in *Anti-Oedipus*, desire is objective and immanent: 'There is no particular form of existence that can be labelled "psychic reality"' (2008: 27). And a few paragraphs later: 'There is no such thing as the social production of reality on the one hand, and a desiring-production that is mere fantasy on the other' (ibid.: 28). Further, and in clear terms, 'desiring-production is one and the same thing as social production' (ibid.: 30). This in turn means that there is no individual fantasy; there are only social fantasies, a revelation that effectively turns psychoanalysis on its head. Deleuze and Guattari refer to such 'material psychiatry' as *schizoanalysis* where the connections and disjunctions operate ad infinitum. As Smith and Ballantyne have recently argued, although 'Freud begins to take us to a field where we can enter a discourse of flow – of novel and intense material connections with that which is non-habitual, non-genital, non-human – unfortunately for Freud there is a "natural" connection and investment; a personalising of desire that ties the ebbs and tides of the libido to the self and the familiar/familial' (2010: 24).

The unleashing of desire is essential for our approach, given that we take the conditions of genesis (production) as the basis of experience to be the very medium of architecture. What distinguishes 'immanent architecture' is that it does not merely fulfil the (pre-given) expectation, it also produces its 'audience': a people yet to come. In contrast to *Anti-Oedipus* – the first volume of *Capitalism and Schizophrenia* – the second volume, *A Thousand Plateaus*, has a much wider range of registers: cosmic, geological, evolutionary, developmental, ethological, anthropological, mythological, historical, economic, political, literary, musical and many more (a thousand plateaus), where every plane is matter unfolding, where relations are effected by specific expressions which, in turn, are events of specific powers to relate.

Despite the introduction of ever more new terms, the abstract machine stays virtually the same: together the passive syntheses at all these levels form a differential field within which stratification takes place as an integration or resolution of that field. As a matter of fact, this machinism dates back to Deleuze's 1968 work *Différence et Répétition*. We find this especially pertinent given that throughout history there has been a prejudicial tendency to set the realm of sensibility against that of reason or understanding. Deleuze was among the first to propose a transformation of transcendental idealism into transcendental empiricism with far-reaching consequences in both metaphysical and epistemological registers:

> If [transcendental] aesthetic appears more profound to us than that of Kant, it is for the following reasons: Kant defines the passive self in terms of simple receptivity, thereby assuming sensations already formed, then merely relating these to the a priori forms of their representation which are determined as space and time. In this manner, not only does he unify the passive self by ruling out the possibility of composing space step by step, not only does he deprive this passive self of all power of synthesis (synthesis being reserved for activity), but moreover he cuts the Aesthetic into two parts: the objective element of sensation guaranteed by space and

the subjective element which is incarnate in pleasure and pain. The aim of the preceding analyses, on the contrary, has been to show that receptivity must be defined in terms of the formation of local selves or egos, in terms of the passive syntheses of contemplation or contraction, thereby accounting simultaneously for the possibility of experiencing sensations, the power of reproducing them and the value that pleasure assumes as a principle. (Deleuze 1994: 98)

Sensibility itself becomes a field of (artistic/architectural) creation and experimentation. Such a thesis invites us, pace Jacques Rancière (2004), to examine 'the distribution of the sensible' in the social field as an issue of social and political individuation.[3] The question is no longer that of the ultimate nature of reality; rather it is the distribution of the sensible and insensible within which we find ourselves immersed. We ought to start by distinguishing *diagrams* from signs, be they vectorial – augmentative powers and diminutive servitudes – or scalar (see Figure 2.1).

Defined diagrammatically [. . .], an abstract machine is neither an infrastructure that is determining in the last instance nor a transcendental Idea that is determining in the supreme instance. Rather, it plays a piloting role. The diagrammatic or abstract machine does not function to represent, even something real, but rather constructs a real that is yet to come, a new type of reality. Thus when it constitutes points of creation or potentiality it does not stand outside history but is instead always 'prior to' history. (Deleuze and Guattari 2004: 141–2)

INDICATIVE	ABSTRACTIVE	IMPERATIVE	HERMENEUTIC
sensory perceptive	retaining selected affective characteristic	effect as end	
physical effect		moral effect	imaginary effect
sensible indices	logical icons	moral symbols	metaphysical idols

Figure 2.1 Four scalar signs of affection: although a sign, according to Spinoza qua Deleuze, can have several meanings, it is always an effect of one body upon another. In 'Spinoza and the Three "Ethics"', Deleuze distinguishes between vectorial and scalar signs. The former are signs of increase and decrease – continuous variations of power – while the latter express one's state at a moment in time, 'a slice of duration'. Affects are irreducible to affections, sensations or perceptions. The figure compares the four principal types of scalar signs that vary according to the contingent nature of assemblage (Deleuze 1997: 138–51).

The significance of the Northern Line is that it 'binds' the undetermined, determinable and (mutually) determined. It is not a given, as Deleuze writes in *Difference and Repetition* (1994: 222), but that by which a given is given. With respect to Architecture, as we hope to show, Cartesian foundationalism does not hold; instead we find the necessity of foundation can only exist for determinable ground, not the final complete determination that remains only ever reciprocally determined. In other words, the system cannot be deterministic and the nature of this 'circle' is to remain radically open, hence diagrammatic.[4]

For Deleuze and Guattari the machine does not conflict with either culture or nature. The machine is not reducible to the mechanics conceived as the protocol of some technical machines or particular organisation of an organism. Machinism therefore designates every system that cuts off fluxes going beyond both mechanism and vitalism: 'The unconscious is a factory and not a stage' (Guattari 1995: 73–4). We will next try to distinguish between the respective desiring machines: the working parts of UNS, the immobile motor of NOX and the adjacent part of OMA and their three forms of energy: 'Libido, Numen, and Voluptas; and their three syntheses: the connective syntheses of partial objects and flows, the disjunctive syntheses of singularities and chains, and the conjunctive syntheses of intensities and becomings' (Deleuze and Guattari 2008: 338) – see Figure 2.2, which we have borrowed and adapted from *Anti-Oedipus*.

FLOW	CODE	STOCK
need to be controlled e.g. water, social, traffic, immigrants, sewage, somatic (blood, urine, milk), *bêtise* (stupidity)	controlling of flow (primarily from economics)	
correlative: no flow without code and vice versa		
transmission or exchange from one pole to another input/output	correlative of flow inscription, recording keeping track of the flows	
uncoded flow: nightmare		
capital/money	code/existence (does NOT pre-exist) e.g. DNA;	possession related as material or juridical (mine = me)
	biological = social it changes, molecular passing along of information	

Figure 2.2 Three cuts: an abstract machine is defined by Deleuze and Guattari as a system of cuts. The figure shows three different kinds of cuts which pertain to the three components of desiring production: (i) flow or the portioning-cut of desiring machines; (ii) code or the detachment-cut from which issues the BwO; and (iii) stock or the remainder-cut that produces the nomadic subject (Bogue 2003: 63).

Manimal: Paranoiac Machine

At the first level of synthesis, the Body without Organs stands opposed to its desiring machines, repelling them in the manner of a 'paranoiac machine' (Deleuze and Guattari 2008: 9). This can be regarded as analogous to what Deleuze called the 'pure present' in *Difference and Repetition*, since the paranoiac machine immediately erases whatever appears on its surface in order to allow for something new to appear. The passive perceptual syntheses of imagination are preceded by a myriad of passive syntheses at the organic level, making the organism 'the primary habit it *is*' (1994: 74). Habit (*Habitus*) is therefore a contraction of habitual contractions that occur on multiple levels. The synthesis of habit, in turn, precedes the memory and recollection of conscious thought. The contraction is not a reflection (ibid.: 91). It provides a 'rule' in the form of sensory-motor responses to present stimuli that anticipate the future on the basis of the past.[5] At this level a (physical) organism could be said to be ruled by instinctual response. The 'connective syntheses of production', through which linear sequences of the 'and then' form are constituted, remains undetermined. However, as Deleuze and Guattari point out (2008: 309, 323), it captures an aspect of the intensive, the machinic assemblage, by connecting or coupling heterogeneous 'partial objects' through the emission of 'energy flows'.

If there is a plane of composition that has marked the *œuvre* of UNS, then it is the Manimal, a computer-generated image of the hybridisation of a lion, a snake and a human. To be clear, the Manimal is neither figural nor structural but machinic: 'As a technique, it excites because it has been produced in a manner radically different from all pictorial techniques that have been previously employed by artists' (van Berkel and Bos 1999b: 80). We can formulate this equation as: Manimal = lion AND snake AND man. According to Ben van Berkel and Caroline Bos, there are three main aspects that make the hybridising technique of the Manimal architecturally interesting; these concern the relations of the technique with the author, time and mereology. The first concerns the ambiguity of authorship, given the plurality of 'sometimes invisible' participants (not excluding the software programmers). The relation to time is one of continuous variation or 'a sequence that could, in principle, run indefinitely'. Accordingly, UNS openly express anxiety over 'freezing architecture in time' given that, according to them, only change exists. Most importantly, with regard to the Part-to-Whole relation, the unity of the Manimal as an image is not disrupted by the diversity of its ingredients, which is what most distinguishes the technique from the traditional technique of collage:

> This is the most radical choice for architecture to face. The totalising, decontextualising, dehistoricising combination of discordant systems of information can be instrumentalised architecturally into one gesture. [. . .]
>
> The architecture of hybridization, the fluent merging of constituent parts into an endlessly variable whole, amounts to organisation of continuous difference, resulting in structures that are scale-less, subject to evolution, expansion, inversion and other contortions and manipulations. Free to assume different identities, architecture becomes endless. (1999b: 83)

Ever since its appearance the Manimal has been the *spiritus movens* of UNS and continues to feature prominently in their discourse. Its genealogy is well known by now: from the 'fragmented organisation of disconnected parts' to the 'displaced organisation of connected parts' to the 'seamless organisation of disconnected parts' or the 'portrait of becoming', where van Berkel and Bos express that they 'have never had a lot of faith in interpretation' (Birnbaum and Lynn 2002: 15). The first 'fragmenting' paradigm is illustrated by the exploded view of Le Corbusier's Villa Savoye, accompanied by the Bauhausian mannequin head adorned in the technique of collage as a seam: stitching together separate parts that retain their respective identities. By contrast, the second 'displacing' paradigm is exemplified by the formal analogy between Francis Bacon's figural (neither figurative nor abstract) portrait and a piece of architectural metabolist megastructure (architecture cum urbanism). It is presented as a transition phase towards the endless (and, and, etc.), best illustrated by the Möbius Strip as well as the Manimal itself. The fascination with the 'production of production' ranks UNS among the leading architects of the flow in the very precise sense of the libidinal form of energy. Aaron Betsky points out in 'Unfolding the Forms of Unstudio' (2002: 9, 11) that, from the beginning, UNS have used the body as a model (and metaphor):

> Up to this point, the architects had argued for the emergence of form out of the manipulation of physical material. They proposed what they called the 'invisible detail'. They articulated this detail in opposition to either the articulated meeting of materials that structural expressionism would champion, or the smooth making of enclosed forms that would seek to deny the physicality of the object. Instead, they thought that details should drink in the difference between materials, make possible their meeting, allow the form to be folded, and then disappear. (Cf. van Berkel and Bos 1994: 176–81)

Their *Move* (1999) opens up not only with kaleidoscopic images but also chains of seemingly unrelated terms.[6] However, this uncompromising decontextualising and dehistoricising strategy comes at a price. When asked how to negotiate the difference between (anthropocentric) scale-dependency and (geocentric) scalelessness, the conceptual persona remains utterly consistent in failing to give an answer.[7] This is simply not an issue for UNS given their theoretical and practical agenda. The Manimal, as we see it, stands not for keeping track of the flow, but for the flow itself, any flow; UNS refer to such a 'non-reductionist' approach as 'Deep Planning'.[8] The ease with which a myriad of 'partial objects' is handled by this 'paranoiac machine' proves the point: 'Move introduces inclusiveness in the design approach [. . .] Inclusiveness allows fragmentation and difference to be absorbed into a coherent, continuous approach, abandoning the strategies of fragmentation and collage' (van Berkel and Bos 1999a: 15). They later conclude: 'The inclusive model is anti nothing' (ibid.: 221). What UNS also unapologetically abandon is history: 'We have already forgotten history, shaken off the metaphors belonging to wood, bricks and steel. We have already seen emptiness. Now it is time to redefine materiality' (ibid.: 156–7). And redefine it they did. Not according to its chemical composition, or vis-à-vis sensibility, but on the basis of performativity in the emergence of the project. For UNS, 'between art and airports', only the present matters, and entire processes are rendered visible.[9] Its favourite colour is blue, the colour which, according to the trend forecaster Edelkoort, 'dissolves contrasts and wipes out details [. . .] and undoes form' (2002: 96–7).

D-Tower: Miraculating Machine

Corresponding to the constitution of a 'pure past' are the disjunctive syntheses by which whatever is produced through the connective syntheses is recorded on the surface of the Body without Organs. BwO therefore functions as a gigantic memory or pure past (Mnemosyne). This past is 'pure' in the sense that it does not contain entities open to representation; it also makes the present pass, as it were.[10] Deleuze and Guattari (2008: 11) show that this 'miraculating machine', which attracts rather than repels the desiring-machines that populate it, becomes determinable (although not determined).[11] The 'disjunctive syntheses of recording' have the form of 'either . . . or . . . or'. At this level a life form can engage in signifiance – a term that indicates the 'signifying capacity' as the primary effect of a regime of signs within the semiotic register.

In *Creative Evolution* (1907), Bergson claims that what distinguishes the instinctual response from a free response of a thinking organism is that there is a gap between the stimulus and response of the latter.[12] The disjunctive synthesis involves the creation of divergent relations among the series that occur on the Body without Organs (Deleuze and Guattari 2008: 13). It therefore refers to the virtual continuum, 'a pure fluid in a free state, flowing without interruption, streaming over the surface of a full body' (ibid.: 8).

In *Anti-Oedipus*, Deleuze and Guattari present the flow and the code as correlative notions. There is no code without the flow and vice versa. It comes as no surprise that uncoded flow represents a true nightmare from the point of view of any society, for it is quite literally elusive and fleeting. The code, as opposed to the flow, introduces a measure of attraction and zones of convergence. The coding process is therefore not inclusive, but exclusive, which is to say that it is not a matter of the production of production but rather the production of recording. It is no coincidence that Lars Spuybroek, the founder of NOX, is not only well versed in history but also openly critical of the atemporality associated with mainstream modernism.[13] His *D-Tower* from 2003, created in collaboration with the artist Q. S. Serafijn, is a paradigmatic example of the production of recording. The tower is twelve metres tall and made of epoxy. During daytime, it is white-greyish, while at night, from 8 p.m., the tower is lit up by LEDs. It has four colours. The colour of the day is fed by a website where a group of Doetinchem volunteers keep a diary. Each day over the course of six months they answer fifty questions about fear, hate, love and happiness. The computer measures the day's emotions based on the answers. At night, it shows the city's emotion of the day: red stands for love, blue for happiness, yellow for fear, green for hate. In the words of Brian Massumi:

> The tower changes color according to the results, becoming a beacon of the collective mood. Affect has been given visual expression. The predominant affective quality of people's interactions becomes visible. This can undoubtedly reflect back on the interactions taking place in the town by making something that was private and imperceptible public and perceptible. A kind of feedback loop has been created between private mood and public image that has never existed in quite this way before. (Massumi 2006)

Whereas UNS seem to be oblivious to the issues of signifi(c)ance, it is quite the opposite in the case of NOX. The mood of Doetinchem is not red *and* blue (love and happiness), but *either* red *or* blue (love or happiness). It is not the Tower that is the Body without Organs, but the whole of Doetinchem. If anything, the Tower is an ad hoc Organ (without the Body). While UNS are concerned with the 'problem' (of endlessness), NOX seem to be more interested in the 'solution' (or convergence, i.e. singularities), hence the title of *The Architecture of Continuity* (Spuybroek 2008). The polar opposite of this continuity, with a Numenal form of energy – which refers to the coming-together of action-perception-construction (relation) – is not discontinuity but endlessness itself (infinite). Of the three conceptual personae, it is NOX that most explicitly embrace the Northern Line, although, in this particular case, 'Gothic' can be read as a synonym for Northern Line (Spuybroek 2011: 46–7). In an interview entitled 'The Aesthetics of Variation' (2007: 142–3), Spuybroek cites liberally from Worringer:

> 'The Ceaseless Melody of the Northern Line' is one of the chapters in [Worringer's] book *Formprobleme der Gotik* (1911) – in English, *Form in Gothic*. Let's just start off with: 'in Northern ornament repetition does not bear this restful character of addition . . .' – and with this he means classicist symmetry – '[. . .] but has, so to speak, a character of multiplication. The intervention of any desire for organic moderation and serenity here is lacking.' A shot right between the eyes of Alberti. Symmetry replaced by repetition, by serial rhythms of multiplication. Nobody really understood at the time how Worringer could have done this book on the gothic three years after his famous *Abstraction and Empathy* (1908), which became the bible of early abstract painters. But it's the same expressionism: 'the Northern Line does not get its life from any impress which we willingly give it, but appears to have an expression of its own, which is stronger than life.'

What sets NOX apart is the attention to what is going on (genealogy) in what happened (archaeology) or the attention to the distribution of singularities on the Body without Organs: 'Life Constructs. Agency builds' (Spuybroek 2008: 19). The vagueness of BwO is not to be taken as a lack of logic, but quite the opposite. According to Lars Spuybroek, it is precisely that which constitutes relations. Most importantly, these relations are exterior to their terms. It is the relations that create the Whole, and not the Part or finalities as Spuybroek calls them. Finality, in turn, is the polar opposite of generality: 'things are necessarily vague [not ambiguous], since they are one and many at the same time' (2008: 23–4). It is for this reason that diagramming is still the most important innovation in architecture, claims Spuybroek in 'Motor Geometry'. On a techno-cultural level, diagramming signifies a move toward metadesign or 'Designing the way of designing itself' (Spuybroek 1998: 50).

Naked Boxer Eating Oysters: Celibate Machine

Finally, the conjunctive syntheses give rise to the 'celibate machine', which, as the practical equivalent of the 'pure future' (Nietzschean Eternal Return), unites the repulsive tendency of the paranoiac machine and the attractive tendency of the miraculating machine.[14] The 'eternal return' is defined by Deleuze in a very formal manner, as summed up by James Williams (2011: 16) in the following proposition: *only difference returns and never the same*. This, in turn, means that novelty is always an expression of pure differences in new events. The three machines – paranoiac, miraculating and celibate – are strictly non-sequential. The 'last' one is the locus of *jouissance* and affirmation: *sentio ergo sum*. The 'conjunctive syntheses of consumption' take the form of a reciprocally determined mode of existence by (retroactively) concluding 'so it's . . .' (Deleuze and Guattari 2008: 12). This is a 'larval subject', beyond the human, who affirms life by evolving with (rather than within) an unrepresentable time, 'a strange subject with no fixed identity, wandering about over the body without organs [. . .] being born of the states that it consumes' (ibid.: 16). The conjunctive synthesis therefore involves the creation of convergent relations among series, an operation which forms 'individuation fields' that already prefigure the intensive pre-actualisation.

If the interest of UNS lies in the physiological register and that of NOX in the register of significance, then OMA could be said to have an ongoing interest in the psychological, with Voluptas as its form of energy.[15] The Downtown Athletic Club from Koolhaas's *Delirious New York* (1978) provides for (metropolitan) conditions that engender (larval) subjects that consume them. According to the architectural historian Hans van Dijk, Koolhaas does not use the Club's section only as a corrective intervention in order to resist the banality of the high-rise, or for mere program distribution, as that would amount to the ordinary and reductive use of a diagram. Rather, the Club's section becomes a deliberate *design device* to employ the 'abstract machine', which produces the skyscraper and makes it susceptible to the unforeseen (van Dijk 2005: 72).

We have located the 'Naked Boxer Eating Oysters – Celibate Machine' in *Delirious New York*. Here Koolhaas studied how the programmes of the thirty-eight-storey Downtown Athletic Club subverted the usual uniformity of the blank-faced tower to become the 'apotheosis of the Skyscraper as instrument of the Culture of Congestion'. The Club harbours a sometimes surreal collection of activities – squash courts, a swimming pool, a colonic centre and an indoor golf course – united only by the circulatory core of thirteen elevators that unite and feed all the floors. The ninth combines a room full of punching bags with an oyster bar. 'Eating oysters with boxing gloves, naked,' says Koolhaas, 'such is the "plot" of the ninth story, or, the 20th century in action'. According to Jeff Kipnis (2005: 103), the free-section is the necessary invention:

> [A] recasting of the metropolis's vertical infrastructure into a building device to achieve the unregulated anonymities – and thus stage the unfettered behaviors – that are not possible in free-plan [in order to] detach the subject in a building from the regime of immediate experience, with its emphasis on satisfied expectations and phenomenological, haptic, aesthetic, and symbolic pleasures, in order to place them elsewhere as subjects of a different spatial regime, one with other pleasures, other expectations, other politics.

This makes OMA an expert in the 'production of consumption or consummation', both libidinal and political, which is virtually the same.[16] However, by no means does the (quasi) subject come ready-made only to be detached; rather, it is *reciprocally* determined.[17] It can therefore only declare (in retrospect) 'so that's what it was'. It is a 'celibate machine'. As Arie Graafland writes in *Architectural Bodies*:

> Koolhaas describes The Downtown Athletic Club in Manhattan (DAC) as a [bachelor] machine where the New York 'bachelor' brings his body into peak condition. To find that original idea which was ultimately realized in America, we must turn to a second machine ['the culture of congestion' a.k.a. Ginzburg's 'social condenser' being the first], that of Marcel Duchamp, who a few years previous to DAC had realized his *La Mariée mise à nu par ses célibataires, même* [The Bride Stripped Bare by Her Bachelors, Even]. [. . .] Indeed, from Beckett to Duchamp, this is an important impulse in the thinking of a number of intellectuals at the beginning of this [twentieth] century.[18] (1996: 44)

As we have seen, Deleuze rejects the Kantian restriction of synthesis to the active 'I think' and the relegation of the passive self to receptivity. That is to say that the bachelor or celibate machine is not the same thing as the willing machine. The bachelor is a playful suitor, as with Duchamp, hovering on the border between the respectable and the unknown, and hence suspect: that is, forever produced as a new alliance between the paranoid and the miraculating, between desiring machines and the Body without Organs. The celibate machine consequently creates the nomadic subject as a residue, something left over. This subject can be an individual, text, practice, architecture or an institution.

It is an offshoot of a particular constellation of forces. The opposition between the forces of attraction (continuum) and repulsion (endlessness) produces an open series of intensive positive elements that are never to reach the state of equilibrium of a system. Instead, they express a variety of metastable states, which a (larval) subject undergoes. It is worth repeating that – contrary to popular belief – a nomad does not move but stays put. Instead of changing his *habitat*, like a migrant or a sedentary, a nomad changes his *habit*. The nomadic subject 'consumes and consummates each of the states through which it passes, and is born of each of them anew' (Deleuze and Guattari 2008: 20).[19] As Fadi Abou-Rihan suggests, the conjunctive synthesis is 'quasi traumatic' in that it acts as the 'signpost of a radical shift in the subject's thought, perception, and experience'; in other words, a shift in the very manner in which the subject deploys 'itself for itself and for others' (Abou-Rihan 2011: 73). He further explains the significance of this ontogenetic imbroglio:

> Through the conjunctive (it's me and so it's mine . . .) synthesis, Deleuze and Guattari are effectively redefining insight and in the process rearranging the terms if not the relevance of the debate here. The synthesis in question is ostensibly a 'so that's what it is!' moment of insight and a clarity identified by its effect to reorganize radically not only delirium (thought) but hallucination (perception) and intensity (experience) as well. The 'so that's what it is!' is not so much a revelation or an uncovering of the subject to itself but the making of a subject. (2011: 72–3)

While the subject does depend on the interaction between *I experience*, *I think* and *I see*, Abou-Rihan continues, 'it is not the sum total of all three moments or modes [intensity, delirium and hallucination]; it is an offshoot and a side-effect rather than a unity precisely because it is constantly disrupted by its nature as a subject in *jouissance*' (ibid.: 71). In this way Deleuze and Guattari manage to rebut a long tradition in both philosophy and psychoanalysis that has insisted on inscribing the subject as primarily grounded in thought (Descartes) or language (Lacan). Such fetishistic subjects have deluded themselves into thinking in the mode of the ready-made that is at the centre of its various experiences and understandings, *separate* from the constellation of intensities that it undergoes.

This revelation sheds a new light on the critique of Koolhaas's alleged regressive strategy of frequent reference to retroactivity. Take, for example, his report on a student field trip to Berlin in the early 1970s. Under the subtitle *Reverse Epiphanies*, Koolhaas admits to the following 'negative revelation': 'The [Berlin] wall also, in my eyes, made a total mockery of any of the emerging attempts to link form to meaning in a regressive chain-and-ball relationship' (Koolhaas 1995: 214–33). The wall's meaning, according to him, appeared to change almost daily or even hourly, often depending on remote events and decisions. 'So, that's what it was.' It turned out that its significance, as a piece of architecture, was in fact marginal. Koolhaas, by his own admission, would never again believe in form as the primary vessel of meaning. How could he, given the ubiquitous capitalist machine that decodes flows and deterritorialises the socius, only to conjoin them anew on its immanent field in order to extract a surplus value? The question arises of whether the energy released via production (of consumption) can be reclaimed as Voluptas, that is to say not in the sense of 'regressing' to the wall (any wall – metonym for architecture) as a territorial sign (coding), and not by overcoding: enter celibate machine. While conscious investment generates subjugated groups who privilege power over desiring-production in their attempt to change the socius, unconscious or libidinal investment generates subject groups whose programless politics subordinates the socius to pure desire with no interest, cause or teleology.[20] At their most experimental, art and architecture have the capacity to escape their historical moment. This is the sine qua non of the project of defatalisation. Upon receiving the Pritzker Prize in 2000, Koolhaas was interviewed by one of the editors of *S, M, L, XL*, Jennifer Siegler. In some of his answers we find an almost uncanny resonance with the 'production of production, recording and consummation' thesis that we put forward:

Jen: That must be why you make people nervous. You take in everything. People feel that.

Rem: I can't ever be oblivious. I wrote a sentence today: 'The tyranny of the oblivious . . .' My whole life has been about envying the tyranny of the oblivious. And feeling the vulnerability of the . . . recorder.

Jen: Of the what?

Rem: Of those who record.

Jen: You call yourself a recorder.

Rem: The thing is that I have a really intense, almost compulsive need to record. But it doesn't end there, because what I record is somehow transformed into a creative thing. There is a continuity. Recording is the beginning of a conceptual production. *I am somehow collapsing the two – recording and producing – into a single event.* (Koolhaas 2000; emphasis added)

A People is Missing

It goes without saying that our triad appears too neat.[21] However, it bears repeating that it is never exclusive. Each of the respective conceptual personae/aesthetic figures discussed above is a product of a specific machinism and the (desiring) machines are part of the same continuum. This means that the three syntheses are irreducible. It is also impossible to circumvent any of them. Yet, according to our (schizo)analysis, a difference of emphasis appears nevertheless.[22] We will refer to it as style. This style is not an effect, but a quasi-cause. It may be argued that Dutch architects such as Claus and Kaan and MVRDV have an exquisite style. By contrast, we would argue that UNS, NOX and OMA have no style. Rather, thanks to the abstract machine or the Northern Line, it is style that has them. Let us reiterate that the 'schizophrenia' Deleuze and Guattari embrace is not a pathological condition. For them, as Massumi explains (1993: 1), 'the clinical schizophrenic's debilitating detachment from the world is a quelled attempt to engage it in unimagined ways. Schizophrenia as a positive process is inventive connection, expansion rather than withdrawal.' What sets our triad apart – as potential proponents of 'immanent architecture' – is the ambition not to fulfil the desire of a ready-made audience but to produce its own audience and quite literally so. Thus we emphasise passive syntheses with the clear architectural agenda of forcing the shift from the design of form to the design of experience. We proceed from the premise that the individual is not form but power.[23] What we refer to as the 'mapping of agency', which is complementary but antecedent to the well-known 'agency of mapping', is best explained by Deleuze qua Klee in *A Thousand Plateaus*:

> The artist opens up to the Cosmos in order to harness forces in a 'work' (without which the opening onto the Cosmos would only be a reverie incapable of enlarging the limits of the earth); this work requires very simple, pure, almost childish means, but also the forces of a *people*, which is what is still lacking. (2004: 337)

Consider the juxtaposition with the architecture theorist Robert Somol's 'active', that is representational (social constructivist), historical triad, where he starts by questioning the stability of form (see Figure 2.3). By contrast to our 'passive' triad, this *logocentric* triad found that form was not 'neutral', but constructed by linguistic and institutional relations. According to Somol, the agenda was first broached in Robert Venturi's deployment of *collage* as a deviation of form to become information or sign, which was not merely compositional but would include both text and 'low-brow' references. By contrast, Peter Eisenman's deviation would move to the trace, the missing index of formal processes, stressing the absence and the conceptual. Finally, John Hejduk would investigate the theatrical construction of form through highly orchestrated relations and instructions, both linguistic and contractual. Somol's 'three-pronged critique' variously foregrounds: *context* with Venturi (framing mechanisms outside form); *process* with Eisenman (active procedures within formation); and *usage* with Hejduk (form's relation to a subject). For Somol (1999), with the neo-avant-garde, 'form would be precisely subjected to the functions of its linguistic descendants: in*form*ing, trans*form*ing, and per*form*ing'. But as Somol professes, yet fails to live up to, working diagrammatically is not to be confused with simply working with diagrams. That is to say, the (non-formal/subrepresentational) mapping of agency is not to be conflated with the agency of mapping (in/trans/per-forming). Abstract machines do operate within concrete assemblages, but they make the territorial

(i) Hauptmann/Radman	PARANOIAC machine *libido*	MIRACULATING m. *numen*	CELIBATE machine *voluptas*
	UNS	NOX	OMA
	partial objects (p.o.)	resonance b/w p.o.	pure intensities
	percept	thought	experience
	hallucination	delirium	intensity
(ii) Somol	IN*FORM*ING	TRANS*FORM*ING	PER*FORM*ING
	Venturi	Eisenman	Hejduk
	context	process	usage
	icon	index	symbol
(iii) Hays	IMAGINARY (I)	SYMBOLIC (S)	REAL (R)
	Rossi	Eisenman	Hejduk (IR) Tschumi (SR)
	analogy	repetition	encounter spacing (*différance*)
	arch. big Other signif.	impossibility of signif.	absence code

Figure 2.3 Three architectural triads: a comparative analysis between the (i) authors' passive, (ii) Robert Somol's 'active' and (iii) Michael Hays' Lacanian systematisation. The difference that marks the first is the dissolution of the self-identical subject: first, in the contraption of habit by the Paranoiac Machine; second, in the memory of the pure past by the Miraculating Machine; and finally, in the third synthesis by the Celibate Machine, time is witnessed as pure form without content, demented, 'out of joint'. In contrast to the model of recognition adhered to by Somol and Hays, the encounter is captured only on the basis of the involuntary thought. It emits signs and intensities that are (empirically) imperceptible, sub-representational yet affective.

assemblage open onto assemblages of another type (molecular, cosmic) that constitute becomings.

By contrast, Koolhaas in his seminal 'Generic City' (1995: 1248) suggests that '[Molar] Identity is like a mousetrap in which more and more mice have to share the original bait, and which, on closer inspection, may have been empty for centuries.' In other words, what makes abstract machines abstract is that they know nothing of forms and substances. Form is never *subjected* to anything.[24] Nor is it *representation* of the real as in Michael Hays's Lacanian systematisation (third triad: imaginary – symbolic – real). Despite their apparent opposition, 'projective' Somol and 'critical' Hays, they share a *correlationist* stance: philosophy of access and access to access (Radman, forthcoming). For schizoanalysis, as opposed to psychoanalysis, the Real = Desiring-production.[25] In *Anti-Oedipus* Deleuze and Guattari consider that 'the machines of desire [. . .] no longer allow themselves to be reduced to the structure any more than to persons. (They thus) constitute the Real in itself, beyond or beneath the Symbolic as well as the Imaginary' (2008: 52). Every abstract machine is nothing but a consolidated aggregate of (un-formed) matters and (non-formal) functions, that is *phylum* and *diagram*. It is singular and creative, real yet non-concrete, actual yet non-effectuated. That is precisely why abstract machines can be dated and named: UNS paranoiac machine, NOX miraculating machine and OMA celibate machine. Not that they refer to architects or to architecture (effectuating moments). On the contrary, it is the names and dates that refer to the singularities of the machines, and to what they effectuate.

Notes

1. If we make an analogy with Deleuze and Guattari's 'conceptual persona', who is not the thinker's representative but rather the reverse, we could say that the architect is only the envelope of her principal 'aesthetic figure'. Deleuze and Guattari explain the reversal as follows: 'Aesthetic figures and the style that creates them have nothing to do with rhetoric. They are sensations: percepts and affects, landscapes and faces, visions and becomings' (1994: 177).
2. Deleuze describes passive synthesis as one which 'is not carried out by the mind, but occurs in the mind'. They are *passive* as they do not presuppose an active agency on the part of the self-identical subject governed by a principle of 'common sense'. Beneath active syntheses of thought there are passive syntheses of perception and farther beneath them still there are passive organic syntheses of metabolism; see Protevi (2010) and Deleuze (1994: 71, 73).
3. Rancière writes: 'Aesthetics is central to politics as the social and political systems are founded on the distribution of the sensible (aesthetic regimes): forms of visibility, ways of doing and making and ways of conceptualising.' We

agree with Katharine Wolfe's assertion that – despite Rancière's denunciation of Deleuze's philosophy in general and his theory of 'imperceptibility' in particular – he is much closer to Deleuze than generally thought; see Wolfe (2006).

4. 'What holds an assemblage together [what gives it consistency] is not the play of framing forms or linear causalities but, actually or potentially, its most deter-ritorialised component' (Deleuze and Guattari 2004: 374); see also Williams (2000: 211–12).

5. See Tamsin Lorraine: 'Deleuze derives a notion of the living present as a contrac-tion or synthesis of time from Hume: two moments (for example the tick-tock of a clock) are impressed upon the imagination which acts as a kind of sensitive plate that retains one moment (or one case of two moments) as the next appears. This results in a living present that is a synthesis of the past (the retention of preceding moments or cases, say two tick-tocks) and the future (anticipation that the next moment or case will be like the past, the expectation that yet another tick-tock will follow)' (Lorraine 2003: 34).

6. 'Sex, Warhol, Television, Disney, Fellini, Resonance, God, Pornography, Therapy, Tarkowski, Politic, XTC, Money, [. . .]' (van Berkel and Bos 1999a: 10–11).

7. See van Berkel (2011).

8. See van Berkel and Bos (2002: 38–9). The *Midtown (NY) cross-section* diagram is illustrative of the approach: flow of passengers into Manhattan, flow of pas-sengers (subway), flow of goods into Manhattan, actual building horizon, build-ing height permitted by zoning. Cf. van Berkel and Bos (2002: 46–7).

9. 'Such is our inconsistency and impatience, which you could also say is an irre-pressible belief in the imagination. This is why the unlikely coupling of art and airports to us represents a new statement, a figment, an appeal to an imagination that is both public and private and that cannot be ignored'; see Birnbaum and Lynn (2002: 21) (in conversation with Ben van Berkel and Caroline Bos).

10. 'When the present is a dimension of the past the process relating the two is different from when the past is a dimension of the present. With the past as prior, processes of making pass and changing relations in the pure past come to complement the process of contraction in the living present. There is therefore an extraordinary richness and potential for experimentation and applications in Deleuze's philosophy of time' (Williams 2011: 14).

11. 'The organless body attracts the organs, appropriates them for itself, and makes them function in a regime other than the one imposed by the organism, in such a way that each organ is the whole body – all the more so, given that the organ functions for itself and includes the functions of all the others. The organs are thus "miraculously" born on the organless body, obeying a machinic regime that should not be confused either with organic mechanism or with the organization of the organism' (Deleuze 2006: 20).

12. 'Instinct perfected is a faculty of using and even of constructing organized instru-ments; intelligence perfected is the faculty of making and using unorganized instruments' (Bergson 1998: 140).

13. 'The new doesn't come from the future, it comes from the past. That's what potentiality is: a mating of old existing events patterning into tendencies, an unfolding of events' (Spuybroek 2008b: 164).

14. In Nietzsche's notion of the eternal return, all events communicate and no predi-cate is excluded in the event of events. This is a synthetic affirmative disjunction which spells death to the self, the world and God 'to the advantage of divergent series as such, overflowing now every exclusion, every conjunction, and every connection' (see Deleuze 1990: 176).

15. In Roman mythology, *Voluptas* or *Volupta* was the beautiful daughter born from the union of Cupid and Psyche. She is one of the Charites, or Three Graces, and is known as the goddess of 'sensual pleasures' whose Latin name means 'pleasure' or 'bliss'.

16. See Arie Graafland's introduction to *Architectural Bodies* (Graafland 1996: 8–9). See also the statement by Deleuze and Guattari (2006: 88): 'Our view presupposes only one economy [political *and* libidinal], and hence the problem [. . .] is to show how unconscious desire sexually invests the forms of this economy as a whole.'

17. 'If there is to be a "new urbanism" [. . .] it will no longer aim for stable configurations but for the creation of enabling fields that accommodate processes that refuse to be crystallized into definitive form; it will no longer be about meticulous definition, the imposition of limits, but about expanding notions, denying boundaries, not about separating any identifying entities, but about discovering unnamable hybrids; it will no longer be obsessed with the city but with the manipulation of infrastructure for endless intensifications and diversifications, shortcuts and redistributions – *the reinvention of psychological space*' (Koolhaas 1995: 961–9; emphasis added).

18. 'Deleuze and Guattari characterized the bachelor machine as a machine of consumption, a gratification that could be called auto-erotic [auto-affective]. This mechanical eroticism proclaims a new connection. A new power [Voluptas] is liberated' (Graafland 1996: 64).

19. It is also important to recognise that for Deleuze and Guattari, '[T]he lived state [comes] first, in relation to the subject that lives it' (Deleuze and Guattari 2008: 40).

20. Whereas the *socius* is used to indicate social organisation at the level of the social-libidinal mode of production in *Anti-Oedipus*, in *A Thousand Plateaus* it is further refined to indicate a set of analytic tools that include: strata, instruments of capture, war-machines and regimes of signs. For an account of the socius situated in a critique of Koolhaas, see Graafland (2000: Part One).

21. Peirce coined the term 'triadomany' for such an over-reliance on trichotomies; see Peirce (1994: CP 1.569 Cross-Ref: ††).

22. It may be said that what distinguishes these approaches – connective, disjunctive and conjunctive – is at once their strength and weakness in respect of each other. That is to say that they become more susceptible to potential co-option by the dominant regime and fetishisation: the first via the physical, the second via the semiotic and the third via the psychic.

23. The logic of relations is founded on this premise – the individual as power (*puissance*) – as well as on the independence of relation in relation to its terms; see Deleuze (1981).

24. 'Abstract machines are always at work upon stratified territories, constantly "setting things loose", but at the same time, that which is deterritorialised, the "new" which is invented from the diagram, is constantly being put back to work, productively employed and "enveloped" again by the strata that surround it. Hence there is in fact, contra Somol and Whiting, no absolute opposition between the indexical/territorial and the diagrammatic/abstract . . .' (Spencer 2009: 13; see also Kehne and Turko 2009).

25. While psychoanalysis settles on the imaginary and structural *representatives* of reterritorialisation, schizoanalysis follows the machinic *indices* of deterritorialisation; see Smith (2004: 635–50).

References

Abou-Rihan, F. (2011), *Deleuze and Guattari: A Psychoanalytic Itinerary*, London: Continuum.

Bergson, H. ([1907] 1998), *Creative Evolution*, New York: Dover Publications.

Betsky, A. (2002), 'Unfolding the Forms of Unstudio', in B. van Berkel and C. Bos, *UN Studio – Unfold*, ed. V. Patteeuw, Rotterdam: NAi Publishers, pp. 6–13.

Birnbaum, D. and G. Lynn (2002), 'In conversation with Ben van Berkel and Caroline Bos: "Digital Conversation"', in B. van Berkel and C. Bos, *UN Studio – Unfold*, ed. V. Patteeuw, Rotterdam: NAi Publishers, pp. 14–21.

Bogue, R. (2003), *Deleuze on Literature*, London: Routledge.

Deleuze, G. (1981), *Cours Vincennes:* 'Spinoza' (17 February 1981), <http://www.webdeleuze.com/php/texte.php?cle=38&groupe=Spinoza&langue=2> (accessed 20 June 2012).

Deleuze, G. ([1969] 1990), *The Logic of Sense*, New York: Columbia University Press.

Deleuze, G. ([1968] 1994), *Difference and Repetition*, New York: Columbia University Press.

Deleuze, G. ([1993] 1997), 'Spinoza and the Three "Ethics"', in *Essays Critical and Clinical*, Minneapolis, MN: University of Minnesota Press, pp. 138–51.

Deleuze, G. (2006), *Two Regimes of Madness: Texts and Interviews 1975–1995*, ed. D. Lapoujade, Los Angeles: Semiotext(e).

Deleuze, G. and F. Guattari ([1991] 1994), *What Is Philosophy?*, New York: Columbia University Press.

Deleuze, G. and F. Guattari ([1980] 2004), *A Thousand Plateaus*, New York: Continuum.

Deleuze, G. and F. Guattari ([1972] 2008), *Anti-Oedipus: Capitalism and Schizophrenia*, New York: Penguin.

Edelkoort, L. (2002), 'In Free fall', in B. van Berkel and C. Bos, *UN Studio – Unfold*, ed. V. Patteeuw, Rotterdam: NAi Publishers, pp. 96–7.

Graafland, A. (1996), *Architectural Bodies*, Rotterdam: 010 Publishers.

Graafland, A. (2000), *The Socius of Architecture: Amsterdam, Tokyo, New York*, Rotterdam: 010 Publishers.

Guattari, F. (1995), 'In Flux', in *Chaosophy/Félix Guattari*, ed. S. Lotringer, Los Angeles: Autonomedia/Semiotext(e), pp. 69–89.

Hays, K. M. (2010), *Architecture's Desire: Reading the Late Avant-garde*, Cambridge, MA: MIT Press.

Kehne, H., and J. Turko (eds) (2009), *Relational Skins: Chronicling the Works of Diploma Unit 12 at the AA School London*, Diploma 12, London.

Kipnis, J. (2005), 'Moneo's Anxiety', *Harvard Design Magazine: On Criticism*, pp. 97–104, available at <http://davidrifkind.org/fiu/library_files/14.%20On%20Criticism-23.pdf> (accessed 6 October 2012).

Koolhaas, R. (1978), *Delirious New York: A Retroactive Manifesto for Manhattan*, New York: Monacelli Press.

Koolhaas, R. (1995), *S, M, L, XL*, eds OMA with Bruce Mau, New York: Monacelli Press.

Koolhaas, R. (2000), 'Interview by Jennifer Sigler', *Index Magazine*, <http://www.indexmagazine.com/interviews/rem_koolhaas.shtml> (accessed 20 June 2012).

Lorraine, T. (2003), 'Living a Time Out of Joint', in P. Patton and J. Protevi (eds), *Between Deleuze and Derrida*, New York: Continuum, pp. 30–46.

Massumi, B. (1993), *A User's Guide to 'Capitalism and Schizophrenia': Deviations from Deleuze and Guattari*, Cambridge, MA: MIT Press.

Massumi, B. (2006), 'Transforming Digital Architecture from Virtual to Neuro: An Interview by Thomas Markussen and Thomas Birch', *intelligent agent*, 5: 2, <http://www.intelligentagent.com/archive/Vol5_No2_massumi_markussen+birch.htm> (accessed 20 June 2012).

Peirce, C. (1994), *Collected Papers of Charles Sanders Peirce: The Electronic Edition 1994*, reproducing Vols I–VI [1931–5], eds C. Hartshorne and P. Weiss, Cambridge, MA: Harvard University Press.

Protevi, J. (2010), 'Deleuze, Jonas, and Thompson: Toward a New Transcendental Aesthetic and a New Question of Panpsychism', Montreal: SPEP, <http://protevi.com/john/research.html> (accessed 20 June 2012).

Radman, A. (forthcoming), 'Architecture's Awaking from Correlationist Slumber: On Transdisciplinarity and Disciplinary Specificity', *Footprint*, 11.

Rancière, J. ([2000] 2004), *The Politics of Aesthetics: The Distribution of the Sensible*, trans. G. Rockhill, London: Continuum.

Smith, C. and A. Ballantyne (2010), 'Flow: Architecture, Object and Relation', *Architectural Research Quarterly*, 14: 1, 21–7.

Smith, D. W. (2004), 'The Inverse Side of the Structure: Žižek on Deleuze on Lacan', *Criticism*, 46: 4, 635–50.

Somol, R. (1999), 'Dummy Text, or The Diagrammatic Basis of Contemporary Architecture', in P. Eisenman, *Diagram Diaries*, New York: Universe Publishing, pp. 6–25.

Spencer, D. (2009), 'The Critical Matter of the Diagram', in H. Kehne and J. T. Spencer (eds), *Relational Skins*, London: Lulu, pp. 9–21.

Spuybroek, L. (1998), 'Motor Geometry', *Architectural Design*, 68: 5–6, 48–55.

Spuybroek, L. (2007), 'The Aesthetics of Variation' (an interview by Arjen Mulder), in J. Brouwer and A. Mulder (eds), *Interact or Die!*, Rotterdam: V2 Pub./NAi, pp. 132–51.

Spuybroek, L. (2008), *The Architecture of Continuity: Essays and Conversations*, Rotterdam: V2/NAI Publishers, pp. 12–31.

Spuybroek, L. (2011), *The Sympathy of Things: Ruskin and the Ecology of Design*, Rotterdam: V2 Pub./NAi.

van Berkel, B. (2011), 'The New Understanding', *Kenzo Tange Lecture at Harvard University, Graduate School of Design*, 3 March, <http://harvard.vo.llnwd.net/o18/gsd/03032011_Berkel.mp4> (accessed 20 June 2012).

van Berkel, B. and C. Bos (1994), 'Corporal Compactness', in K. Feireiss (ed.), *Ben van Berkel: Mobile Forces = Mobile Kräfte*, Berlin: Ernst & Sohn, pp. 176–81.

van Berkel, B. and C. Bos (1999a), *Move: (1) Imagination: Liquid Politic*, Amsterdam: UN Studio & Goose Press.

van Berkel, B. and C. Bos (1999b), *Move: (2) Techniques: Network Spin*, Amsterdam: UN Studio & Goose Press.

van Berkel, B. and C. Bos (2002), 'Deep Planning', in B. van Berkel and C. Bos, *UN Studio – Unfold*, ed. V. Patteeuw, Rotterdam: NAi Publishers, pp. 38–9.

van Dijk, H. (2005), 'Critical Project or the Project of Criticism?', in H. Bekkering, D. Hauptman et al. (eds), *The Architectural Annual 2003–2004*, Rotterdam: 010 Publishers, pp. 68–75.

Williams, J. (2000), 'Deleuze's Ontology and Creativity: Becoming in Architecture', *Pli*, 9, 200–19.

Williams, J. (2011), *Gilles Deleuze's Philosophy of Time: A Critical Introduction and Guide*, Edinburgh: Edinburgh University Press.

Wolfe, K. (2006), 'From Aesthetics to Politics: Rancière, Kant and Deleuze', *Contemporary Aesthetics*, 4, <http://www.contempaesthetics.org/newvolume/pages/article.php?articleID=382> (accessed 20 June 2012).

Chapter 3

Why Deleuze, Why Architecture

Marko Jobst

Deleuze's thought has been inscribed into the histories of architectural theory at least since the 1980s; its influence on contemporary architectural discourse is evident and has been enduring, though not always acknowledged. To discuss this I will critically interrogate several key publications, primarily Kate Nesbitt's *Theorizing a New Agenda for Architecture: An Anthology of Architectural Theory 1965–1995*, A. Krista Sykes' *Constructing a New Agenda: Architectural Theory 1993–2009*, and Harry Francis Mallgrave and David Goodman's *An Introduction to Architectural Theory 1968 to the Present*, published in 2011. I also address Jorge Otero-Pailos' *Architecture's Historical Turn: Phenomenology and the Rise of the Postmodern* in order to indicate a more specific set of questions on the position of phenomenology relative to Deleuze's philosophy within the field of architectural theory.

Locating Deleuze

In 1996 Nesbitt edited a book of architectural theory which aimed to cover the emergence of its contemporary form in the 1960s and the various subsequent developments. The volume was seminal for the format it employed and its aim to systematise architectural theory while placing it within a broader historical context. Gilles Deleuze's name appeared in two texts, and only the second would go beyond a mere mention, Peter Eisenman's 'Vision's Unfolding: Architecture in the Age of Electronic Media'. In the introduction to the text Nesbitt states that Eisenman borrowed the concept of the fold from Gilles Deleuze, 'a contemporary French film and cultural critic' (Nesbitt 1996: 555). Besides the vagueness of this qualification this entry is notable for the stress it placed on the digital realm that Eisenman's text concerned itself with. This wasn't the first time Deleuze was discussed in the context of the digital – Greg Lynn's highly visible *AD* Special Issue *Folding in Architecture* had appeared in 1993 – but it is indicative that digital architecture was the line along which Deleuze's name would enter a collection of this sort.

In 2010 Sykes edited what can be identified as a companion volume to Nesbitt's anthology, *Constructing a New Agenda: Architectural Theory 1993–2009*, which examined the succeeding period of architectural theory. By this point Deleuze's name appears in five texts (Lynn, Rajchman, Speaks, Martin, McMorrough), with at least another eight owing part of their conceptual scope, method and sometimes vocabulary to Deleuze (Kwinter, Allen, Somol and Whiting, Picon, Vidler, Hays, Chu, Reiser+Umemoto); most of these were associated with the early or middle reception of Deleuze into architecture, as Simone Brott demonstrates in 'Deleuze and the "Intercessors"' (Brott 2011: 15–36), the first chapter of her *Architectures for a Free Subjectivity*. But a different peculiarity emerges: despite the fact that his philosophy appears to have influenced, even infiltrated, at least half of the texts on offer, Deleuze is made all but invisible, both by Krista Sykes and K. Michael Hays, the author of the afterword.

In the introduction Sykes writes of a 'myriad tendencies' that had emerged since Nesbitt's collection, claiming that they were characterised by a 'lack of a single theoretical discourse during the period in question' (Sykes 2010: 12). Critical theory represented the dominant mode of inquiry in the period when theory itself was formulated in architecture, she claims, but the current moment is marked by the absence of an 'overarching concept' – since critical theory had entered a period of being 'in transition, if not in crisis' (ibid.: 15–16).

Sykes identifies a 'pro-practice' movement of the 1990s as the force behind this push away from critical theory. The 2000 event and subsequent exhibition at MoMA, 'Things in the Making: Contemporary Architecture and the Pragmatist Imagination', she posits as one of the key moments in the transformation toward projective, design-based research; but while she identifies the crucial role of the pragmatism delivered by John Rajchman, there is no mention of the role of Deleuze's philosophy in Rajchman's own writing. 'Despite its philosophical origins, pragmatism, with its various emphases on experimentation and experience, holds the promise of practical application, of action, of tangible product', Sykes writes (2010: 17). The implication is that architecture bears an irrefutable link to all things 'pragmatic', whatever the specific definitions of pragmatism – a valid point, but one missing the corollary that this is a discipline that should therefore be at the forefront of the feedback loop into any philosophy that concerns itself with the question of immanence, as Deleuze's does. Architecture is already given special status in Deleuze and Guattari's *What Is Philosophy?*, but the point they make still remains largely overlooked in architectural theory.

Along with other key events that mark the decline of critical theory, Sykes identifies the closure of publications such as *ANY* and *Assemblage*, followed by the appearance of new journals which placed architectural practice in 'more direct correspondence' with its discourses (2010: 20). The missing aspect of the assessment is once again the role the previous generation of publications had in disseminating Deleuze-influenced architectural writing, which is clear from Sanford Kwinter's interview with Simone Brott (Brott 2011: 25) in which he points out that even *Assemblage*, which despite its fortuitous name was initially anti-Deleuze, eventually became a vehicle for the dissemination of the philosopher's ideas.

Brott characterises this 1990s reinscription of Deleuze into architectural discourse (after the initial phase in the 1970s and 1980s) as one that largely evacuated the political aspect from Deleuze and Guattari's work by focusing on somewhat narrow readings of 'time, virtuality and movement' (Brott 2011: 7). Seemingly driven by the exhaustion of architectural theory, this turn away from it, about which Sykes also writes, appears to have been concurrent with the partial re-introduction of Deleuze to architecture. As is evident from Sykes's collection this would ultimately lead to the erasure of Deleuze's tracks and the reformulation of the question of pragmatism (to take but this one theme) as self-emergent within the architectural discourse. If this 'official' story is to be believed, the turn to pragmatism was primarily the result of the need of architectural practice to reassert its importance over theory; instead, I would argue that it was the outcome of theory's encounter with Deleuze's philosophy. Sykes concludes that:

> Theory can no longer occupy its previous role, and thus it too has started to shift – in some cases away from utopian ideals, the declarative rejection of the status quo, and heavy-handed cultural critiques toward . . . what? What is the architectural end game at this moment in time? There is no clear or easy answer; indeed, the texts collected here, dating from 1993 through the present day, situate themselves along different trajectories. Auspiciously, these paths all point forward. (2010: 27)

In fact, there aren't that many trajectories, if one looks at the influence of Deleuze on the overall 'theoretical' landscape presented by the collection. Sykes makes the options appear open-ended, but if they are so, it is in a distinctly Deleuzian sense of thinking the novel, the productive and the uncharted. The thinking behind a substantial number of texts in the collection owes its existence to Deleuze and Guattari one way or another; far from charting out an emergence of anti- or post-theory, the writing in fact shows the ambiguous position architectural theory currently holds vis-à-vis philosophy, and Deleuze's philosophy in particular.

The afterword written by K. Michael Hays is equally telling in terms of Deleuze's peculiar (non-)presence: Hays's vocabulary seems to be in tune with Deleuze's to a surprising degree, yet the latter's name doesn't merit a mention. Hays writes of architecture as an 'intimate blend of sensing, imaging, and conceptualizing' (Hays 2010: 472) and states that:

> Were an architectural ontology of the nineties and noughts possible, [. . .] it would have to be an ontology of the atmospheric – of the only vaguely defined, articulated, and indeed perceptible, which is nevertheless everywhere present in its effects. (2010: 473)

It is hard not to see this omnipresent yet 'vaguely perceptible' realm as a nod in the direction of the Deleuzian virtual, a question that would have been circled by both the first and the second generation of writers on Deleuze in architecture (Rajchman, Kwinter, then DeLanda and Lynn). However, Hays still links this 'new paradigm' to the digital technologies and 'computer programs that coordinate and synthesise multiple parameters and different sorts of data into smooth, frictionless flows' (2010: 473).

The 'sensing, imaging, and conceptualising' of which Hays writes, which in an earlier period of architectural theory might have merited the conceptual vocabulary of 'experience', 'representation' and 'theory', appears to bring the 'post-theoretical' discourse into tune with the vocabulary of sensation, immanent imaging and the creation of concepts which constitute the backbone of Deleuze and Guattari's work in *What Is Philosophy?*, without acknowledging the operation. The 'smooth, frictionless flows' can be traced back to the discussions surrounding the smooth and the striated, which Sanford Kwinter identifies as crucial for the first period of introduction of Deleuze to architectural theory (Brott 2011: 26) and which 'stimulated' the 1990s discourse once again, as Brott too suggests (2011: 26–7), while the question of flows itself resurfaces, for example, in 2012 with the clear Deleuzian tint given to *Architecture in the Space of Flows*, edited by Andrew Ballantyne and Chris L. Smith.

Hays continues in similar vein:

Writing the new architecture means writing with the body as much as the mind, apprehending the atmospheric and the ecological as feeling and affect as well as thought – folding and refolding the situation, thickening and articulating it into narrative structures, squeezing it to yield its social precipitate. The mode of writing we now have recourse to is not inscription (with its implication of certainty) but diagramming. (2010: 474)

Affect, fold, diagram – this is Deleuze utilised yet unnamed, even silenced. As will be discussed in the next section in more detail, Deleuze's book *The Fold: Leibniz and the Baroque* was closely associated with architecture from 1993 onwards, primarily through the work of Greg Lynn – a troubled connection itself, as Anthony Vidler indicates in *Warped Space* (2002: 219), Hélène Frichot reiterates in 'Stealing into Gilles Deleuze's Baroque House' (2005: 72–4) and Simone Brott confirms in *Architecture for a Free Subjectivity* (2011: 27). The concept of the diagram would have been championed by John Rajchman (see the already mentioned 'A New Pragmatism?' in Sykes for one) as well as Peter Eisenman in his *Diagram Diaries* in 1999 and has as such found its way into Mark Garcia's AD Reader *The Diagrams of Architecture*, where Garcia identifies Deleuze and Guattari as the key source for 'the definitions of the diagram in architectural and other spatial design theories', alongside Michel Foucault (Garcia 2010: 23); as for affect, in *Chaos, Territory, Art*, Elizabeth Grosz (2008) discusses sensation in relation to Deleuze and Guattari's *What Is Philosophy?*, a rare study committed solely to teasing out the ideas laid out in that text.

Regarding Hays's assertion that 'the new architecture means writing with the body as much as the mind', this should be seen as the presence of another unvoiced, underlying philosophical question – that of immanence, which might just turn out to be the single 'overarching concept' that Sykes is on the lookout for, but is unable to identify (Sykes 2010: 15).

How can a single philosophical presence seem so influential within the architectural discourse yet remain hidden from view at crucial junctures? Part of the answer lies doubtless with the exhaustion of a number of concepts developed by Deleuze and Guattari (associated primarily in architectural discourse with *A Thousand Plateaus*) that were imported into architecture – rhizome, territorialisation and deterritorialisation, the smooth and the striated, and so on – which have been markedly on the wane. While concepts like these might have had a crucial influence on the thinking of the first generation of architectural writers who came in contact with Deleuze's philosophy (see again Kwinter's account in Brott 2011: 8–10), without the broader philosophical context they showed themselves easy to render ineffective, and appropriate for the discourses that led to the supposed 'demise' of architectural theory. The construction of a 'philosophy of architecture' has as yet to offer a viable alternative in the aftermath of that apparent demise. As John Rajchman wrote in *Constructions*, even at the end of the nineteenth century the Swiss art critic Heinrich Wölfflin expressed 'astonishment' that there was as yet no such thing (Rajchman 1998: 78). Rajchman indicates that a philosophy of architecture is one of the most promising aspects of Deleuze's *oeuvre* where architecture is concerned: to create productive connections between architecture and philosophy, with the specifics of the discipline of architecture informing the creation of new philosophical concepts, which in turn could affect philosophy itself.

Deleuze famously proclaimed theory to be 'like a tool box' (Deleuze and Foucault 2004: 208) from which concepts can be picked according to need, but Gregg Lambert gives a telling qualification when he writes, in *Who's Afraid of Deleuze and Guattari?*, that this notion of a conceptual tool box 'led to many misunderstandings' due to the misappropriation of the concepts used (Lambert 2006: 6).

In other words, Deleuze's name might remain deliberately unspoken, in part as a gesture of the ultimate 'utilisation' of his work – after all, what could seem more in keeping with Deleuze, who wrote to Rajchman that he didn't like people who wrote about him (Brott 2011: 17) and suggested that a philosopher be given 'a child that would be his own offspring, yet monstrous' (Deleuze 1995: 6)? But I also want to argue that Deleuze's philosophy hasn't been utilised to its full potential, either in its promise regarding the understanding of architecture in the context of immanence, or in the way his and Guattari's conceptual palette has been used.

The Fold and the Digital

In the spring of 2011 Harry Francis Mallgrave and David Goodman offered the next instalment in this series of assessments of half a century of architectural theory, a history notable for its aim to relate theory to architectural practice and the new paradigm of design practice research every step of the way. Here we witness an attempt to map the importance of Deleuze's philosophy in architecture, in the section on the 1990s under the title 'From Derrida to Deleuze' – a move telling in that it names that other 'poststructuralist' philosopher whose ideas infiltrated the realm of architecture while simultaneously retaining their status as philosophy 'proper'. However, it is the approach to summarising Deleuze's influence that is of note here.

Mallgrave and Goodman write that the appearance of *The Fold: Leibniz and the Baroque* in 1993 in English translation was 'propitious in that it would provide a framework to build a post-deconstruction platform' (Mallgrave and Goodman 2011: 164). They summarise Deleuze's take on the Baroque as 'unconnected to any specific moment in history', literal when 'found in baroque clothing' and 'metaphysical when it mediates the exterior world of mass and matter with the interior world of the soul' (ibid.). As might have been expected, 'architects tended to focus their attention on the literal and physical folding – the idea of formal continuity' (ibid.). This assessment of the potential superficiality of appropriation of philosophical concepts in architecture seems just; however, the fact that *The Fold* did become one of the key texts for Deleuzian interpretations in architecture, while understandable considering it was one of Deleuze's few forays into architecture, offset the importance of his broader philosophical project.

The obvious reference point here is the work of Lynn, who is also responsible for the introduction of the other major theme Deleuze has been linked with in architecture since the early 1990s, the allegedly paradigm-shifting importance of the digital realm. While the aim was valiant – to 'allow architects to represent complex and "anexact" form rather than pure or "eidetic" form', and question architecture's assumed status as a 'totalizing and exact discipline' in the process – the emphasis remained squarely on the digital and its relation to form, however obliquely the latter might have been understood (Mallgrave and Goodman 2011: 164–5). As Mallgrave and Goodman point out, this also relied on a problematic underlying technological determinism, something that has, in various forms, recurred throughout the history of modernity in architecture (2011: 165).

Closely associated with this issue was the notion of parametric architecture. Here, once again, the Deleuzian angle was used to offer a way of addressing the unpredictable nature of outcomes driven by the parametrically governed design processes. The problematic implication is that architecture is understood to be unable to be in touch with the *not-as-yet-known* unless it does so via a complex computational process. In other words, the virtual in its Deleuzian sense is brought to overlap with the virtual of the digital realm.

In the European context, Mallgrave and Goodman continue, the appropriation of Deleuze took on a somewhat different route, manifesting itself in a series of projects that blurred the distinction between figure and ground:

> It is possible to trace this line of thinking back to Deleuze, as we can see in these projects a continuous surface that folds, like the Leibnizian conception of the universe, if not to infinity, then at least to the very limits of the site. Here, one presumes, the only thing stopping the inexorable spread of the building would be the cold logic of the property line. (2011: 171)

Here it is then, Deleuze's current place in architecture, both in terms of design practice and its various theories and histories, as identified by Mallgrave and Goodman: the philosopher of a dehistoricised baroque, responsible for inspiring architectural experiments in design through the building of formal and spatial continuities, and the key source for explaining invention within the digital realm. Most definitely a terrain no other philosopher could have helped with in the 1990s, considering the overwhelmingly 'textual' heritage of most of the architectural theory of the period following the influence of Derrida's philosophy of deconstruction, but the characterisation is a grave reduction of Deleuze's scope and an act of stunting the potential importance of his philosophy for architecture.

In this same period the landscape of architectural theory did not remain completely silent on the question of the potential reach of Deleuze's philosophy within the discourse. In 2005 Andrew Ballantyne published *Architecture Theory: A Reader in Philosophy and Culture*, which was followed by *Deleuze and Guattari for Architects* in 2007. However, by Ballantyne's own admission in the preface to the former:

> I have made use of ideas drawn from Deleuze and Guattari in trying to understand and explain what is going on, but I have not tried to present their ideas systematically. My use of their concepts is opportunist and pragmatic. Most of the time I have avoided the metaphysical aspect of their work, and have preferred their pragmatic side, which will give an impression of them being less finely nuanced than in fact they are. (Ballantyne 2005: ix)

For this very reason, Ballantyne's books, while filled with insight, failed to make a more extensive impact on the field of architectural theory. In a review of *Deleuze and Guattari for Architects* Robert Harbison openly claimed to be baffled by the concept of faciality, which Ballantyne had utilised (Harbison 2008). What Harbison and others in the non-Deleuzian architectural academe would have been missing was a more comprehensive explanation of the way signification is conceptualised in Deleuze and in his work with Guattari, or indeed that key aspect of his philosophy, which Miguel De Beistegui has proposed was the key principle orienting Deleuze's thought and his philosophical project: the question of immanence (De Beistegui 2010: 192–5).

Beyond Phenomenology

Zooming out of these histories of architectural theory and their implicit mappings of Deleuze's philosophy in the context of architecture, I will now look at a strand of thought that played a crucial role in the development of architectural theory itself after the Second World War in order to argue that the reintroduction of Deleuze into architectural discourse might need to take place primarily within the territory today still claimed by architectural phenomenology.

In *Architecture's Historical Turn*, Jorge Otero-Pailos identifies architectural phenomenology as 'one of the major unexamined intellectual sources of postmodern architectural thought' (2010: xii). He claims that phenomenology was initially responsible for the notion that 'meaning' in buildings was inextricable from their 'direct' physical experience (ibid.: xiii). This represented, Otero-Pailos writes, an emergence of a 'distinctly new theoretical kind of history by architects and for architects' (ibid.).

Otero-Pailos identifies three strands that helped phenomenology connect sensory experience to architectural history: the theme of experience, with its 'conviction that the senses were not historically determined', which would ultimately lead to the essentialisation of bodily experience; the theme of history which 'involved the modernist belief that historical buildings were expressions of a deeper structuring reality, which was thought to remain constant across time'; and the third theme, that of theory, which Otero-Pailos sees as an 'early instance of interdisciplinarity' (ibid.: xxxiii). Through these themes architectural phenomenology also hit its limit: the so-called second generation of architectural phenomenologists would accuse the first of 'mishandling the postmodern themes of history and theory and [. . .] essentializing both into a specious notion of universal human experience' (ibid.: xix).

As Otero-Pailos writes:

> Once this younger group displaced the earlier 'conservatives', they began instituting a 'nonfoundational' approach to phenomenology, which prepared the ground for the introduction of poststructuralist theory. More significantly, the emphasis on a nonfoundational architectural theory was code for the autonomy of theory from its traditional 'foundation' in practice. The architect-historian began to turn into the figure of the autonomous architectural theorist. (Ibid.: 259)

From the position of the current debates surrounding the supposed demise of architectural theory, Otero-Pailos's book offers insight into a potentially crucial historical moment. This 'autonomous architectural theorist' of the 1990s will ultimately be cast as a problematic figure and the link between architectural theory and practice re-examined once more. What Otero-Pailos clearly shows is that the role of the theorist grew out of a particular inability of architectural phenomenology to survive the tasks set before it – not least the question of the relation of various forms of experience to thought, as it would have been discussed within philosophy decades prior to this architectural reckoning (and in the various reassessments of phenomenology, including those by Deleuze).

Most importantly for this discussion, Otero-Pailos writes that 'although its centrality in architectural theory has been much diminished, architectural phenomenology continues to be the primary discursive mode for dealing with the questions of perception and affect' (ibid.: 261) – a fair assessment and one of some significance when discussing the positioning of Deleuze within the broader field of architectural thought and writing. These 'questions of perception and affect', and with them a specific understanding of experience in architecture, are still seen to be an area of thought 'naturally' associated with phenomenology, since whatever discussions of 'percept' and 'affect' might be happening in Deleuze studies in relation to architecture, they are still predominantly tied up with the digital realm.

Once this poststructuralist ushering in of autonomous theory took place phenomenology devolved even further, to the point that 'today, architectural phenomenology undergirds the sensualist neomodernist fantasy of an essential experiential origin to architecture' (2010: 262). If this question of 'experiential origin' is to be redefined, that is experience in architecture claimed from an angle that does not involve an 'essentialising' position, the relationship between experience and 'origins' might rise to the surface once again – and the germ of this is already present in Deleuze and Guattari's *What Is Philosophy?*

Deleuze and Guattari write that 'art begins not with flesh but with the house. That is why architecture is the first of the arts' (1994: 186). They go on to elaborate that architecture 'can be defined by the "frame", by an interlocking of differently oriented frames, which will be imposed on the other arts, from painting to the cinema' (1994: 186) and that these 'frames and their joints hold the compounds of sensations' (1994: 187).

Elizabeth Grosz expanded on this in 2008 in *Chaos, Territory, Art: Deleuze and the Framing of the Earth*, a project that focused on the importance of the way architecture is defined in *What Is Philosophy?*, as already mentioned. She wrote that: 'Art is, for Deleuze, the extension of the architectural imperative to organise the space of the earth' (Grosz 2008: 10) and that 'art, developed alongside of the territory-house and house-territory systems, is what establishes the emergence of pure sensory qualities' (2008: 10). There are two important repercussions to this: first, architecture is assigned special status with regard to how the arts should be understood; and second, the primacy of sensation is clearly established as key when defining architecture's disciplinary 'origins'.

'Architecture is the most elementary binding or containment of forces', Grosz writes with regard to Deleuze and Guattari's proposition in *What Is Philosophy?*, 'the conditions under which qualities can live their own life through the constitution of territory' (Grosz 2008: 16). The constitution of territory is itself 'the fabrication of the space in which sensations may emerge, from which a rhythm, a tone, coloring, weight, texture may be extracted and moved elsewhere, may function for its own sake, may resonate for the sake of intensity alone' (2008: 12). The emphasis on sensation in architectural theory, as seen in Otero-Pailos, is still commonly perceived to be the domain of architectural phenomenology, but Grosz's is a Deleuzian project, and hence based on a very clear critique of the phenomenological strand. Regarding the understanding of the body, for instance, Grosz writes:

> Sensations, affects, and intensities, while not readily identifiable, are clearly closely connected with forces, and particularly bodily forces, and their qualitative transformations. What differentiates them from experience, or from any phenomenological framework, is the fact that they link the lived or phenomenological body with cosmological forces, forces of the outside, that the body itself can never experience directly. (Grosz 2008: 3, note 2)

In *Architecture for a Free Subjectivity* Simone Brott elaborates on this question in some detail. For her project, one of reinscribing the question of subjectivity (the process of 'subjectivisation') into the architectural discourse, it is important to note that Deleuze criticises 'phenomenology [. . .] as still engaging a classical (Cartesian) notion of subject as individual or free agent, a form of subjectivity premised on the separation of the subject and the object of that subject's attention' (Brott 2011: 1). And when developing her own conceptual vocabulary revolving around architecture's 'impersonal effects', Brott's project becomes 'phenomenological insofar as they [impersonal effects] situate the architectural encounter as the locus of subjectivity' (2011: 45). In other words, phenomenology is in Brott's work identified as one of the key strands to address in architectural theory, and a failed project to overcome.

What is at stake here then is the reinscription of a more challenging conception of the subject into what both Otero-Pailos and Brott portray as the 'weak' phenomenological discourse, which retained its hold on architecture via an uncritical approach to the question of sensation. Equally, this is the opportunity to rescue Deleuze's philosophy from its post-1990s stress in architectural theory on the digital realm, which Brott associates with the 'neo-liberal architectural discussion surrounding Deleuze' she finds characteristic of the period (Brott 2011: 8). If we go back to *What Is Philosophy?*, at the root of this lies the question of percepts and affects, of 'blocs of sensation' that art and architecture 'preserve' (Deleuze and Guattari 1994: 164). 'By means of the material, the aim of art', and therefore architecture, if it is to be understood as the first of the arts, 'is to wrest the percept from perceptions of objects and the states of a perceiving subject, to wrest the affect from affections as the transition from one state to another: to extract a bloc of sensations, a pure being of sensations' (1994: 167).

If 'perception and affect' still belong to the vocabulary of phenomenology in architectural theory, as Otero-Pailos argues, and percept and affect are the key notions that Deleuze and Guattari associate with art and architecture, then this is where the Deleuzian project should re-examine its relation to architectural theory, with all its political and ethical implications in tow.

The First of the Arts

The primary focus here has been to indicate that the way Deleuze is currently being written into the histories of architectural theory is problematic: his philosophy is reduced to a handful of concepts and linked with a few very specific approaches to architectural design, with a strong emphasis on the digital realm still in place. While taking a few architectural theory surveys might seem like a reductive approach considering the wealth and variety of publications within the architectural discourse, it is nevertheless necessary, since such sources represent the first port of call for students of architecture, architectural practitioners unfamiliar with the wilder shores of architectural theory, or indeed anyone who comes from beyond the field of architecture. As such, it offers a set of discourse-defining milestones, which inadvertently steer the discussions surrounding Deleuze, and the uptake of his and Guattari's thought, within architecture.

It is therefore at the level of such broad discursive paths that I aim to suggest that the reinscription of Deleuze into architectural theory (in its third wave, the 2010s?) might need to cast itself broadly over the territory that is still associated – even among those whose interest in architectural theory is all but non-existent – with architectural phenomenology and its engagement in questions revolving around sensation.

In terms of the philosophical discourse, the schema laid out in *What Is Philosophy?*, which distinguishes the plane of art from those of science and philosophy, places architecture clearly on the side of art, yet doesn't seem to account for the aspects of the discipline that surpass art. In effect, this means that architecture as a discipline potentially unsettles the clarity of Deleuze and Guattari's tripartite division – they write that 'if art preserves it does not do so like industry, by adding a substance to make the thing last' (Deleuze and Guattari 1994: 163) which, in the case of architecture, is clearly complicated by its dual role as art *and* industry – and retains its 'primary' yet undeveloped role in the definition of the arts. This means, ultimately, that accounting for architecture from within Deleuze's philosophy might pose an interesting challenge to his thought, possibly one that proves crucial for furthering the understanding of the arts outlined in *What Is Philosophy?*, their interrelations, as well as their relations to philosophy and science.

The key point with regard to architectural discourse, however, would be that even if Deleuze is not written or spoken of, and his name erased from the discourse – which, after all, might be a more 'Deleuzian' project than any that insists on codifying his thought and chiselling it into the edifice of the academic canon – he will be fed back into the discourse via the writing in the arts, whether architecture's role be currently acknowledged in them or not. In this sense, it is illustrative that Stephen Zepke and Simon O'Sullivan write in the introduction to *Deleuze and Contemporary Art* that 'perhaps Contemporary art is a field of production [. . .] that ignores the line Deleuze and Guattari draw between concepts and sensations' (2010: 1), as well as that 'Deleuze and Guattari did nothing much more than mention contemporary artists in passing' (ibid.: 2). This makes the connection between Deleuze and Guattari's thought and contemporary art problematic from the outset, yet in equal measure full of promise. The very question of the insertion of art into everyday life, as the key aesthetic problem noted by Deleuze in *Difference and Repetition* (Zepke and O'Sullivan 2010: 4), poses a number of potentially contradictory answers, and one of the approaches Zepke and O'Sullivan indicate might be the return to the question of sensation or, as they put it, 'critical sensation' (ibid.: 4–5).

Such questioning of distinctions between concept and sensation from within the discourses of art indicates the potential for bringing under scrutiny the exact disciplinary distinctions outlined in *What Is Philosophy?*, a challenge that architectural discourse interested in Deleuze will have to take up due to the very definition of architecture given by Deleuze and Guattari, locating architecture so squarely with the arts. But also, if we pursue this line of inquiry regarding the insertion of art into life, it seems unlikely that architecture, in all its ubiquitous material presence, can ever be avoided by the 'other' arts – even if it is not their primary focus from the outset.

A survey of recent publications that tackle the question of the overlap between art and architecture – in their spatial, institutional, urban or indeed material manifestations, all of which form the facets of the discipline of architecture – shows that there is a steady interest precisely in the zone where art meets the everyday through the 'frame' of the built environment (see Rendell 2010, Whybrow 2010 or Foster 2011, to name but a few). But these studies don't make much use of Deleuze. Meanwhile, within the field of Deleuze studies, glimpses of architecture can be seen on the outskirts of discourses of art. This constant expansion of focus in the arts is inadvertently constructing architecture's Deleuzian discourse, yet indirectly, without bringing the discipline centre-stage or addressing head-on the many questions raised by architecture's existing theoretical discourses. The 'first of the arts' will simply have to contend with a more careful inquiry into sensation, and the question of immanence that underlies it, if it is to make use of Guattari and Deleuze – before their names can be made obsolete in architectural discourse.

References

Ballantyne, A. (2005), *Architecture Theory: A Reader in Philosophy and Culture*, London: Continuum.

Ballantyne, A. (2007), *Deleuze and Guattari for Architects*, London: Routledge.

Ballantyne, A. and C. L. Smith (eds) (2012), *Architecture in the Space of Flows*, London: Routledge.

Brott, S. (2011), *Architecture for a Free Subjectivity: Deleuze and Guattari at the Horizon of the Real*, London: Ashgate.

De Beistegui, M. (2010), *Immanence: Deleuze and Philosophy*, Edinburgh: Edinburgh University Press.

Deleuze, G. (1995), 'Letter to a Harsh Critic', in *Negotiations 1972–1990*, trans. M. Joughin, New York: Columbia University Press, pp. 3–12.

Deleuze, G. and F. Guattari (1994), *What Is Philosophy?*, trans. G. Burchell and H. Tomlinson, London: Verso.

Deleuze, G. and M. Foucault (2004), 'Intellectuals and Power', in *Desert Islands and Other Texts 1953–1974*, trans. M. Taormina, Los Angeles: Semiotext(e), pp. 206–213.

Eisenman, P. (1999), *Diagram Diaries*, New York: Universe.

Foster, H. (2011), *The Art-Architecture Complex*, London: Verso.

Frichot, H. (2005), 'Stealing into Gilles Deleuze's Baroque House', in I. Buchanan and G. Lambert (eds), *Deleuze and Space*, Edinburgh: Edinburgh University Press, pp. 61–79.

Garcia, M. (ed.) (2010), *The Diagrams of Architecture*, Chichester: Wiley AD Reader.

Grosz, E. (2008), *Chaos, Territory, Art: Deleuze and the Framing of the Earth*, New York: Columbia University Press.

Harbison, R. (2008), '*Deleuze and Guattari for Architects* Book Review', *Architects' Journal*, 227: 19 (15 May), 110–11.

Hays, K. M. (2010), 'Afterword', in A. K. Sykes (ed.), *Constructing a New Agenda: Architectural Theory 1993–2009*, New York: Princeton Architectural Press, pp. 472–5.

Lambert, G. (2006), *Who's Afraid of Deleuze and Guattari?*, London: Continuum.

Mallgrave, H. F. and D. Goodman (2011), *An Introduction to Architectural Theory 1968 to the Present*, London: Wiley-Blackwell.

Nesbitt, K. (ed.) (1996), *Theorizing a New Agenda for Architecture: An Anthology of Architectural Theory 1965–1995*, New York: Princeton Architectural Press.

Otero-Pailos, J. (2010), *Architecture's Historical Turn: Phenomenology and the Rise of the Postmodern*, Minneapolis, MN: University of Minnesota Press.

Rajchman, J. (1998), *Constructions*, Cambridge, MA: MIT Press.

Rendell, J. (2010), *Site-Writing: The Architecture of Art-Criticism*, London: I. B. Tauris.

Sykes, A. K. (ed.) (2010), *Constructing a New Agenda: Architectural Theory 1993–2009*, New York: Princeton Architectural Press.

Vidler, A. (2002), *Warped Space: Art, Architecture, and Anxiety in Modern Culture*, Cambridge, MA: MIT Press.

Whybrow, N. (2010), *Art and the City*, London: I. B. Tauris.

Zepke, S. and S. O'Sullivan (eds) (2010), *Deleuze and Contemporary Art*, Edinburgh: Edinburgh University Press.

PART II

CONSTRUCTING

Chapter 4

Deleuze and the Story of the Superfold

Hélène Frichot

The story of the superfold is one that can be told in the wake of the exhaustion of the material and conceptual procedure of folding as a technique used in architecture.[1] Below I will revisit aspects of a tale concerning the uptake of the compelling method of folding materials and concepts toward novel architectural ends, which emerged in the early 1990s of the last millennium. As with all stories this one owns a genealogy that precedes its acceptance and popularisation through the glossy pages of architectural journals, whose influence should not be underestimated. I want to begin with the end, which may also spell out the end of 'man', and introduce at once the thought-figure of the superfold. In Gilles Deleuze's appendix to *Foucault*, entitled 'On the Death of Man and Superman', the concept of the superfold is briefly presented in its relation to new configurations of life, labour and language, or biology, political economy and linguistics (Deleuze 1988a: 127), that is with how 'man' is a living being, a working individual, and a speaking subject (ibid.: 97). The superfold also displaces a former classical sense of the infinite as that which raises relations all the way to infinity, and in its place introduces an unlimited finitude wherein 'a finite number of components yields a practically unlimited diversity of combinations' (ibid.: 131; see also O'Sullivan, 2005: 104–6). Caught up amid these finite delimitations, which are unlimited in their combinations, 'man's' life, labour and language perpetuate through the modulations of what Deleuze has called societies of control (1995). This chapter examines the role of the superfold in relation to the 'constructions' of architectural design and discourse, with an emphasis on how to *follow the material* amidst 'ultrarapid forms of apparently free floating control' (Deleuze 1995: 178), and how far control can be creatively resisted.

To elaborate upon the concept of the superfold Deleuze gives examples such as the constructive foldings of genetic code, the potential of silicon in third-generation machines and the agrammatical contours of the sentences of modern literature (1988a: 131). The exemplary form of the superfold, or else the best known example according to Deleuze, is the double helix (ibid.: 132), by which he appears, at least in passing, to privilege what is at work in genetic coding. Deleuze concludes that the problem remains as to whether the advent of this new form, the superfold, will prove better or worse than what came before (ibid.). Through the finite, yet unlimited recombinations of the superfold, how will 'man' and his environments be altered? This temporal register of the advent of the superfold also signals the shift from disciplinary societies to societies of control (Deleuze 1995), which are 'continuous and unbounded' (ibid.: 181), and in which individuals become coded 'dividuals' whose material relations and freedom of movement in their given environment is modulated and whose self-improvement is a perpetual work in progress. An exemplary site where a small part of the story of the superfold might be told is alongside the fast-paced, ever-modulating, contemporary history of the emergence of the fold as an architectural design process, which inaugurates the 'digital turn' in architecture and, more recently, new forms of 'material computation' (Menges 2012). The superfold in architecture alerts us to how new techniques and technologies may well transform 'man' and his environments beyond recognition, as contemporary avant-garde architects claim that one day soon buildings will respond to life criteria by becoming something akin to building-organisms (Hensel et al. 2004, 2006, 2010; Hensel and Menges 2007). Furthermore, the superfold is a story told not of a past, but a story imagined for a future, a coming people, and new approaches to material and immaterial admixtures, new kinds of subjects and objects, even new hybrids of biological and machinic parts that are post-anthropomorphic in scope. The superfold anticipates a biotechnogenesis of the human condition, but we cannot yet know what this means or what kind of peoples and things and what kind of post-human landscapes will emerge. With this chapter I suggest that a projective history or a story of speculative post-human futures can be told by recourse to the superfold and the way it promises to capture the productive forces of architecture in relation to architecture's outside, an argument I will develop below in relation to the line of the Outside.

A Return to Folding

Despite the seeming exhaustion of folding in architectural practice and amidst the institutional, pedagogical context of countless architectural design studios, I will begin with a return to the fold. What is the fold, or what does *folding* entail? An emphasis needs to be placed immediately on processes of folding, and an understanding of the fold as one briefly identified formal moment along a continuum of continuous variation of folding. Perhaps it is best to commence from the detail of the fold and work outwards, for the thing about the fold is that when you look and feel more closely you see that an initial fold reveals further folds, and folds within folds, a veritable 'swarming' of folds (Deleuze 1993: 37). The undulations of the fold show how the texture of material aggregates varies depending on your point of view, close or distant, and depending on the distribution of the material at hand. On the one hand there are the folds in the soul that emerge out of the process of actualisation of the virtual, and on the other hand, there are the folding creases and pleats in matter, which realise what is possible. That is to say, the process of folding is animated by immaterial forces, as well as producing material effects; folding entails *material expressivity* as well as pertaining to concrete, *formed materiality* (DeLanda 2008: 164).

Following the material implications of folding, a number of examples can be presented. A sheet of paper, or even a handkerchief, can be used by way of an example, it can be folded and folded again, even crumpled in one's pocket, and through this process formerly distant points that have been marked across its field will be drawn into the neighbourhood of each other (Deleuze 1993: 37; Serres and Latour 1995: 60–1). The fold does not allow for the specification of ordinary points, but operates in the neighbourhood of points. It follows, on Deleuze's account, that the smallest element of matter is not given as an ordinary point, but as a fold, which can divide into smaller and smaller folds, as though all the way to infinity. Deleuze is also keen to stress that folding and unfolding do not constitute opposing actions, unfolding is not contrary to folding but 'follows the fold up to the following fold' (1993: 6). And yet, as matter is presumably exhausted through over-folding, we also see that this only apparently infinite potentiality is something more akin to an unlimited set of possibilities derived from a delimited or finite material. We come to realise that the fold, after all, does not unfold all the way to infinity, but instead operates rather like a superfold, whereby unlimited combinations of finite components are facilitated. This process can be organised through the logic of algorithms and their dynamical rational patterns, processes and functions, lending themselves to the combinatorial interactions that drive computation, as I will elaborate below (Chu 2004: 89).

The development of an embryo or egg (Deleuze 1993: 6) is a further example, one that allows us to see that the fold bears a relation not only to the arrangement of inorganic stuff, but to organic, biological matter. There is an affinity of matter with life, Deleuze insists, and it is important that the force of the fold relates to both the inorganic and the organic and how they fold in and through each other (ibid.: 7). Deleuze further explains that the relation between the organic and the inorganic pertains to the relationship between an organism and its environment: the inorganic is an exterior site that enters the organic body (ibid.: 9), which is at the same time undertaking its own action of folding and unfolding according to its genetic information. 'To explicate is to evolve, to involve is to implicate', the one unfolded is manifested in many, and the many infolded is expressed in the one (Deleuze 1992: 16). There is in a world, let's say an ecological niche, an action of exterior material surroundings, and a folding influence of interior organic forces so that the outside is drawn into the inside, achieving an invagination of the outside (Deleuze 1992: 8). The masses or the inorganic forces that lay out the organism's environmental niche facilitate its development as it folds and unfolds through involution and evolution (ibid.: 10). Thus folding, and superfolding too, suggest ways to approach ecological concerns.

What forms and environments have architects composed on encountering the forces aroused through folding? As architects well know, the fold can be applied to both planar, thin surfaces, such as card or paper, and thick surfaces, such as dough, and blob-like, seemingly amorphous forms, like the fits and starts of the developing embryo (see Lynn 2000). Much like the brief set of examples I have offered above, architects move from a planar, paper or handkerchief treatment of folding, through to organic or biomimetic folds, via an increased immersion in digital techniques and technologies and a turn toward a new biotechnological agenda in architecture (Hensel et al. 2004, 2006, 2010). It is through this development that the fold shifts in its relation to the infinite and produces instead practically unlimited combinations; specifically, *superfolding* can be pursued 'practically' indefinitely in order to continue producing new forms.

Diagramming the Fold 1: The Baroque House and Classical Thought

I will present two crucial diagrams used by Deleuze to discuss this central concept of folding and how a future of superfolding is in the midst of tentatively emerging. The first diagram is included in Deleuze's

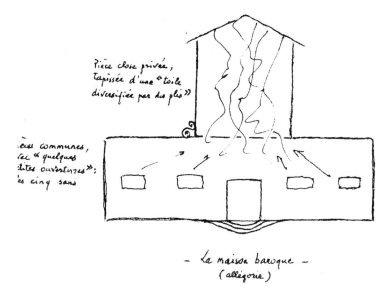

Figure 4.1 Baroque House: analogy. From Deleuze, G. (1988). Le Pli: Leibniz et le Baroque. Paris: Les Éditions des Minuit. Reproduced with permission from Les Éditions des Minuit, Paris.

The Fold: Leibniz and the Baroque, and conceptually arranges what the philosopher calls an analogy of a Baroque House, revealing that folding is not such a contemporary phenomenon after all, as its genealogy can be traced back to the baroque period, if not earlier (see Figure 4.1). The second diagram is included in Deleuze's book *Foucault,* where he discusses the folds of subjectivation in relation to a seemingly ungraspable 'outside' (see Figure 4.2 later). Both diagrams tell us something of the relation between different orders of infinity, including finitude, as well as the crucial interplay between material and immaterial forces.

As Deleuze explains with respect to the baroque period and its material instantiations, including clothing, sculpture and architecture, the fold of classical thought unfurls all the way to infinity. The Baroque House presents two orders of infinity which subsequently multiply. On the lower floor are the folds or pleats of sensory matter, and on the upper floor the conceptual folds in the soul. The two floors communicate through a third fold, in between floors, which like a tympanum or ear-drum transfers vibrations between these chambers or apartments. The expression of ideas (upper floor) and the material and sensory impressions of mixtures of bodies (lower floor) rise up and plunge down, as can be seen from the falling draped lines and upward shooting arrows that Deleuze has drawn. There is much toing and froing between floors, and it cannot be said where one begins and the other ends: it is a complicated interleaving of the sensible and the intelligible (Deleuze 1993: 128). Deleuze then deliberates on further orders of infinity, all of which pertain to classical thought. Seventeenth-century texts, he explains, are concerned with distinctions between different orders of infinity: 'the infinity of grandeur and the infinity of smallness in Pascal; the infinite in itself; the infinite in its cause and the infinite between limits of Spinoza; all the infinities in Leibniz, and so on' (Deleuze 1988a: 125; 1993: 57). Between these orders of infinity 'a whole play of passages and transformations of principles' (1993: 58) ensues, which is to say one and the same world also offers an infinite variety of differences.

An intuition of the infinite and the raft of problems that infinite magnitudes pose has fascinated philosophy at least since the ancients – consider Zeno's paradox. Deleuze explains that already with the Greeks the geometrical problem of how to determine curves and curvilinear surfaces had 'led them to invent a special method called the method by exhaustion [which] allowed them to determine curves and curvilinear surfaces in so far as it gave equations of variable degrees, to the infinite limit' (Deleuze 1980). It was through the invention of the calculus, and infinitesimal calculus, independently of but soon after Isaac Newton, that Leibniz hoped to create a plan for a universal symbolism, which would account for thought and replace controversy with calculation and a systematic form. As Karl Chu argues, Leibniz's *Monadology* sought to describe a system of principles to generalise the nature of the world from an abstract point of view, and his work proved fundamental to a future history of the development of computation, for each of Leibniz's monads can be figured as a *bit* of information (Chu 2004: 87). Chu further stresses that Leibniz's work can also be seen to contribute to 'an architectural theory of world making' (ibid.: 87).

Where classical thought continuously loses itself in infinity, the nineteenth century witnesses the emergence of the forces of finitude, which brings man to the realisation of his own finitude, and through this the 'man-form' is composed as distinct from the 'God-form' which had prevailed before. Constituting a thickness and a hollow 'the forces within man fall or fold back on this new dimension of in-depth finitude, which then becomes the finitude of man himself' (Deleuze 1988a: 128). As Foucault famously argues in *The Order of Things*, man is a 'recent invention', a brief rift in the order of things, and he will disappear as soon as a new form of knowledge and power emerges (1970: xxiii). Where the unfold, a force of unfurling, designates classical thought raised all

the way to infinity, the nineteenth century grapples with forces of finitude, or the fold, and how things are ordered and life develops along
ever bifurcating passages of transformation and upon an 'evolutionism'
based on the impossibility of convergence (Deleuze 1988a: 129). With
the speculative, precarious emergence of the superfold conceived as a
formation of the future, 'biology takes a leaps into molecular biology
. . . and the genetic code'; modern literature, exemplified by Mallarmé,
Artaud, Roussel and Burroughs, enters into atypical forms of expression
that mark the limits of language as such (ibid.: 131); and labour grapples
with the exhaustion of its materials. Silicon supersedes carbon, genetic
components supersede the organism, agrammaticalities supersede the
signifier. Another way of instantiating this last shift concerning language
is in the recognition of the shift to a politics of affect, wherein today's
language is no longer necessarily directed toward meaning, but toward
channelling the subtle shifting of emotional registers, often with political
ends (Thrift 2008; Massumi 2002; Gregg and Seigworth 2010). It is a
developed sense of the infinite that Deleuze describes when he presents
the superfold, that is an infinite redefined as unlimited combinations of
finite materials (Deleuze 1988a: 131). The unfurling of the baroque fold
all the way to infinity shifts to become the unlimited combinations of
the superfold. The question that follows is, how can we continue to fold
that which is finite, and follow the limited material resources we have
available to us?

Diagramming the Fold 2: The Superfold and Posthuman Thinking

This brings us to Foucault's diagram, the diagram of the fold (see
Figure 4.2), or, as I have previously analysed it, one discrete section of
the superfold (see Deleuze 1988a: 120; also Frichot 2009, 2011). Here
it would appear that the upper story of Deleuze's Baroque House has
evaporated into the unthinkable, unrepresentable realm of the Outside,
which nevertheless animates all thinking and doing as well as the possibility of resistance to oppressive power formations (Blanchot 1993:
45–8; Deleuze 1988a: 90). Where the Baroque House diagrams the
dynamics of classical thought, the section-like diagram of the superfold
maps a thinking yet to come that emerges out of disciplinary societies
and their increased organisation via the flows and cul-de-sacs of information into societies of control. Between the Baroque House and the
superfold a shift occurs so that 'either it is the fold of the infinite, or
the constant folds of finitude which curve the outside and constitute the

inside' (Deleuze 1988a: 97). What I am calling the superfold diagram annotates the animated, peristaltic movements of the line of the Outside. It is crucial to stress that the line of the Outside is not a fixed limit but 'a moving matter animated by peristaltic movements, folds and foldings that together make up an inside: they are not something other than the outside, but precisely the inside of the outside' (ibid.: 97). Importantly, the line of the Outside manifests as a manifold of multifarious folds (see also Frichot 2009, 2011). Beneath this line there is sheltered a strategic zone, where power relations are distributed, and beneath that again the strata or collected archives of knowledge, where habit, opinion and cliché come to be sedimented and the common knowledge of 'man' accumulated. Over time the strategic zone accumulates as strata, and as they settle into place they 'have the task of continually producing levels that force something new to be seen or said' (Deleuze 1988a: 120). Plunging through these layers is the fold, or rather plural folds of subjectivation, with their privileged access to the Outside, which has now hollowed out countless, sheltered interiors. And so we move from the classical thought of the Baroque House, which unfolds all the way to infinity, to the diagram of the superfold and its unlimited combinations of finitude and manifold folds of subjectivation.

The Digital Turn and Its Manifolds

The architectural approach to the fold is popularised in the 1993 edition of the journal *AD* (*Architectural Design*), edited by Greg Lynn and called *Folding in Architecture*. The backstory of the superfold proceeds from the mechanical applications of the fold through schematic sketches and diagrams, and results in forcing the fold as a formal model or mould onto what is conceived to be *inanimate* material. This could be called the hylomorphic model, that is 'a form that organises matter, and a matter prepared for the form' (Deleuze and Guattari 1987: 369; see also Simondon 1992: 299 and Thomas 2007: 4). A form, for instance, the fold, is impressed upon what is assumed to be a mute, receptive material, which then results in some substantial built artefact. Even though there is a celebration of a rediscovered curvilinearity, a viscosity and fluidity of form, and a pliability that supposedly responds to contingent circumstances and landscapes, the experiments remain limited to a literal foldedness. Many of the early aesthetic results are somewhat reified versions of the fold; folding procedures forcibly inflicted on conventional materials and contexts, which sometimes only obscured the pliable materiality, the infinitely porous, peristaltic movements, whorls

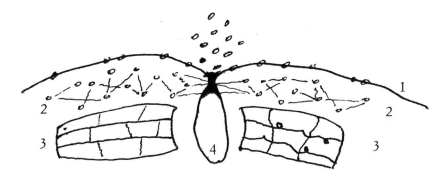

1. Ligne du dehors   2. Zone stratégique   3. Strates   4. Pli (zone de subjectivation)

DIAGRAMME DE FOUCAULT

Figure 4.2 Foucault's diagram (the superfold). From Deleuze, G. (1988), Foucault, trans. S. Hand, Minneapolis, MN: University of Minnesota Press. Reproduced with permission from Les Éditions des Minuit, Paris.

and maelstroms, and worlds within worlds, offered up by this concept. As the design process of 'folding' developed and became more nuanced it seemed somehow inevitable that its aesthetic qualities would continue to rely on smooth, continuous curvilinearity.

With the republication of *Folding in Architecture*, in 2004, Lynn's emphasis shifts, and he argues that, less than the will to curvilinearity and its suggestion of organic form and process, it is the calculus and its implementation by architects that fascinated him in Deleuze's *The Fold*. Quite simply, 'You need differential calculus when you find yourself faced with the task of determining curves and curvilinear surfaces', says Deleuze (1980). Lynn remarks that the work of the practices collected in the first edition of *Folding in Architecture* is work undertaken 'at the instant before they would become completely transformed by the computer'(Lynn 2004: 10). They are perched at a moment of inflection in their fold of thinking-doing architecture, as though at the crest of a wave, before they plunge head first into the realm of the superfold. In 1993 the focus had been on 'compositional, organisational, visual and material sensibilities', and yet, Lynn suggests, the architectural works effectively pre-empted what would emerge over the following ten years and beyond. Not only is CAD (computer-aided design) commonplace in the office, but a further paradigm shift has occurred which means that architects not only use computer programs to represent their schemes, they use computation to generate architectural projects and find novel form, and their techniques are supported by what Lynn has called a calculus-based medium. Architects, rather than mechanically applying the fold by inflicting a form imagined a priori onto a mute material, begin to recognise ways in which they can follow the fold conceived as a material force, and in this, through computation, they begin to privilege the models that biology, as a logic of life, uses in its attempts to understand how life develops. To achieve this requires an investment in the algorithmic codes that underlie computer software, and these algorithms are themselves often derived from the algorithms biology as a discipline deploys to model life and living systems, at the scale of genes, organisms, species and even ecological niches (Chu 2004).

Meanwhile time has passed, and the digital turn, as Mario Carpo describes it (2011), has developed and its tropes have become more easily identifiable. Carpo tells the story in the reverse direction in his recent introduction to Bernard Cache's book, *Projectiles*. He explains how Deleuze's *The Fold*, which relied on a crucial conceptual exchange between Deleuze and his student Cache – specifically, between Deleuze's interest in the history of the calculus and Cache's expertise as an architect with a background in mathematics – laid the conceptual ground for much of what would develop in the domain of 'digital architecture' for the next twenty years. This theoretical influence would have gone unnoticed, according to Carpo, if it were not for Peter Eisenman, who in turn introduced the writings of Deleuze to his student Greg Lynn (Carpo 2011: 6–8). At the same time, as Karen Burns has demonstrated, other minor histories risk becoming occluded, such as the feminist story of the influence of Luce Irigaray's work on Lynn (Burns this volume). A thought for a possible future: what might be the implications of a new woman-form? Is a woman-form and altered forms of practice possible to imagine across the plane of composition that is architecture? I cannot follow this line of argument here, but will save it as a promise to future work.

The Precarious Emergence of a New People and a New Earth

By addressing the projective thought-image of the superfold, which Deleuze constructs as a complement to such figures as Friedrich Nietzsche's *Übermensch* (simply, if comically, translated as 'superman'), the superfold is not merely aesthetic, but political, calling forth what Deleuze and Guattari have described as a people yet to come and a new earth. And to mix one oft-cited conceptual refrain from the Deleuzian lexicon with another: we do not yet know what a new people and their new earth can do. From the Dutch philosopher Spinoza, Deleuze identifies the ever-varying power of our mode of being to affect and be affected, to enjoy joyful affects and then sad passions, and how this open-ended affective register suggests we do not yet know what a body can do. This oft-repeated formula can be neatly coupled with the quasi-utopian call Deleuze and Guattari make when they speculate on a future form, a new earth and a people who do not yet exist (Deleuze and Guattari 1994: 108, 218), a people that presumably supersedes the so-called man-form with a becoming-imperceptible, a becoming-woman, a becoming-other, even an anticipation of hybrid, post-anthropic forms. Or else, a future form that risks returning to an altered God-form, whereby man presumes to supersede the powers he once attributed to God. We risk a refold into older sovereign forms, as 'it may be that older means of control, borrowed from old sovereign societies, will come back into play, adapted as necessary' (Deleuze 1995: 182).

In his 2004 essay 'Metaphysics of Genetic Architecture and Computation', Karl Chu incants the 'Promethean rumblings' of the convergence of computation and biogenetics, which I argue has already been suggested in Deleuze's discussion of the superfold and its unlimited finitude. Chu likewise draws attention to how 'man' is taking into 'his' possession what was once presumed to belong to the power of god, and that is the ability to create new forms of life (Chu 2004: 76). Today an investment in the logic of the living is being made by avatars of computation adept at scripting, such as *R&Sie*, *Biothing*, *Terraswarm* and Karl Chu's studio *Metaxy*. These representatives of the proliferating phenomenon of collective design intelligence (Speaks 2002; Hight and Perry 2006) weave evolutionary algorithms into webs of affect and percept without apparent scale or purpose, but with an increasingly recognisable aesthetic or 'feel', which calls on an aesthetics of the infinitesimal (or at least an intimation of infinite variations of form), while being arranged through finite combinatorials. This means a more exacting involvement on the part of the architect in programming and algorithmic and parametric processes, so as to escape the constraints of the meta-level of design held by some invisible programmer who has predetermined the parameters of off-the-shelf modelling and animation software. Through an intimate and doubled articulation, digital experimental architects are not just investing in the arrangement of bits of information toward novel formal ends, but they are also concerned with how a body, or let us say some material aggregate or mass, emerges out of delimited algorithm-based rules. They are engaged in how to follow the materials of language, labour and life toward novel forms. If 'true novelty' lies not only in the generalisation of design systems but also in 'materials and beyond them nature as an engineered reality' (Picon 2004: 120), and if materiality is intrinsically linked to how we experience the world as distinct and at the same time as connected to us, then digital technologies promise to transform our definitions of materiality with an emphasis on the production of sensory affects (Picon 2010: 12). Picon also reminds us that we increasingly conceive of matter in terms of information: 'bio-technological creations are ultimately DNA manipulations analogous to coding and decoding practices' (2010: 143). Material computation (see Menges 2012) not only manages the innovative interface between computer code and material output, by way of CNC milling, 3D printing and so forth, but also promises a future in which semi-living materials can be managed. For digital architects the exhortation is to follow material flows, including semi-living ones, and to invent new means to capture language (or code), labour (our modes of practice) and life (our capacity to affect and be affected). There are risks here, in that a delimited understanding of what counts as architectural material may remain restricted by the autonomous concerns that isolate architecture within the sheltered fold of its own internal, disciplinary logic. Architecture's capture of life may overwhelm its ability to pursue a practical ethics and a future history of life will, in turn, capture architecture and engulf it in its folds. Where digital architecture remains in an autonomous field concerned with its own internal logic and recurring rhetorical and formal tropes, the material is perhaps not followed far enough toward an understanding of the politics of affect.

Following Material Foldings

Manuel DeLanda and Brian Massumi, both commentators on Deleuze, are oft-cited sources concerning discussions of new materialities in architecture (Thomas 2007: 07). Rather than focus on the emergent qualities of materials or material behaviour that is 'far from equilibrium' (see Kwinter 2008) and thus apt to transform in unexpected ways (great points of fascination for digital architects), a more useful approach in this context is the use DeLanda makes of Deleuze and Guattari's 'double articulation' between material expressivity (code) and formed materiality (territorialisation) (DeLanda 2008: 164), where he also attempts to rescue the role of materiality from the 'linguistic turn' and its emphasis on discursive formations and textuality. Beyond this parallel and co-productive relation between statements and visibilities, the discursive and the non-discursive, material expressivity and formed materiality, there is also the ethical question of how we *follow the material* (see Deleuze and Guattari 1987: 373). As well as discussing how we should follow the material by allowing it to have a say in the structures we create (DeLanda 2004: 21), DeLanda draws attention to the political aspect of new materialism. He reframes the material relations and scales of operation of individuals, institutions and nation states, so suggesting ways to return to the problems of concrete social entities and their capacities to affect and be affected (DeLanda 2008: 167). If we turn to the recent work of Jane Bennett and the influences she absorbs from both ANT (Actor Network Theory) and Deleuze and Guattari, especially their assemblage theory, another notion of new materials emerges. Bennett is concerned with what she calls 'vibrant matter' and the lively role it plays amid a political ecology of things, to which we could add the products of architecture. Her expanded definition of matter insists 'I am a material configuration, the pigeons in the park are material compositions, the viruses, parasites, and heavy metals in my flesh and in pigeon flesh are materialities, as are neurochemicals, hurricane winds, E. coli, and the dust on the floor' (Bennett 2010a: 112; see also Bennett 2010b), and while we can forensically separate out, analyse and consider abstract definitions of each material, in the end they remain inseparable as their mobile relations determine their very constituency amid atmospheres of affect.

The superfold inaugurates a posthuman future, which is not to say that the human species is entirely dispensed with. The diagram of the superfold understood as an arrangement of relations of power 'stems from the outside but the outside does not merge with any diagram, and continues instead to "draw" new ones' (Deleuze 1988a: 89). In this way the Outside is always an opening onto a future and 'we must take quite literally the idea that man is a face drawn in the sand between two tides: he is a composition appearing only between two others, a classical past that never knew him and a future that will no longer know him' (ibid.). Two directions that Deleuze posits for this new diagram of the superfold are towards genetics and computation. If we conjoin these two experimental tendencies what we have is a new biotechnological paradigm, signs of which are becoming increasingly evident in architecture today as it moves toward novel combinations of material expressivity and formed materiality. The combinatorial is the 'art or science of exhausting the possible' (Deleuze 1998: 153) and its logic proceeds at the expense of physiological exhaustion and the wearing out of human and non-human materials and relations. The double articulation of material expressivity (language, or else code in all manner of combinations) and formed materiality (including human and non-human labour and material resources and their associated territories) extends beyond the materials that architecture generally busies itself with. Timber, concrete, steel and a panoply of materials that promise to combine organic and inorganic stuff in surprising ways toward potentially semi-living architectures do not reside in closed-off laboratories of digital thinking and experimentation, but seep out into possible worlds and across mental, social and environmental ecologies at all scales (Guattari 2000), and at all levels of interconnectivity, impacting upon atmospheres of affect in positive and negative ways. In his *Postscript on Societies of Control* (1995), Deleuze warns of the ways in which the informatics of our daily lives will facilitate our material and conceptual freedom of movement from one fold of our capsularised existences to another (De Cauter 2004), right up until the moment we discover the way is inexplicably barred to us and our pass key has expired. We exit the family unit so as to enter school, which in time we exit so as to enter the next zone of segmentarity, whether that be the army, the factory, the office: 'all kinds of clearly defined segments' (Deleuze and Parnet 1987: 124). As we shift from the segmentary, modular organisation of disciplinary societies into control societies, our human matter must also be apprehended as so much material to be biopolitically managed, as well as the ways we express ourselves through this matter and the practices we employ to get by, get a better job, make a break, discover a line of escape.

Existence is a physical or chemical test that allows us to analyse our precarious compositions (Deleuze 1988b: 40–1). To follow the material as an ethical gesture in the field of architecture is to recognise the economies, the labour, the handling and shaping, the wearing down and final disposal of all those goods and services we comfortably enfold ourselves in (Thomas 2007: 2). Katie Lloyd Thomas speaks of a need to open up architecture to questions that progress beyond the autonomous concern of form and new material research, and into questions about how we practise and the social and political implications of our modes of practice. In conclusion, I offer again a brief definition of the superfold conceived as unlimited finitude, wherein 'a finite number of components yields a practically unlimited diversity of combinations' (Deleuze 1988a: 131). Practically unlimited, importantly, is not the same as infinite, and does not unfurl all the way to infinity. Unlimited, through repetition and exhaustive recombination, leads us eventually to the exhaustion of the (hu)man-form and materials, our expressive modes of subjectivation and our non-renewable resources.

Notes

I want to thank Deborah Hauptmann, Andrej Radman and my colleague Oliver Tessman, KTH Architecture, all of whom kindly took time to read and offer comments on drafts of this chapter. Thanks to Dr Tessman for alerting me to the recent edition of *AD: Material Computation*, and to Lee Stickells and Michael Tawa who helped me source French copies of the figures used here.

1. As stressed in our introduction to this volume, exhaustion can also be considered a methodology, which is developed in detail in Deleuze's essay on Samuel Beckett, *The Exhausted*, found at the closure of *Essays Critical and Clinical* (1998: 152–74).

References

Bennett, J. (2010a), *Vibrant Matter: A Political Ecology of Things*, Durham, NC: Duke University Press.

Bennett, J. (2010b), 'A Vitalist Stopover on the Way to a New Materialism', in D. Coole and S. Frost (eds), *New Materialisms: Ontology, Agency, and Politics*, Durham, NC: Duke University Press.

Blanchot, M. (1993), *The Infinite Conversation*, Minneapolis, MN: University of Minnesota Press.

Carpo, M. (2011), 'Introduction', in B. Cache, *Projectiles*, London: AA Publications.

Chu, K. (2004), 'Metaphysics of Genetic Architecture and Computation', *Perspecta: The Yale Journal of Architecture*, 35.

De Cauter, L. (2004), *The Capsular Civilization: On the City in the Age of Fear*, Rotterdam: NAi Publishers.

DeLanda, M. (2004), 'Material Complexity', in N. Leach, D. Turnbull and C. Williams (eds), *Digital Tectonics*, London: Wiley Academy.

DeLanda, M. (2005), *Intensive Science and Virtual Philosophy*, New York: Continuum.

DeLanda, M. (2008), 'Deleuze, Materialism and Politics', in I. Buchanan and N. Thoburn (eds), *Deleuze and Politics*, Edinburgh: Edinburgh University Press.

Deleuze, G. (1980), *Le Cours de Gilles Deleuze: Leibniz Seminar*, 24 September, <http://www.webdeleuze.com> (accessed 25 November 2009).

Deleuze, G. (1988a), *Foucault*, trans. S. Hand, Minneapolis, MN: University of Minnesota Press.

Deleuze, G. (1988b), *Spinoza: Practical Philosophy*, trans. R. Hurley, San Francisco: City Lights.

Deleuze, G. (1992), *Expressionism in Philosophy: Spinoza*, trans. M. Joughin, New York: Zone Books.

Deleuze, G. (1993), *The Fold: Leibniz and the Baroque*, trans. T. Conley, Minneapolis, MN: University of Minnesota Press.

Deleuze, G. (1995), 'Postscript on Societies of Control', in *Negotiations*, trans. M. Joughin, New York: Columbia University Press, pp. 177–82.

Deleuze, G. (1998), *Essays Critical and Clinical*, trans. D. W. Smith and M. A. Greco, London: Verso.

Deleuze, G. (2001), *Pure Immanence: Essays on a Life*, trans. A. Boyman, New York: Zone Books.

Deleuze, G. (2003), *Francis Bacon: The Logic of Sensation*, trans. D. W. Smith, Minneapolis, MN: University of Minnesota Press.

Deleuze, G. and F. Guattari (1987), *A Thousand Plateaus*, trans. B. Massumi, Minneapolis, MN: University of Minnesota Press.

Deleuze, G. and F. Guattari (1994), *What Is Philosophy?*, trans. G. Burchell and H. Tomlinson, London: Verso.

Deleuze, G. and C. Parnet (1987), *Negotiations*, trans. H. Tomlinson and B. Habberjam, New York: Columbia University Press.

Duffy, S. (2006), 'The Differential Point of View of the Infinitesimal Calculus in Spinoza, Leibniz, and Deleuze', *Journal of the British Society of Phenomenology*, 37: 3, 286–307.

Duffy, S. (ed.) (2006), *Virtual Mathematics: The Logic of Difference*, Bolton: Clinamen Press.

Foucault, M. (1970), *The Order of Things: An Archaeology of the Human Sciences*, English trans. London: Tavistock.

Frichot, H. (2005), 'Stealing into Deleuze's Baroque House', in I. Buchanan and G. Lambert (eds), *Deleuze and Space*, Edinburgh: University of Edinburgh Press.

Frichot, H. (2009), 'On Finding Oneself Spinozist: Refuge, Beatitude and the Any-Space-Whatever', in C. J. Stivale, E. W. Holland and D. W. Smith (eds), *Gilles Deleuze: Image and Text*, New York: Continuum Press, pp. 247–64.

Frichot, H. (2011), 'Drawing, Thinking, Doing: From Diagram Work to the Superfold', *ACCESS*, 30, 1–10.

Gregg, M. and G. Seigworth (eds) (2010), *The Affect Theory Reader*, Durham, NC: Duke University Press.

Guattari, F. (2000), *The Three Ecologies*, trans. I. Pindar and P. Sutton, London: Athlone Press.

Hensel, M. and A. Menges (eds) (2007), *Morpho-Ecologies: Toward Heterogeneous Space in Architecture Design*, London: AA Publications.

Hensel, M., A. Menges and M. Weinstock (eds) (2004), *AD: Emergence: Morphogenetic Design Strategies*, Chichester: Wiley Academy.

Hensel, M., A. Menges and M. Weinstock (eds) (2006), *AD: Techniques and Technologies*, Chichester: Wiley Academy.

Hensel, M., A. Menges and M. Weinstock, (eds) (2010), *Emergent Technologies and Design, Towards a Biological Paradigm for Architecture*, London: Routledge.

Hight, C. and C. Perry (eds) (2006), *AD: Collective Intelligence in Design*, Chichester: Wiley Academy.

Kwinter, S. (2008), *Far From Equilibrium: Essays on Technology and Design Culture*, Barcelona: Actar.

Lazzarato, M. (2006), 'The Concepts of Life and the Living in the Societies of Control', in M. Fuglsang and B. M. Sørensen (eds), *Deleuze and the Social*, Edinburgh: Edinburgh University Press, pp. 171–90.

Lynn, G. (ed.) (1993), *AD: Folding in Architecture*, London: Wiley Academy.

Lynn, G. (2000), 'Greg Lynn: Embryological Houses', in *AD: Contemporary Processes in Architecture*, 70: 3, 26–35.

Lynn, G. (ed.) (2004), *AD: Folding in Architecture*, revised edn, London: Wiley Academy.

Massumi, B. (2002), *Parables for the Virtual: Movement, Affect, Sensation*, Durham, NC: Duke University Press.

Menges, A. (ed.) (2012), *AD: Material Computation*, March–April 2012, Profile No. 216, Chichester: Wiley Academy.

O'Sullivan, S. (2005), 'Modulation: "Fold" + Art and Technology', in A. Parr (ed.), *The Deleuze Dictionary*, Edinburgh: Edinburgh University Press.

Picon, A. (2004), 'Architecture and the Virtual: Toward a New Materiality', *Praxis: Journal of Writing and Building*, 6, 114–21.

Picon, A. (2010), *Digital Culture in Architecture*, Berlin: Birkhäuser.

Serres, M., and B. Latour (1995), *Conversations on Science, Culture, and Time*, Ann Arbor: The University of Michigan Press.

Simondon, G. (1992), 'The Genesis of the Individual', in J. Crary and S. Kwinter (eds), *Incorporations*, New York: Zone Books, pp. 296–319.

Smith, D. (2006), 'Axiomatics and Problematics as Two Modes of Formalisation: Deleuze's Epistemology of Mathematics', in S. Duffy (ed.), *Virtual Mathematics: The Logic of Difference*, Bolton: Clinamen Press, pp. 145–68.

Speaks, M. (2002), 'Design Intelligence and the New Economy', *Architectural Record*, 190: 1, 72–5.

Thomas, K. L. (ed.) (2007), *Material Matters: Architecture and Material Practice*, London: Routledge.

Thrift, N. (2008), *Non-Representational Theory: Space, Politics, Affect*, London: Routledge.

Chapter 5

Objectile: The Pursuit of Philosophy by Other Means?

Bernard Cache with Christian Girard

Introduction: A Conversation between Bernard Cache and Christian Girard

There is much to be said concerning the work of the French architect Bernard Cache, both retrospectively and prospectively, in relation to the philosophical thought of Gilles Deleuze. As the author of *Earth Moves: The Furnishing of Territories* (*Terre Meuble*) (1995), Cache's writing and practice is incontestably located in a privileged position between the philosophy of Deleuze and the discipline of architecture. More recently a collection of his essays has been published under the title *Projectiles* (2011), in an AA Publications series called *Architecture Words*. Below we present some of Cache's reflections on his philosophical relation with Deleuze in conversation with Christian Girard, a French architect and Professor of Architecture at the École Nationale Supérieure d'Architecture Paris Malaquais. This conversation serves to introduce Cache's chapter for this volume.

> *Christian Girard (CG)*: You have known Gilles Deleuze, what was the nature of your relationship with him?
>
> *Bernard Cache (BC)*: In the first instance, Gilles Deleuze was my professor at the University of Vincennes, Paris. In that experimental university context the contact between students and professors was very direct, because, in the first year, rather than exams, students already begin to plan for their thesis (*mémoire*), for presentation in the third year of one's studies. Deleuze had an immediate and profound effect on me. It was in the framework of this influence that I began writing a series of texts that would eventually be published as *Earth Moves (Terre Meuble)*.[1] After I had completed my thesis Deleuze and I remained in touch through correspondence, and through visits I paid to him at his home. Over time we became friends on the basis of shared philosophical intuitions. Though

we were working in different theoretical disciplines, we both shared a particular interest in the fold (*le pli*). Deleuze was working on his Leibniz lectures, while I was working on my furniture and interior design projects, through which I perceived the idea of a geographical fold brought from the outside, into the inside, through the frame of architecture.

Today the geographical surfaces I have taken an interest in would go by another name: 'Free Shapes', which through the advent of the computer and computation are now composed with more ease. When I first commenced work on these problems I was doing so without the aid of the computer. In a very concrete and material way, and before the advent of CNC (computer numerical control) milling, I manipulated complex surfaces with sanding tools. This was well before my architectural design studio *Objectile* (with Patrick Beaucé) became a serious enterprise. The name *Objectile* was based on a word invented by Deleuze (Deleuze 1993: 19).[2]

CG: Deleuze has been utilised in all sorts of ways by architects. It is possible to name at least three kinds of instrumentalisation of Deleuze's thought in architecture. First, there is the erudite approach, based on a profound understanding of the philosophy of Deleuze; for example, John Rajchman. Second, there is the productive approach, which can be associated with Manuel DeLanda. Third, there is the cosmetic use of Deleuze's philosophy whereby concepts such as the 'rhizome' have been reduced to clichés, and due to their conceptual exhaustion such concepts can no longer be recuperated. It would also be possible to compile a catalogue of all the misrepresentations architects have perpetrated through sampling Deleuzian concepts for the purposes of presenting projects, accompanied by an iconography as contrived as can be. For you, what are the instrumentalisations of Deleuze that you consider legitimate and productive, those that you believe deserve to be attributed to the thought of Deleuze?

BC: In fact, I do not believe I know these works commenting on Deleuze well enough to speak seriously on this matter. Moreover, the approach of instrumentalising Deleuze in architecture does not really interest me, especially as Deleuze was a philosopher who did not want to form a school or to have followers. For me his texts instead provide points of departure for other things. In fact, my research interest in antiquity was first aroused on encountering the two texts that conclude Deleuze's book, *The Logic of Sense*, 'Plato and the Simulacrum' and 'Lucretius and the Simulacrum'. I almost become a Platonist, which would have been quite an unexpected outcome for a Deleuzian, though I would have been a Platonist of a special kind, who used tools of calculation, sampled weaving and interlacing techniques, and explored undecidable propositions.

CG: Since the publication of *Earth Moves* in 1995, is there still some

Deleuzian resonance that persists in your work? For instance, in your research on Albrecht Dürer, which you are completing at the moment, and on which you will speak more here? Or else, your work on Vitruvius, who you wrote about over two years ago now, a work that still remains unpublished?

BC: I continue to see resonances everywhere. For example, between machines and machinism (see Deleuze and Guattari 1983, 1987; Deleuze and Parnet 2007: 104). Machining Plato: that is much better than reversing Platonism. This is surely what the Greek mathematician Eutocius achieved when he credited Plato with the invention of an instrument for calculating continuous proportions. Although this attribution is in fact false, it demonstrates that during the time of Antiquity some lectures of Plato were compatible with such instrumental calculation. Another concept of Deleuze is that of the diagram (Deleuze 1988c, 2003; Deleuze and Guattari 1987), which is fundamental to Dürer's *Underweysung der Messung* (*Instructions for Measurement*). The notion of the serpentine line also belongs to Dürer, which is a line that relates to other animal lines, such as the snail, or the spider. It goes without saying that the serpentine line also relates to the concept of inflection (Deleuze 1993: 14). Although I almost never cite Deleuze directly, I frequently surprise myself by discovering Deleuzian themes in my own work, such as the war machine. One could reread all of Vitruvius in order to suggest that he understood the Greek temple as a kind of war machine. Because, in his real life, rather than being a builder of edifices, Vitruvius was actually a builder of war machines, and his *De Architectura* (*On Architecture*) concludes with a book on mechanics. Whether or not there is any sense in saying one is a Deleuzian or a Platonist, this should not stop one from finding concepts in one or the other, even from moving away from one philosopher only to rediscover him in another.

CG: In relation to these thoughts, and taking into consideration the work of Deleuze and Guattari, one can see how their philosophy has anticipated the evolution of capitalist societies, especially with respect to power relations. It appears that their sombre prognosis of capitalism is being realised on a global scale. You are political – do you see any effective application of Deleuzian philosophy with respect to political concerns today?

BC: Unfortunately Deleuze and Guattari had good reason to deliver such a sombre prognosis, and you have good reason to highlight the importance I also place on politics, but great care must be taken as to the implications of this politics. The role of the intellectual is not to represent the working classes. There is already enough to fight for within the various intellectual practices, where conflicts and battles often end up connecting to the major fracture that is the struggle between classes. I believe that the difficult challenge is that we must return to the diagnosis of Marx and yet discover other solutions. What I am saying here is not really new, but resumes a theme that has been framed by Foucault and Deleuze in conversation (Foucault and Deleuze 1977). One of the most pertinent intellectuals today is certainly Paul Krugman, who delivers his political conclusions on the basis of a thorough knowledge and critique of his own discipline, that is economics. In particular, Krugman shows that the austere policies implemented across Europe today take root in a distorted memory of German history. Indeed, what brought Hitler into power was not at all the inflation that followed the First World War, because fortunately this hyper-inflation was cured by 1924, which allowed Germany to benefit from a buoyant economy from 1925 to 1929. What paved the way to Nazism and the Second World War were the austerity measures taken by Chancellor Brüning, which only worsened the consequences of the 1929 financial crisis on the German economy. In his last book *End this Depression Now* (2012b), Krugman regularly complains about the oblivion of history, which enables the construction of false memories, such as the story of inflation in early twentieth-century German history. Intellectuals must fight on their own field, and from my point of view the classics are more than ever a field of political struggle, not least to fight against the dissemination of a conservative vision of art history.

The work of Albrecht Dürer, upon which I have been undertaking research, offers a good example of what I mean. The peasant revolution broke out in Germany in 1525, the same year that Dürer drafted the *Instructions for Measurement*. Using every means available to him, the German art historian Erwin Panofsky attempted to neutralise the importance of this historical context in relation to Dürer's work (Panofsky 1945). Panofsky accused the rioters of being iconoclasts, communists and polygamists. He suggested that the placing of a peasant at the top of the memorial column in book three of the *Instructions for Measurement* (1528) could only be the expression of the scornful attitude of Dürer towards the rioters. By projecting his own conservative opinions on Dürer, Panofsky also obscured the meaning of a note that the painter had placed at the base of an aquarelle two weeks after the massacre of one hundred thousand insurgents, by translating the German word *Grausamkeit* as 'violence' rather than 'cruelty', thereby shifting Dürer's sense. In his historical account of Dürer's work, Panofsky does not even mention the name of a close collaborator of Dürer, Georg Pencz, who was banned that year alongside two other godless (*gottlos*) painters. Dürer was so close to Pencz that he had entrusted him with the execution of a fresco in the town hall of Nuremberg in 1521. Without necessarily making a proletarian hero of Dürer, it is crucial to stress this historical context in relation to the *Bauernkrieg* (Peasants' War), which was the first grand European revolution of its kind, and which has marked the political history of Germany since 1525!

Panofsky was a profoundly conservative intellectual who strategically used his erudition in three books. In his commentary on Dürer's engraving *Melancholia* (1514), Panofsky emphasises the geometry of polyhedrons, despite the fact that what Dürer was interested in was the serpentine line, which is so variable and owns so few polyhedral qualities. This interpretation by Panofsky is based on a neoplatonic reading of the *Timaeus*, which Dürer doesn't seem to have adhered to. Let us remember that the so-called platonic polyhedrons do not play a major role in Plato's philosophy, and that the dodecahedron only pops up in one single sentence of the *Timaeus*. Although these polyhedrons are described in the last book of Euclid's *Elements* (*c*.300 BC), they do not constitute the end or the horizon of the whole of geometry as Panofsky would have it. The title itself of the *Elements* indicates that this treatise was just a prelude to a more elaborate geometry (Cache 2011: 31–59). This higher geometry engaged in how curves can be drawn with instruments other than the compass and the ruler was to be built upon elementary geometry, and it was precisely this form of geometry that interested Dürer. For that reason, Dürer makes only two demonstrations in his treatise, precisely on the fundamental topic of superior geometry, namely the duplication of the cube. Thus one sees how it is necessary to return to a critique of these classical texts in order to reconstruct a tradition that is more open. This is also true of two other works of Panofsky in relation to architectural issues. For instance, rather than a symbolic form, perspective has been a long-standing mutual misunderstanding between artists, architects and mathematicians across several centuries. Or else, concerning French Gothic architecture, how could one not see, with Roland Bechmann, that the ogival arch is an approximation of an ellipse? As a result these vaults are not ruled but warped, self-supporting surfaces, with no other definition than that of their border edges. These Gothic vaults are located at as great a distance from both the scholasticism of Panofsky and the rationalism of Viollet Le Duc. Hence the work of Panofsky is a good example of the kind of research that neutralises history. It is necessary to reconstruct a form of critical knowledge to rediscover the possibilities of the depth of historical time in the heart of our contemporary moment.

CG: Since you put an end to the company *Objectile* in 2010, at least in terms of its services and its public face, is that a loss of the project *Objectile* for you? Have you renounced all interest in the sphere of architectural production?

BC: I have no obsession with the cubic volume of concrete, nor with building totemic signifiers of architecture, even if, in effect, the architectural panels produced by my firm *Objectile*, and their multiple counterfeits, cover a lot more area in terms of square metres than if I had worked as an architect within the constraints of a conventional architectural firm.

Now, I have to make a virtue out of necessity. In the 1980s there were serious shortcomings in design in general, hence my interest in instruments that could allow an escape from a narrow rationalist design, and my desire to form a company that offered another, very 'machinic' way to practise as an architect. Today what is most lacking is not the ability to draw, or to create extravagant architectural bubbles, it is long-term thinking, reason and an engagement in history.[3] If *Objectile* emerged out of my engagement with philosophy, today I would invent a philosophy that extended the concept objectile by other means. The cessation of the work of my design firm *Objectile* is a kind of cataclysm that I must survive. Yet aspects of this have worked out in my favour, as I have now accumulated a great deal of material to work on and much to write. Hence, I should now write another text whose title should be: 'Philosophy: The Pursuit of Objectile by Other Means'.

The simple fact of returning to antiquity has proved very productive because most of today's inventions are ultimately related to inventions of the past. For instance, in mathematics, many researchers continue to read Euclid today (Cache 2011: 46–7). What I would most like to do is to reconstruct a classical culture for the purposes of today's world. To achieve this, a return to the original texts is necessary, as much as their transposition by way of computation. Many ancient concepts are susceptible to new readings due to developments enabled through this form of digital transposition. The best example would be the serpentine line of Dürer. This is the central object of the *Underweysung der Messung*, and yet, when the artist introduces the instrument that describes it, he refrains from drawing the line itself. This is very curious for someone whose job it is to produce images. Now, it is by modelling this instrument and generating its variety of curves that one can understand what was at stake in Dürer's geometry: how to find a way to regulate the power of variation.

Objectile: The Pursuit of Philosophy by Other Means?

Perhaps I'd best begin by unpacking the title of this essay. Objectile was the name given by Gilles Deleuze to the research I am carrying out with Patrick Beaucé and others into the development of industrial means of producing non-standard objects.[4]

By this, I mean objects that are repeatable variations on a theme, such as a family of curves declining the same mathematical model; *objects* in flux, inflected like the signal modulating a carrier wave; or lines and surfaces of variable curve, such as the folds of Baroque sculpture or the decorative bands of plant motifs whose capacity for transformation was so convincingly demonstrated in Alois Riegl's history of ornament

(Riegl 1993). The 'pursuit of philosophy' refers to philosophy engaged as a mode of production – and not as a contemplative activity, and even less as an instrument of communication. 'Pursuit by other means?' The phrase consciously alludes to Carl von Clausewitz, reminding us not only that philosophy *is* a machine for waging war on any kind of apparatus, but also that our aims can easily be distorted by the means we use to achieve them – something that troubled the Prussian general (an avid reader of Kant). A neo-finalism as a philosophy of distortion – here, perhaps, is cause for celebration!

How is it that philosophy is subject to such distortion? There are probably many reasons, and there seems to be no shortage of either causes or opportunities. Yet, like most, I detect one overriding factor: the computer. This is hardly a new denaturing force, however, for the seeds of the computer were not planted by Gaspard Marie Riche de Prony (1755–1839), who wanted to manufacture logarithms 'as easily as pins', or even by Charles Babbage (1791–1871), who found a way to mechanise the calculation of mathematical tables. Nor was it conceived during the Second World War – in the calculating rooms where the trajectories of ordnance were plotted – or even more latterly, in the garages of Silicon Valley. Rather, it took a philosopher like Leibniz to anticipate everything that contemporary computer science is only now beginning to realise. It was Leibniz who stated, clearly and brilliantly, that any form, no matter how complex, can be calculated. And it is this statement which validates our current attempts to design digitally – to conceive of 'objectiles' as declinations of parametric surfaces.

Philosophy as a calculation of reason and of forms, then. Having stated this goal, we now need to consider the means – systematic as well as material – required to achieve it. In terms of system, mention should be made of a largely forgotten giant of the history of science, Joseph Fourier (a contemporary of Charles Fourier), whose theorem made it possible to break up any periodic function into a series of trigonometric functions. It was Fourier who discovered the application for realising Leibniz's program. All that remained was to implement the algorithms in high-performance silicon in order to automate the otherwise laborious calculation of series – FFT: Fast Fourier Transform. A French engineer, Didier LeGall, set up shop in the US, and his C-Cube Inc. developed the first digital compression circuits. The MPEG or H.261 video coding standards that underpin developments such as digital television and the videophone are nothing other than ultra-high-speed executions of Fourier transformations by integrated circuits. So one has to ask: how have these integrated circuits managed to distort a philosophical affirmation by processing a theorem in a fraction of a second behind our screens? This is just the kind of problem – related to the speed and the slowness of thought – that Gilles Deleuze loved to pose (Deleuze 1988a: 124–7).

So let us rejoice in the face of this algorithmic Fourierism, for it signals, perhaps, that we have come to a turning point. We have to make the most of the fact that mathematics has effectively become a manufactured object, and when its components become photonic rather than electronic, the brakes will come off the speed of calculation. But the question is no longer simply one of the speed of calculation, which is potentially unlimited; what we now have to confront is the power or potency of calculation. Ought we to believe, then, the prophets of artificial intelligence who foresee a time when machines will think in our stead, and who claim that our consciousness is nothing but an epiphenomenon, more or less a parasite of algorithmic calculation? Is machinic thinking reducible to information processing? Are we on the threshold of a consciousness of a third kind, verging on that absolute or lightning speed of thought described by Gilles Deleuze in relation to the Fifth Book of Spinoza's *Ethics* (Deleuze 1992)? Or are we heading instead towards a kind of explosion of thought where, having broken the calculation barrier, we soon discover a world in which algorithms no longer have any currency? In broaching these questions, one has to begin by saying that a computer does essentially two things: it calculates and it memorises. Calculation and Memory – not so different from Bergson's *Matter and Memory* ([1896] 1991). Let us examine each of these aspects in turn, starting with calculation.

Turing himself had already shown that there is a set of problems for which no algorithmic solution exists. As an example, we can cite a problem that is ostensibly very simple: 'Out of a set of polygons, which ones are suitable for tiling a plane?' This is a problem for a tiler or a mason, almost child's play. 'How do you cover a surface with a small number of basic shapes without leaving gaps or creating overlaps?' But it is also close to being a philosophical problem: 'How do you construct (a) space out of shapes rather than points?' Atomism posed the problem of constructing space on the basis of the point, understood as the means of reaching the limit of a shape so small that it has neither form nor parts. What daring! It is clear to us today that the problem is already very complicated when you start with divisible components, that is components with actual extension and form. Even if you restrict yourself to very simple elements – the juxtaposition of identical squares – there is no algorithmic solution to the problem of tiling a plane and worse still, a space, because of the occurrence of non-periodic elements. Such combinations of squares, known as polyominos (James and James 1992),[5] will not form infinitely repeatable basic patterns, allowing one to tile a plane correctly. It was the British mathematician Roger Penrose who pointed out that the impossibility of solving tiling problems algorithmically was demonstrated by the fact that there was no general procedure for deciding when to 'switch off' a Turing machine. There are completely deterministic models of the universe, with well-defined rules of evolution, which are impossible to encompass algorithmically. Penrose then adds that the understanding of mathematics cannot be reduced to computation, and that comprehension is itself a non-algorithmic activity of the mind or brain. The most important consequence of Gödel's theorem is not the existence of unprovable propositions but rather the uncomputable element of thought, which can only be revealed in the most formalised domain, namely that of mathematical invention. Penrose builds on an argument advanced by John Searle: suppose that I manage to communicate, step by step, the basic elements of computer programming to someone who understands nothing about the field – partisans of artificial intelligence would claim that the computer 'understands' the algorithms it is processing, whereas it is clear that the user, even though he is the one who has written the program, persists in understanding nothing at all. This leads Penrose to propose the following:

1. Intelligence requires understanding.
2. Understanding requires an immediate knowledge of a different order from the writing of an algorithm.

In light of this, we might wonder whether the real achievement of the invention of computers has been to liberate thought from algorithms and the need to memorise things. André Leroi-Gourhan has talked about how the act of standing upright freed human jaws from prehensile and utilitarian functions, thus opening the way for the vocalisation of sounds to become the articulation of speech. In a similar fashion, *homo cyberneticus* seems well on the way to developing the strange new faculties of an amnesiac and analgorithmic consciousness. Gilles Deleuze was very much a philosopher of the twentieth century, in the sense that he knew how to ford this stream of mnemonic and algorithmic unconsciousness, picking his way from one stepping stone to the next – from Bergson to Ruyer – finding in them confirmation of the value of a 'surveying' consciousness (*conscience de survol*) (Deleuze and Guattari 1994: 21).

What the twenty-first century may well reveal is that the strangest thing about thought is this *consciousness*. We may be about to perform a tremendous philosophical somersault that will lead to a revival of interest in consciousness – not in any role as the seat of Reason, but rather as the locus of an irreducible *unreasonableness*. Let us not forget that Enlightenment thinkers made Reason a conscious act, and equated a lack of Reason with a lack of conscious awareness, unbounded in law but in reality limited. Then came the Romantics who intuited only too well the intrinsic limits of consciousness in face of an irrationality that would soon be relocated in the unconscious. Freud would attempt to salvage the situation by explaining that the unconscious is itself a second form of Reason, long before the structuralists came along to tell us that this unconscious is not only the reason for a troubled conscience, but is Reason itself: Engram with a capital E, and Algorithm with a capital A. Nevertheless, what annoyed Gilles Deleuze about psychoanalysis was not so much its take on the unconscious as the absolute reign of the engram and of the algorithm – of the infantile memory and, later, of linguistic, anthropological and mathematical structuralisms. Say we accept that there is an irreducible unreasonableness at the heart of consciousness. What then? The next step is to oppose the ideology of Information with a philosophy of Incarnation. For an algorithm has first to be incarnated before it can be processed. Telecommunications engineers are well aware that source coding is only half the story. Any image, no matter how complex, can certainly be sampled and reduced to a highly compressed digital series thanks to Fourier transformations, but this digital series still has to be supported by a physical platform. The source coding has to be backed up by a channel coding. In fact any text, any sound, any image may in future be reduced to a digital series, but a bit-stream – a series of ones and zeros – is nothing until it is recomposed in a given platform at a predetermined dock time. This is how a digital series can effectively become a sound on a stereophonic membrane or an image on a video screen; this is how the digital word is made analogue flesh. And this is how the new digital montages are created: no longer is a given sound coupled to a given image, as in the good old days of cinematography; instead, sounds are visualised or images heard in a chiasmus of perceptions.

For even the smallest perception is itself already composed of a multitude of vibrations. Bergson reminds us that the simple fact of seeing a colour or hearing a sound is already an act of memory which contracts a quantitative multitude into a qualitative multiplicity. But this is something entirely different from the engram-memory of our computers. The engram is nothing but a sequence of bits, whereas memory-contraction is the act by which we constitute our presence in the world by condensing a series of moments into the thickness of a duration. It is the act whereby a bit of information is incarnated through a perceptual support – retinal persistence, or after-images of our consciousness – and number becomes sound or image. Yet this process is impossible to understand unless one makes matter itself the object of the kind of distinction that is applied to memory. For matter is also dualistic. Bergson commended Berkeley's 'immaterialism'; 'matter has no inside, no underside . . . it hides nothing, holds nothing . . . possesses neither power, nor virtuality of any kind . . . it extends as surface and coheres at every moment in everything it gives' (Deleuze 1988b: 41, translation modified). Matter is thus simultaneously that by which everything is given, reducible to pure quantity, like Lucretius' black atoms, as well as that which constitutes the most relaxed membrane, the qualitative residue without which quantity does not exist. It is the minimal colour without which there is no black or white, the fundamental noise without which there is no signal.

The computer forces us to rethink the boundary not just between the two major Bergsonian concepts of matter and memory, but also between the two Leibnizian stages that Gilles Deleuze used to explain the fundamental difference between the pairings of virtual/actual and possible/real (Deleuze 1988b: 42–3; Deleuze 1993: 105). These two stages no longer separate monads from bodies, nor matter from memory; instead, they create a chiasmus which allows us to place algorithm and engram together, on the side of Information, while coupling membranes and temporal frequencies on the side of Incarnation. Thus you have on one side all that can be computed and written, and on the other elements which appear non-computable and non-samplable – to put it in negative terms – but which take on a positive aspect as Duration and Membrane. This works so well that we are tempted to propose a new version of the diagram sketched by Gilles Deleuze in *The Fold*, where he juxtaposes two very different processes: the actualisation of the virtual and the realisation of the possible. When it comes to the engram and the algorithm anything is possible – at least, so IT experts keep telling us. And possibilities press to become realities, subject only to rules of economic optimisation as calculated by the invisible hand of the market, which, as an added bonus, promises to select only the best of all possible worlds. However, this overlooks the fact that there are algorithms that cannot be determined, and therefore propositions of which it is impossible to say whether they are contradictory or not, or, more exactly, whether they are compatible or not with another set of propositions. This is the irreducibly uncomputable. On the other hand, the possible cannot become real without becoming corporeal, without incarnating itself in a membrane and undergoing a change in its nature in accordance with the temporal stimulus driving it to realisation. 'That which cannot be divided without changing nature' (Deleuze 1988b: 40) is how Deleuze described this second process, whereby the possible cannot become real without something of the virtual becoming actual. This is why Duration has its own thickness, and the reality cannot be anticipated in the possibility.

Membranes and frequencies: these are the singular figures through which the virtual is actualised at the same time as the possible becomes real, without any guarantee that the best will be selected. Kandinsky used the term resonance to designate what is spiritual in art. He also clearly perceived the advent of information technology: 'As these means of expression [abstract forms] are developed further in the future . . . Mathematical expression will here become essential' (Kandinsky 1982: 544), he announced in *Point and Line to Plane*. He also warned, 'There is, however, the danger that mathematical expression will lag behind emotional experience and limit it. Formulas are like glue, or like a "fly paper" to which the careless fall prey. A formula is also a leather arm chair, which holds the occupant firmly in its warm embrace' (ibid.). Written in 1923, Kandinsky's remarks sound like a warning to those of us who spend our days in front of a computer screen.

To be sure, computation enables us to design forms as modulations of abstract surfaces whose frequency and membrane remain indeterminate for a time. After Kandinsky, we take Leibniz at his word when he says that all forms are computable. And the only means we need to achieve this are the ones prescribed by Fourier, that is series of trigonometric functions. And when we want to design volumes, we use whole periodicities which cause surfaces to curl up on themselves. In this first stage, therefore, we make mathematical models that allow us to calculate the infinite permutations of the possible. In order to approach these 'worlds', whose functions are comprised as much of dimensions as of parameters, we have developed exploratory tools that generate series of video images corresponding to trajectories within these multi-dimensional universes. Objects generated by this process initially resemble still frames from video footage.

But in order to move from these virtual possibilities to actual realities, we have to switch scanning techniques and replace the electronic remote control that activates the pixels on our video screen with a digital command router that manufactures any material. If we hear the term virtual reality so often, it is because video scanning appears to be the minimal machinic operation of the extremely ductile, supple membrane that is the video screen. We have to insist on the dual nature of this operation: first, it is already an incarnation, and second, the screen is just one membrane among many others. Hence video sequences are only a primary or first actualisation, which is why we can effectively speak of virtuality. The mathematical models that we are exploring still belong to the order of the possible and hold no surprises, except to the extent that our power of calculation remains limited. On the other hand, what we will never be able to predict is the relation between a frequency and a membrane. Selecting a still image requires us to assign a value to the parameters of our periodic functions in order to manufacture singularities in a series of objects in a specified material. Should the modulations on the surface of wooden panels be made larger or smaller in a given architectural context? Would a different modulation curl into a three-lobed volume in the middle of a room? How will the phase difference of an electron ripple relate to the texture of a predetermined membrane? Solutions to these problems cannot be anticipated, for in each case the actualisation differs in nature from all others, and in no case can the selection be optimised.

In a certain sense, none of this is really new. In fact, Mersenne's *Harmonie Universelle* of 1636 already asked whether one could compose the best song imaginable on the basis of an exploration of combinatorial principles. Mersenne concluded that it could not be done, because the number of possibilities was just too great – for example, the number of foreseeable melodies with 23 non-repeating notes already runs to the factorial of 23. Another example of combinatorics is the game of chess, where the number of permissible moves stands at 10 to the power of 56, a figure so large that it exceeds the number of electrons in the universe. The calculation of all of these moves thus remains unfeasible as long as computers are driven by electronic technology. If today's computers perform relatively well against flesh-and-blood opponents, it is because they use software programmed with heuristic devices that simulate a player's intuition on the basis of probabilistic hypotheses that limit the field of possibilities. But this does not count for much, since we can envisage that one day we will have quantum computers that will be unbeatable because they will be able to calculate all the possibilities. In essence, the problem of chess remains simple and eminently computable: it is a purely algorithmic problem based on a comparison of different possibilities with a view to selecting the best outcome – and thus purely a problem of realisation. Mersenne's musical problem is something quite different. We have long known that harmony is not defined once and for all, and that two notes which are considered consonant in the soprano range will be dissonant in the bass range, and that a chord which one composer finds dissonant will appear consonant to another. There is still no common basis for comparing musical modulations in the same way that we can weigh up chess moves. Leibniz proposed that the existence of a perfect major chord in one monad implies the existence of a minor or dissonant chord in another. But the procedure for selecting the 'optimum' solution out of all the different possibilities seems to be functioning less and less well. Thus dissonance in one monad no longer implies consonance in another, to the benefit of universal harmony. On the one hand, the uncomputable element of algorithmic possibilities impedes selection by criteria of optimisation; on the other, the virtual cannot become real unless it undergoes a change in the nature of the membrane in which it is incarnated or the frequencies that animate it.

As reality submits to ever more divergent actualisations, worlds jostle each other for space. And from this crush the notion of harmony is emerging as a singularity, rather than something universal. This is the basis of our attempt to put into practice a means of production for the non-standard.

Notes

The opening paragraph has been written by Christian Girard. The translation of the opening conversation between Bernard Cache and Christian Girard was undertaken by Hélène Frichot, and she would like to acknowledge the kind advice offered by Christian Girard and Maurice Frichot. We would like to thank AA Publications, London for permission to reproduce the essay 'Objectile: The Pursuit of Philosophy by Other Means?', in Bernard Cache, *Projectiles*, London: AA Publications, 2011.

1. Although *Terre Meuble* was written in French, it was, in fact, first published in English translation as *Earth Moves*, in the *Writing Architecture* series, edited by Cynthia C. Davidson, for MIT Press. (*Translator's note.*)
2. In *The Fold: Leibniz and the Baroque*, Deleuze invents the concept 'objectile' in direct reference to Bernard Cache. The objectile, following Deleuze's account, can be defined as a special kind of technological object, wherein 'fluctuation of the norm replaces the permanence of a law; where the object assumes a place in a continuum by variation'. See also Cache's essay 'Toward a Non-Standard Mode of Production' recently republished in *Projectiles* (2011). (*Translator's note.*)
3. To further demonstrate how European governments are showing an ignorance of history, read Krugman (2012a, 2012b).
4. The others being principally Jean-Louis Jammot, Charles Claeys and Christian Arber, all software developers at Missler Software.
5. 'polyomino. n. The plane figure formed by joining unit squares along their edges. Polyominos all of which are congruent to a given polyomino that uses four or fewer squares can be used as tiles to cover a plane (ie monominos, dominos, trominos, tetrominos . . .)'. (See James and James 1992.)

References

Bergson, H. ([1896] 1991), *Matter and Memory*, trans. N. M. Paul and W. S. Palmer, New York: Zone Books.

Cache, B. (1995), *Earth Moves: The Furnishing of Territories (Terre Meuble)*, trans. A. Boyman, Cambridge, MA: MIT Press.

Cache, B. (2011), *Projectiles*, trans. C. Barrett and P. Johnson, London: AA Publications.

Deleuze, G. (1988a), *Spinoza: Practical Philosophy*, trans. R. Hurley, San Francisco: City Lights.

Deleuze, G. (1988b), *Bergsonism*, trans. H. Tomlinson and B. Habberjam, New York: Zone Books.

Deleuze, G. (1988c), *Foucault*, trans. S. Hand, Minneapolis, MN: University of Minnesota Press.

Deleuze, G. (1990), *The Logic of Sense*, New York: Columbia University Press.

Deleuze, G. (1992), *Expressionism in Philosophy: Spinoza*, trans. M. Joughin, New York: Zone Books.

Deleuze, G. (1993), *The Fold: Leibniz and the Baroque*, trans. T. Conley, Minneapolis, MN: University of Minnesota Press.

Deleuze, G. (2003), *Francis Bacon: The Logic of Sensation*, trans. D. W. Smith, Minneapolis, MN: University of Minnesota Press.

Deleuze, G. and F. Guattari (1983), *Anti-Oedipus: Capitalism and Schizophrenia*, trans. R. Hurley, M. Seem, H. R. Lane, Minneapolis, MN: University of Minnesota Press.

Deleuze, G. and F. Guattari (1987), *A Thousand Plateaus: Capitalism and Schizophrenia*, trans. B. Massumi, Minneapolis, MN: University of Minnesota Press.

Deleuze, G. and F. Guattari (1994), *What Is Philosophy?*, trans. G. Burchell and H. Tomlinson, London: Verso.

Deleuze, G. and C. Parnet (2007), *Dialogues II*, trans. H. Tomlinson and B. Habberjam, New York: Columbia University Press.

Dürer, A. (1528), *Vier Bücher von menschlicher Proportion*, Nuremberg.

Foucault, M. and G. Deleuze (1977), 'Intellectuals and Power', in *Language, Counter-Memory, Practice*, trans. D. F. Bouchard and S. Simon, Ithaca, NY: Cornell University Press, pp. 205–17.

James, R. C. and G. James (eds) (1992), *Mathematics Dictionary*, London: Chapman & Hall.

Kandinsky, W. (1982), 'Point and Line to Plane', in K. C. Lindsay and P. Vergo (eds), *Kandinsky: Complete Writings on Art, Volume II, 1922–1943*, Boston: G. K. Hall, pp. 524–699.

Krugman, P. (2012a), 'The Great Abdication', *New York Times*, 24 June. See <http://www.nytimes.com/2012/06/25/opinion/krugman-the-great-abdication.html>.

Krugman, P. (2012b), *End This Depression Now*, New York: W. W. Norton.

Panofsky, E. (1945), *The Life and Art of Albrecht Dürer*, Princeton, NJ: Princeton University Press.

Riegl, A. (1993), *Problems of Style: Foundations for a History of Ornament*, trans. E. Kain, annotations, glossary and introduction by D. Castrioti, preface by H. Zerner, Princeton, NJ: Princeton University Press.

Chapter 6

The Architect as Metallurgist: Using Concrete to Trace Bio-digital Lines

Mike Hale

'It is quite possible to project whole forms in the mind without recourse to the material.' (Alberti 1998: 7)

disegno – (Italian Renaissance): 'to design is to draw from mind to matter' (Sheil 2005: 15)

Against hylomorphism

When design privileges thinking before doing, by determining solutions a priori or in advance, we can say that the conceptual realm transcends the materials and methods that are subsequently used to construct the built version of the idea. This is precisely the sense we are given above in the translation of the Italian word for design, *disegno*, which draws mental designs first before imposing these conceptual and often idealised forms upon matter. The composition transcends the means of construction in the sense that once a design is conceived there may be numerous ways to build a representation of the theoretical or formal solution being proposed. What matters in this case is not necessarily the specific details of how the design is realised, which are often seen as incidental or 'practical' concerns, but the disassociation of the ideas from the materials, processes and built results that ensue. If we design a box with a sloping roof as the best solution to an architectural problem, then its image and function is what generates the translation into built form. We then add in the practical constraints that determine how we might build it: for example, we might decide to use steel, concrete, masonry, timber or perhaps a combination of these depending on a variety of factors like cost, availability, skills, performance and so on. No matter what influences the translation or how the specifics of a material might try to inform the process, we will still build a box with a sloping roof that resembles the formal plan generated by the original idea.

The selection and practical use of materials follows and is secondary to the predetermining design idea. Formalism dominates materialism. Of course this is a simple example that belies the complexity that usually informs the translation of design ideas into buildings and the myriad of smaller decisions made along the way. Nevertheless, the design idea transcends these 'practicalities' and determines the form first and irrevocably, which sets a linear one-way process in motion. There is no room for a more fluid exchange of feedback and alteration to the design ideas that the materials themselves might suggest. Instead, architects struggle to manipulate the materials through successive compromises to represent the predetermining design ideas. Matter according to this schema is essentially inert, non-vital, dumb and made to conform to formal arrangements in order to reflect the master 'plan'. The resemblance of the result to its originating design concepts takes priority over all else and as a consequence the influence of any feedback that arises during the construction phase has little or no effect on the design ideas. One could push this further to argue that any material feedback encountered is often seen as a hindrance to the completion of the design idea, which must be overcome, suppressed or generally resisted. As a result, this approach blocks the possibility of considering matter in any way as informative, vital or otherwise interactive with design, other than at best in terms of its structural and outwardly aesthetic capacities. Matter here is understood and used according to a hylomorphic principle. Hylomorphism is the philosophical doctrine that physical objects result from the combination of matter (Gk. *hulē*) and form (*morphē*). It assumes that 'order displayed by material systems is due to the form projected in advance of production by an external producer, a form which organises what would otherwise be chaotic or passive matter' (Protevi 2005: 296). Therefore matter is 'dumb' and secondary to the ideas that precede and transcend it.

In the plateau '1837: Of the Refrain' in *A Thousand Plateaus*, Deleuze and Guattari develop a critique of hylomorphism in order to break with the problem of ideas preceding actions and the implications this has for our use of matter. If matter is not inert, then for Deleuze and Guattari the alternative is found in a reconception of matter as living and creative. Hylomorphism is replaced with the concept of a vital materialism. From an architectural perspective, we might ask how such a challenge to the traditional model of form–matter relations could suggest a different mode for us to practise. John Protevi neatly summarises Deleuze and Guattari's alternative as a non-hylomorphic or artisanal theory of production. In this theory, forms are developed by artisans out of potentials of matter rather than being dreamed up by architects and then imposed on passive matter. In artisanal production, the artisan must therefore surrender to matter, that is follow its potentials by attending to its implicit forms and then devise operations that bring forth these potentials to actualise the desired properties. (Protevi 2005: 296–7)

One of the most striking challenges to the traditional architectural model of design being made here is not simply the argument that matter itself should be regarded as vital, but also the suggestion that architects should use and understand material properties in a very different way. No longer can we remain at a distance from the materials we specify. Instead, we are required to work with the materials, experiment with what they might do for us, become receptive to the particularities they emit, all in order to develop an alternative approach to design that resists the problem of hylomorphism. The idea of 'following' certain material traits may seem antiquated or otherwise foreign to the modern architectural mind at first, but it can be argued that there is a long-standing counter-history of architecture that has treated the building materials it used in a far more integrated manner than is generally the case today. Deleuze and Guattari use the idea of 'technological lineages' as a way to develop an alternate history of material developments and the effects they have had. Although deserving of a separate discussion in their own right, the ideas of the Metallic line and Gothic line feature prominently in *A Thousand Plateaus*.[1] In each case, a technological line traces the modulation of a specific force–matter relation across time. The Gothic line, for example, charts the evolution of the haptic process of construction used by master masons, each block of stone to some extent having informed the way it was sculpted and installed, which helped to develop a new structural system altering the possible description of space. A simple preoccupation with gravity was transformed into a virtuosic free-flowing vortex of stone, light and space by developing an innovative use of stone which included following its specific traits in order to trace lines of structural force in new ways.

The concept of following material traits in order to make architectural innovations has had a resurgence in some contemporary architectural practices. One of the advantages of the digital age is its capacity to analyse and experiment with new material properties and configurations in greater depth and at higher speeds than before. As much as the new formalism for the most part continues to inflect a hylomorphic approach to architectural design, there are a number of practices that attempt to resist it.[2]

Deleuze and Guattari see the alternative of an 'energetic materiality in movement' altering our conceptual framework from both directions, that is from a formal perspective and from the properties of the matter itself:

> Simondon exposes the technological insufficiency of the matter-form model, in that it assumes a fixed form and a matter deemed homogeneous. It is the idea of the law that assures the model's coherence, since laws are what submit matter to this or that form, and, conversely, realize in matter a given property deduced from the form. But Simondon demonstrates that the *hylomorphic* model leaves many things, active and affective, by the wayside. On the one hand, to the formed or formable matter we must add an entire energetic materiality in movement, carrying *singularities* or *haecceities* that are already like implicit forms that are topological, rather than geometrical, and that combine with processes of deformation: for example, the variable undulations and torsions of the fibers guiding the operation of splitting wood. On the other hand, to the essential properties of the matter deriving from the formal essence we must add *variable intensive affects*, now resulting from the operation, now on the contrary making it possible: for example, wood that is more or less porous, more or less elastic and resistant. (Deleuze and Guattari 1987: 408)

Living matter combining in variable and sometimes unpredictable ways creates opportunities for architects to renew their experiments with the transmission of forces, affects and the resultant spatial compositions they may generate. While at one level this is a question of form and matter relations, in A Thousand Plateaus it is contextualised in other ways that can help to elaborate the relevance this line of thought might have for architects. Deleuze and Guattari address the re-evaluation of material relations along at least two more generally intertwined trajectories that are of direct relevance for architecture: the problem of consistency or consolidation, and the concept of metallurgy. By elaborating these concepts further, my intention is to argue for the development of architectural practices that attempt to avoid the problems of the hylomorphic schema through ongoing variable and adaptive design practices that incorporate the concept of vital materiality as a catalyst for further innovative experimentation.

Metallurgy and Consolidation

> To be an artisan and no longer an artist, creator or founder, is the only way to become cosmic, to leave the milieus and the earth behind. The invocation to the Cosmos does not at all operate as a metaphor; on the contrary,

the operation is an effective one, from the moment the artist connects a material with forces of consistency or consolidation. (Deleuze and Guattari 1987: 345)

The proposition of artisanal production and the 'following' of variable and specific cues from the materials themselves are problems of Metallurgy. In the 'Treatise on Nomadology' plateau we are presented with the figure of the metallurgist as a transformer of material alloys, that is an artisan who experiments with different mixtures and processes in a way that remains creatively open to new material combinations and their effects. Deleuze and Guattari focus on metallurgy because it cannot easily be categorised as either an art form or a science and as such develops a series of openings for us to explore within this variable space of resistance. It is more akin to an experimental practice of manipulation that remains sensitive to the emission of mutations as opportunities for new ways to combine and use materials. In other words, 'Metallurgy in itself constitutes a flow necessarily confluent with nomadism' (1987: 404). Metallurgy remains adaptable, variable and somewhat unpredictable by utilising the flows of vital matter to resist a hylomorphic, law-driven and linear schema of materiality. The metallurgist might discover new material mixtures and interactions with potentially unexplored applications, while at the same time reinventing the processes involved in material experimentation and manipulation needed to do so. This is an opening which could allow architecture to develop alternative responses to its problems by starting out with a foundational shift in its reappraisal of how and what architecture does according to a re-evaluation of materiality along these more fluid lines.

The metallurgist is attuned to the interactive suggestions offered through the active experimentation any material manipulation involves. Architectural practice informed by metallurgy would require us to get our hands dirty, to experiment with different material combinations to see what they suggest we can do differently, according to the vital flows of forces that pulse through matter reconceived. The vitality of matter for Deleuze and Guattari turns not only on its ability to resist homogeneity, but also on its capacity to remain sensitive to variation, adaptable to change and therefore responsive to difference. Taking this on board, the problem of design then modulates away from a recourse to pre-existing templates that cut materials off from their inherently vitalising flows towards the problem of how to become sensitive to the forces that make matter itself vital and the potential for intensive affects, spaces and structures this might unlock for us. As Deleuze and Guattari underline,

'One addresses less a form capable of imposing properties upon matter than material traits of expression constituting affects' (1987: 404).

The primary difference this suggests is the interactive flow of information in any design process, which in turn influences a variable feedback and adaptability to complex and non-homogeneous solutions. Rather than determining a one-way flow of how a design problem can be solved, metallurgy as a creative strategy differs by remaining open to the influence of the material qualities, capacities and modifications themselves at different stages throughout the process of 'design and construction'. This traditional binary division starts to dissolve as we turn towards the potential implications of a non-hylomorphic conception of material relations, which incorporates and responds to different sources of feedback throughout the evolution of an architectural object. It is along this trajectory that the architect as metallurgist might look to the materials themselves in order to innovate, to create new tools with which to sculpt structures and spaces as yet unimagined.

For Deleuze and Guattari architecture is a problem of consistency and consolidation. If we consider materials themselves as vital, that is as aggregations of matter and force that are variable according to their specific mixture and state at any given moment, then in order to use them to build with we need to consolidate them. Architecture is therefore an attempt to develop consistency from chaos, to consolidate the flows of vital matter in ways that develop spatio-material responses to architectural problems. Chaos for Deleuze and Guattari is defined as the incessant and variable flows of matter and force, not as total disorder. For the architect this could suggest a design practice which would seek to consolidate useable mixtures of these vital and differential movements of matter–force. We could therefore argue that architecture seeks to consolidate mixtures of matter and force in order to create spaces that are intended to resolve specific architectural problems. Architectural structures are thus consolidations of variable mixtures of an energetic materiality that use the specific qualities of combinations of force and matter to generate active spaces with variable affects.

In the case of the hylomorphic model of form–matter relations, consistency is developed through the imposition of form from above, from the realm of theory, which may or may not necessarily have any relation to how or what is eventually produced. Composition therefore is understood to occur before construction and almost in spite of its materials, not as a part of it. If we follow the tendency to standardise and repeat the same material forms and procedures of consolidation, how can we expect to entertain an opening towards anything genuinely different at a materially driven level? Having sustained their critique of hylomorphism and offered up the figure of the metallurgist as an illustrator of what an alternative materialism might look like, Deleuze and Guattari have put aside the question of how all of this might unfold in a design process which actually builds something. One way to develop a more detailed response to it is suggested when they make the following proposition:

> It is no longer a question of imposing a form upon a matter but of elaborating an increasingly rich and consistent material, the better to tap increasingly intense forces. What makes a material increasingly rich is the same as what holds heterogeneities together without their ceasing to be heterogeneous. What holds them together in this way are intercalary oscillators [. . .].
> (Deleuze and Guattari 1987: 329)

The definition of a material as something that is rich or intensifies force revolves around how to mix heterogeneous material aggregates in a way that resists any overpowering homogenising tendencies. To 'intercalate' is to make or allow insertions between discrete material entities that facilitate interaction without fundamentally altering their specific traits and characteristics. Insertions in this sense are material pathways of connectivity and communication between different material aggregations. The oscillation of the connecting insertions promotes the concept of a more fluid and variable series of material couplings, allowing for movement and variable interrelation while maintaining a degree of heterogeneity at the same time. Subsequently, this concept turns not only on the different mixings, but on the intermediate binding agents, the insertions between discrete consolidations that allow them to interact, perhaps even communicate, without irrevocably altering their distinct characteristics. Each consolidation itself is creative according to Deleuze and Guattari's 'machinics' of molecular engineering as they call it (1987: 328), and the way we combine and 'intercalate' different substances, structures, forces and so on can alter the resulting properties of materials simultaneously. The example they use to (very briefly) illustrate this proposition is the radical change the intercalation of iron or steel to reinforce concrete had on the evolution and future development of building structures and spaces.

A Concrete Example

At a first glance, one might think that a discussion about concrete has almost nothing to do with metallurgy. However, in their brief description of the intersection between concrete and 'iron' in *1837: Of the*

Refrain (1987: 329), Deleuze and Guattari present us with a useful illustration of how we can identify, use and explore the as yet unknown effects of innovative conjunctions between seemingly disparate or wholly unrelated materials. The example given describes the development of concrete technology and the paradigmatic shift in its potential use that emerged when combined with reinforcing steel. For Deleuze and Guattari this identifies a material combination that changed the ways in which physical structure could subsequently be thought. A transformation of specific material combinations altered potential uses for architects, enabling them to describe space differently by using a new material mixture with different structural capacities. Within the broader discussion of consolidation, Deleuze and Guattari pinpoint the effect the emergence of reinforced concrete had on revising existing responses to force and matter: 'More recently, matters like reinforced concrete have made it possible for the architectural ensemble to free itself from arborescent models employing tree-pillars, branch-beams, foliage-vaults' (1987: 329).

Prior to the development of steel reinforced concrete, we might understand building structures as limited to a simple load-bearing logic of pillar, beam and vault. This paradigm implies a high degree of material homogeneity, of consolidation of the material in a regular, measurable and predictable form and the linear translation of mostly compressive structural forces. Concrete itself is an ancient material combination of cement, stone aggregates, sand and water that has traditionally been used much like a liquid incarnation of stone. The structural logic that has made it useful is its ability to be spread in a liquid flow and then cure into a hard, stone-like load-bearing end product. It is an aggregate material with heterogeneous qualities that can change state from an initial viscous flow to a consolidated aggregate that has been spread, poured or pumped into otherwise inaccessible areas, as well as predetermined shapes or moulds. One could characterise concrete's usefulness at this point in its development as a function of its ability to change state, to alter its rate of flow from fast, as a liquid able to be poured, to slow, in its affinity with stone, once cured. According to the hylomorphic model, concrete is consolidated and used in a particular way according to the one-dimensional transmission of compressive forces in a linear manner, across vault and beam, through pillar to ground. One material, one force tracing one line in one direction.

Deleuze and Guattari see concrete as an inherently heterogeneous material because its consistency is subject to significant variation depending on the contents of the mixture. It is the variability inherent to concrete mixtures that helps to illustrate the experimental importance such a material might have. Concrete's variable plasticity can allow designers to experiment with different structural and spatial arrangements as a direct function of the material mixing and building process. This property has since been utilised and developed through the chemical addition of plasticisers, retardants or accelerants among a plethora of altering admixtures and processes. Moreover, the methods and modes of mixing continue to be developed. The limitation, however, was the restriction of standard or non-reinforced concrete mixes to only perform well under compressive loads. With the insertion of steel reinforcement, concrete is subsequently able to effect an opening through which to escape its structural arborescence, its reliance on the predetermination of the mould and its linear correlation with the load-bearing modular use of masonry. The intercalation of 'iron' in concrete's heterogeneous mixes allows the flow of concrete to become self supporting, the concrete mixture flowing into new forms that are supported through the intercalated rhythm of the reinforcing metal rather than through the external surfaces of the scaffolded moulds or the formwork. Indeed, the modulation of concrete into a self-supporting surface discards its external formwork by internalising it through the intercalation of steel. Where originally concrete was limited to effectively dealing with one type of structural force, this trait is intensified by adding the tensile capacity inherent to steel into the mix. Suddenly the new material mix can better follow multiple structural forces in a way that was previously impossible.

For Deleuze and Guattari, a turning point in material technology helps us to better understand the forces that surround us by altering the way we can trace lines of force in the structures we create. However, this sort of innovative development will not unfold on its own, by limiting ourselves to an a priori conceptual approach. Rather we can only hope to innovate in this way through integrated mixtures of thought and action. This means design is experimentation, testing new material mixtures and combinations according to different arrangements to see what they might consolidate and following these cues. It is precisely this approach to materials that Deleuze's concept of metallurgy points us toward. In this example, what really matters is not just the insertion of metal rods into the concrete mix, rather it is the structural and subsequent spatial transformations such an experiment made possible. All of a sudden concrete had a means to escape the mould in an innovative way and start tracing new structural lines, describing new spatial volumes. It created a new tool that helped architects to develop previously unachievable, perhaps even unimaginable structures and spaces. We could look to Wright's cantilevering horizontal planes over a flowing river below at 'Fallingwater' (1936–9), Utzon's Sydney Opera House with its organic vaulted shell-sails (1957–73) or Calatrava's sinuous skeletal bridges and buildings (1983–present), all of which use reinforced concrete to trace and extend lines of force in previously unachievable ways. It is the manner in which these structures insinuate new lines in themselves, new flows and spaces, that is of particular interest for architects. New material mixes can develop unknown and unexpected openings for architects to explore, releasing them from the predominance of form. Reinforced concrete changed the limit conditions for the creation of space by developing a logic of the *armature* as opposed to traditional load-bearing structure, by exploring the concept of a 'self-supporting surface' that can be manipulated according to an alternate logic. This is understood as a combination of the rhythm of forces resonating through the steel and the fluid heterogeneity of the variable concrete mixes that entomb it. Deleuze and Guattari describe this as follows:

> Not only is concrete a heterogeneous matter whose degree of consistency varies according to the elements in the mix, but iron is intercalated following a rhythm; moreover, its *self-supporting surfaces* form a complex rhythmic personage whose 'stems' have different sections and variable intervals depending on the intensity and direction of the force to be tapped (armature instead of structure). (1987: 329)

At the same time, in opposition to the linearity of the hylomorphic model, we can see that there is a co-determining feedback process being used here, between the ways a material can work and the ideas this suggests to modify its use with a view to describing new spaces. Having an idea and finding a material that can be made to comply with one's will to realise this idea is to remain trapped within the hylomorphic mode. Alternatively, working with the variable singularities of different material aggregates under different conditions, in different states, to see what more they can do, how to otherwise develop structure (or armature) and space, might present us with a more fluid conception of design. This alternative seeks to be open to specific influences, vague essences and otherwise hidden cues that the materials and processes of design themselves can integrate and respond to along the way according to the evolving and variable processes of experimentation. This alternative conception of design then asks if, by following the ideas new material combinations suggest to us, we might more fully explore the limits of what we already have. To design according to the challenge of charting new force lines or adding to existing lines in innovative ways could at the very least suggest new ways to explore the material world.

There are two senses of the word 'armature' that are of relevance here. First, an armature is the metal framework on which a sculpture is moulded with clay or similar material (concrete in this case). Second, in biology an armature is the protective covering of an animal or plant. In the first instance we have the Deleuzian alternative to traditional structure that in concert with heterogeneous concrete mixes allows the steel armature to follow new configurations of force. Second, we have the concept of a self-supporting surface that protects itself, literally protects the underlying steel reinforcement from rust and decay and hence structural failure and the collapse of the surface.[3] This could be developed into a notion of an architectural materiality that protects itself, literally arms itself in order to resist certain forces and thus sustain others.[4] Architecture here literally becomes a war machine, armoured by its use of materials, or propositionally as the inventor of new architectural instruments and techniques that function as affective weapons in the service of a new assemblage.

Tracing Bio-digital Lines

A useful contemporary example of this sort of experimental proposition is the 'Bio-concrete' project undertaken by R&Sie, the design studio of French architects François Roche and Stéphanie Lavaux, where new material compounds of concrete are being experimented with in combination with digitally programmed robotic machines. As a part of their larger architectural research work entitled *Une Architecture des Humeurs*, R&Sie have developed a series of experiments exploring the potential that a combination of new concrete polymers might have for future structural systems that are far more adaptive and responsive than traditional systems.[5] One area of this research looks into the mixtures of synthetic polymers and biological resins combined with concrete filler materials. Experimentation is needed to explore how differing mixtures change key components of the new material, for example viscosity, adherence, curing times and so on. Concurrently, R&Sie investigate different iterations of swirls and braids in order to develop a better understanding of how the new bio-concrete mixtures might perform structurally. These platted extrusions of bio-concrete are designed to be constructed by purpose-built robots that operate according to a complex pattern of algorithmically determined movements that adapt to the adhesion and viscosity profiles of specific bio-concrete mixes. Different levels of inter-material adhesion change the 'stickiness' of the braids, which in combination are added together or 'secreted' by the construction robots to form larger structurally self-supporting aggregates. The new bio-enhanced concrete material in concert with the twisting forms into which it is platted is used as a digitally programmable structural framework. The material is simultaneously the formwork, structure and means of construction. The difference between form and matter dissolves into a variable structural-material experiment that becomes responsive to different human inputs. The intercalation of steel reinforcement has transformed into digital signals programming robotic construction processes. Steel has been replaced by modern bio-polymers, genetic braiding algorithms and dis/assembly robots. Metal remains, however, the conduit that processes and translates the design inputs, via its algorithmic rhythms and the literal armatures of the robots that build the new bio-concrete structures. Deleuze's 'metallic line' continues to evolve outside the literal material as a digital conductor of material information flows, which help aggregate new consolidations. How architects might experiment, explore and exploit the untested possibilities suggested by these contemporary bio-digital lines remains to be fully explored. This prospect offers some hope for architectures-yet-to-come.

This is a truncated synopsis of one part of an architectural research project that is deserving of a much more detailed analysis in order to illustrate the intelligence and experimental creativity that drives it. Nevertheless, it serves as a useful illustration of precisely the sort of innovative architectural practices I am advocating here using Deleuze's concepts of metallurgy and vital materiality. Not only are the different compounds of new composite-based concrete themselves being developed, their development is related to the complex algorithmically based structural 'engineering' robots that secrete the bio-concrete polymers while assembling (and at times disassembling) structures.[6] Arguably it illustrates one cutting-edge iteration of the sort of metallurgical experiments the architect as alchemist after Deleuze can catalyse. On a contemporary stage, the intersection of digital technologies, manufacturing techniques, engineering-based structural mathematics and innovations in material science would appear to neatly illustrate where future architectural experiments may fruitfully lead us. The underlying suggestion here points towards the potential for us to push the development of our architectural work further by embracing these and other multifarious facets of our emerging contemporary metallic line, a bio-digital line that may yet allow us to develop new architectural tools and techniques with which to structure future spaces. One could argue that

R&Sie's bio-concrete experiments in fact remove or displace the metallic element, the literal reinforcing steel, from the concrete and replace it with synthetic bio-polymers, complex algorithmic weaves and digitally determined metal construction robotics. The metal itself thus becomes a virtual element, a digital flow that determines the way the bio-concrete responds to different design constraints, whether or not the robots add to or remove parts of the structure they attend to. So in terms of the armature proposition stated above, the intercalation of reinforcing steel has modulated to bio-synthetic concrete polymer braids, and the biological idea of covering and protection now develops through the literal material composition which incorporates biological materials and algorithmic growth principles.

DeLanda emphasises the variable potential of research like Roche and Lavaux's in a way that allows us to appreciate the importance of the following experiments by identifying the productive connection between new materials and the new traits that they emit, suggesting new ways to use them. He says that with the advent of 'new composites', which have very different and specific 'traits', 'we may need to nurture again our ability to deal with variation (material/structural) as a creative force, and to think of structures that incorporate heterogeneous elements as a

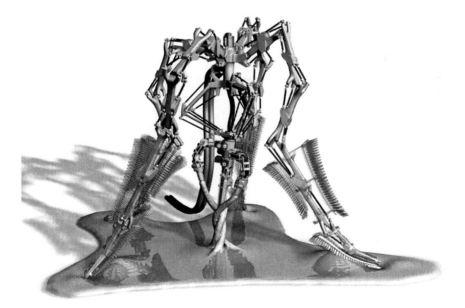

Figure 6.1 Self-supporting surfaces secreted by structural braiding, algorithmically driven robotic bio-concrete construction machines. Reproduced with permission from R&Sie.

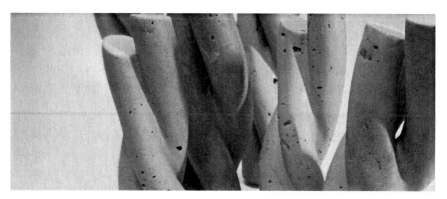

Figure 6.2 Bio-concrete polymer samples: braided armatures. Reproduced with permission from R&Sie.

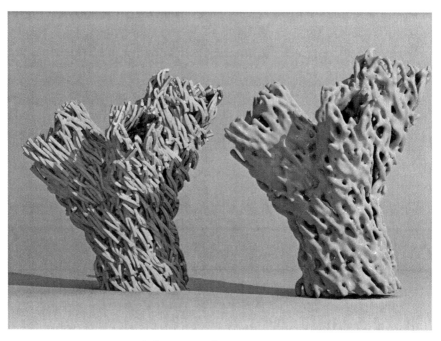

Figure 6.3 Fragment Y (bifurcation), from weaving to coagulation. Structural forms as assemblies of bio-concrete components – testing different mixes, exploring different affects through experimenting with a combination of weave patterns and material viscosity, experimenting with the effects of variable viscosity on structural form and its capacity both to support itself and play a role in a larger structural system. Reproduced with permission from R&Sie.

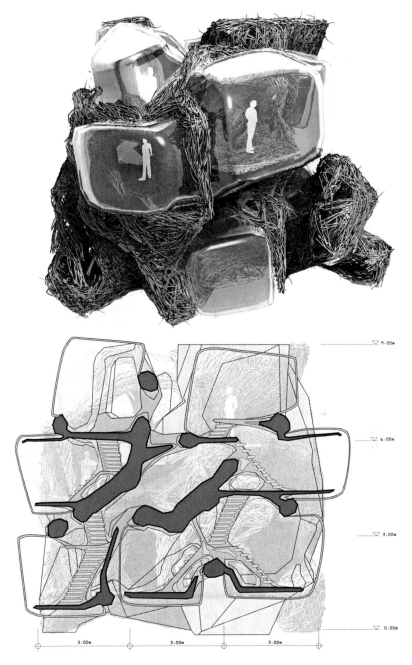

Figure 6.4 Space as a consolidation of a braided matter–energy flow. Structural lines of force encapsulate discrete, perhaps habitable spatial volumes. Reproduced with permission from R&Sie.

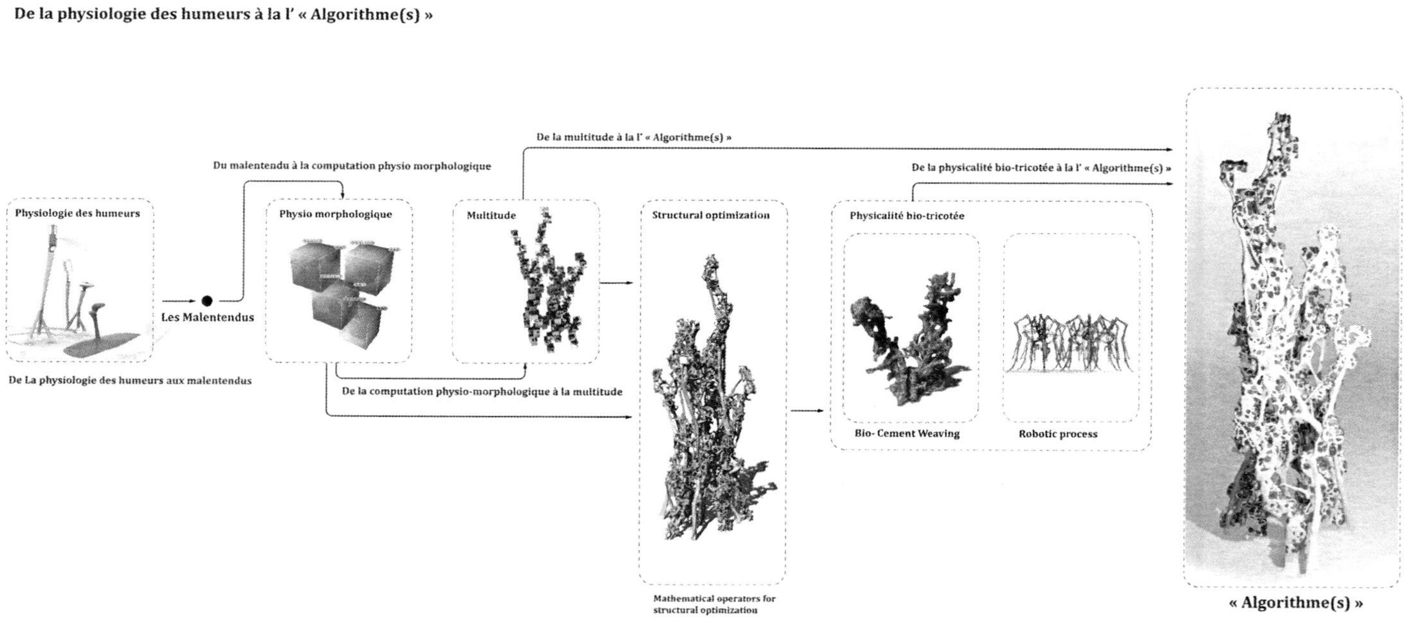

De la physiologie des humeurs à la l' « Algorithme(s) »

Figure 6.5 'From physio to algorithm(s).' Reproduced with permission from R&Sie.

challenge to be met by innovative design' (DeLanda 2004: 21). Simply put, new techniques combined with new compounds and new composites constructed in innovative ways alter the possibilities for material use going forward.

Reinforced concrete is only one modern material among a raft of others including plastics, synthetic polymers, advanced composites like Kevlar and carbon fibre, structural glasses, rubbers and ductile metallic alloys. The list goes on and continues to grow, which attests to the fact that the architect plays an important role in the experimental development of these, trying to search out new ways of creating spaces by pushing materials beyond their limits and testing new material combinations in order to trace out new lines of force. Deleuze and Guattari were sharply aware of this, an observation that goes a long way to explaining why they have exerted a significant influence on some areas of contemporary architectural research. As much as the more easily digestible or perhaps more cynically 'marketable' terminology of 'folding' has taken centre stage in the veneration of Deleuze and Guattari by the architectural media machine, one of the most challenging underlying innovations they made was in proposing a new theory of materiality, characterised here in terms of metallurgical relations. As they say, it is a question of consistencies and consolidation and the manipulation of 'blocks of wrought matter'[7] in order to see where else we might go.

If we can thus extract the notion of the in-between from the example just sketched out, then this suggests at least one way for the architect to proceed. It is to invent new ways of making insertions between heterogeneities, at varying levels and scales from the purely material to the spatial and across their myriad intersections and interactions: connection, not cutting off; cultivating and following the flows of force rather than imposing upon space the sentence of a closed or even 'finished' object for static contemplation or inhabitation. This is done in order to produce spaces that are themselves vital and variable and that maintain a shifting multifaceted connectivity, resisting their opposite in the static, inflexible and non-vital effects of hylomorphism. In some ways the preceding example of reinforced concrete could be construed as a literal form of innovative material combination, in that reinforcement steel is intercalated within the liquid concrete mixture which hardens and develops a symbiotic relation between the 'metallic' and the stone-like flows of concrete. At the same time, it is also illustrative of how a metallic line itself might be traced through the developmental history of a particular building material. It was the introduction of structurally reinforcing metals within concrete flows that produced a new material which over time has been engaged to describe new structural forms, new systems of construction, new ways to elaborate previously unachievable architectural forms. Crucially, this kind of innovation cannot be forced or predetermined; it has to emerge through the experimental testing of these new material mixtures.

Regardless of how immersed we may become in our experiments with materials, we should not lose sight of the fact that we can also use ourselves as weapons in the service of an architectural war-machine. By searching for new modes of practice and connection, we are looking for ways the architect can maintain a vital connectivity to the pulsing multiplicity of force–matter flows without falling back into chaos or becoming trapped by the rigidity of inflexible striations. In order to rise to the complex challenges of our epoch, perhaps now is a better time than ever to revisit our architectural armoury and get to work making new weapons to replenish our stores. This is the challenge a serious engagement with Deleuze's reworked concept of metallurgy suggests to me. The question of how architecture might proceed into the future and remain vital can no longer be hijacked by the superficialities of fashion, ego, power and privilege, or the deadening repetition of unthinking, template-based, formally driven regurgitations of the same failed design responses. Next time you speak to an architect, don't ask them what designs they're working on or how their building works are progressing; ask them what weapons they are using and if they are inventing new ones.

Notes

I would like to thank Paul Patton for his support, encouragement and suggestions both in the research that preceded this chapter while supervising my PhD and in the distillation of the key themes presented here. I would also like to thank Hélène Frichot for her patience, editorial skill and good humour.

1. See plateau '1227: Treatise on Nomadology – The War Machine' (Deleuze and Guattari 1987: 411) and also '1440: The Smooth and Striated' (1987: 492–9) where they discuss the influence of Worringer, the Gothic Line and the material component of the innovations made in that era. For an excellent discussion of the Metallic Line and its relation to Metallurgy, see Deleuze (1979).
2. See, for example, the work of Michael Hensel, Achim Menges and OCEAN (Hensel and Menges 2006), Sean Lally (2009) and Peter Zumthor (2010). Other practices more explicitly cite Deleuze's influence in their attempts to re-evaluate the place of form–matter relations. See, for example, the work of Bernard Cache (1995), Greg Lynn (1998), Foreign Office Architects (FOA 2002) and Lars Spuybroek (2009).
3. Recently the use of steel reinforcement has been replaced in experiments with

hollow carbon fibre reinforcement which, although more expensive, is exponentially stronger and lighter, suggesting a contemporary evolution of the armature of concrete as a self-supporting structure. Carbon fibre reinforcement will not rust and, by being hollow, it can also double as an in-situ cast in service management systems for electrical and other services.

4. This idea of a self-modifying, self-arming or 'healing' concrete has become a reality. A recent development of concrete admixtures uses it is a bacterial 'feed' mix developed by Dutch researchers, which allows the concrete to 'heal' itself. When a crack develops and water ingress occurs, potentially threatening to damage the reinforcing steel and compromise the material and structure, the dormant bacteria in the concrete mix react to the water and 'activate' by producing calcite, which then seals the crack. Further water ingress is prevented, the concrete dries out and the bacteria return to their dormant state. A self-supporting material and a self-repairing one; see Lynch (2010).

5. For more detail on the work of Roche and Lavaux/R&Sie and their *Architecture des Humeurs* research, refer to <http://www.new-territories.com/blog/> (accessed 10 October 2012). For the specific 'Bio Concrete' section, refer to <http://www.new-territories.com/blog/architecturedeshumeurs/?p=108>.

6. Our understanding of the change of status of the object away from 'dumb' matter being forced into a mould according to the 'hylomorphic schema' towards the conception of vital matter in continuous movement and shifting formal arrangements benefits from Deleuze's concept of the event. If matter is in continuous movement according to this idea, then the event is most likely going to be the only way we could define an object according to the way it unfolds differently at any given moment. Every 'snapshot' of an object would be slightly different, which is a radical redefinition of the object, building, space, etc. as rigidly fixed. Where R&Sie's robots remain under a degree of human control, we can with some caution imagine pushing the evolution of this idea further and developing into an architecture that builds itself. This idea, although still embryonic in terms of real-world examples, finds its way into some contemporary science fiction. See, for example, the description of buildings and cities by Alastair Reynolds in his *Revelation Space* series, where the integration of advanced technical machinery and biological systems in buildings (and humans) is infected by a viral plague that causes the buildings to mutate and grow uncontrollably and unpredictably over time (continuous variation and formal development). In describing the onset and effect of the 'Melding Plague' he writes:

> At the time of the plague's manifestation our society was supersaturated by trillions of tiny machines. They were our unthinking, uncomplaining servants, givers of life and shapers of matter, and yet we barely gave them a moment's thought . . . We forged and sculpted matter on the scale of mountains; wrote symphonies out of matter; caused it to dance to our whims like tamed fire. Machines grew our orbiting city-states from raw rock and ice and then bootstrapped inert matter towards life within their biomes [. . .] Machines made Chasm City what it was; shaping its amorphous architecture towards a fabulous and phantasmagoric beauty [. . .] The plague went beyond mere destruction, into a realm much closer to artistry, albeit an artistry of a uniquely perverted and sadistic kind. It caused our machines to evolve uncontrollably – out of *our* control, at least – seeking bizarre new symbioses. Our buildings turned into Gothic nightmares, trapping us before we could escape their lethal transfigurations. We became glistening larval fusions of flesh and machine. (Reynolds 2001: 3–4)

7. Quoting Henry James; see Deleuze and Guattari (1987: 329). Deleuze and Guattari use the idea of 'blocs' with reference to sensation in *What Is Philosophy?* and *Francis Bacon: The Logic of Sensation*. It means an aggregate of affects, or in this case an aggregate of materials that are yet to undergo the metallurgical operations of transformation.

References

Alberti, L. B. (1988), *On the Art of Building in Ten Books*, trans. J. Rykwert and R. Tavenor, Cambridge, MA: MIT Press.

Cache, B. (1995), *Earth Moves: The Furnishing of Territories*, trans. A. Boyman, Cambridge, MA: MIT Press.

DeLanda, M. (2004), 'Material Complexity', in N. Leach, D. Turnbull and C. Williams (eds), *Digital Tectonics*, London: Wiley Academy, pp. 14–21.

Deleuze, G. (1979), 'Cours Vincennes. Anti-Oedipe et Mille Plateaux. Metal, Metallurgy, Music, Husserl, Simondon', trans. C. Stivale, <http://www.webdeleuze.com/php/texte.php?cle=186&groupe=Anti Oedipe et Mille Plateaux&langue=2> (accessed 10 October 2012).

Deleuze, G. (2003), *Francis Bacon: The Logic of Sensation*, trans. D. W. Smith, Minneapolis, MN: University of Minnesota Press.

Deleuze, G. and F. Guattari (1987), *A Thousand Plateaus (Capitalism and Schizophrenia)*, trans. B. Massumi, London: Athlone Press.

Deleuze, G. and F. Guattari (1994), *What Is Philosophy?*, trans. G. Burchell and H. Tomlinson, London: Verso.

Foreign Office Architects (FOA) (2002), *The Yokohama Project*, Barcelona: Actar.

Hensel, M. and A. Menges (2006), *Morpho-ecologies*, London: Architectural Association.

Lally, S. (2009), *Energies: New Material Boundaries*, London: Wiley Academy.

Lynch, D. (2010), 'Dutch develop self-healing bio-concrete', *New Civil Engineer*, 9 September, <http://www.nce.co.uk/news/structures/dutch-develop-self-healing-bio-concrete/8605735.article> (accessed 10 October 2012).

Lynn, G. (1998), *Folds, Bodies & Blobs: Collected Essays*, [Brussels]: La lettre volée.

Protevi, J. (ed.) (2005), *The Edinburgh Dictionary of Continental Philosophy*, Edinburgh: Edinburgh University Press.

Reynolds, A. (2001), *Chasm City*, London: Gollancz.

Sheil, B. (ed.) (2005), *Design Through Making*, Special Issue of *Architectural Design*, 75: 4, London: Wiley Academy.

Spuybroek, L. (2009), *Research & Design: The Architecture of Variation*, London: Thames & Hudson.

Zumthor, P. (2010), *Thinking Architecture*, Basel: Birkhäuser.

Chapter 7

Assembling Architecture

Kim Dovey

The concept of 'assemblage' emerges in the work of Deleuze and Guattari (1987), primarily in *A Thousand Plateaus*, and has been developed by DeLanda (2006) and others into a more transparent and practical social theory. This chapter explores the application of assemblage thinking to architecture and urbanism. In parallel with words like 'design', 'housing' and 'building', 'assemblage' is at once verb and noun. An assemblage is a whole that is formed from the interconnectivity and flows between constituent parts – a socio-spatial cluster of interconnections wherein the identities and functions of both parts and wholes emerge from the flows between them. Assemblage is at once material and representational, it defies any reduction to essence, to textual analysis or to materiality. It is also multi-scalar with smaller assemblages (rooms, families, events) enmeshed in larger ones (cities, societies, states) without reduction of the smaller to the larger. Assemblage is a useful way of rethinking theories of 'place' in terms of process, identity formation and becoming, but without the Heideggerian essentialism. A building or a place is neither object nor a collection of parts – rather it is an assemblage of socio-spatial flows and intersections. Assemblage thinking has a capacity to move architecture away from a focus on fixed form towards process and transformation; from an expression of architecture as Being-in-the-world towards a more Deleuzian becoming-in-the-world. While appearing abstract and often opaque, the conceptual apparatus of assemblage thinking is eminently pragmatic in terms of both design and research. This will be illustrated through a discussion of the design of new school buildings where adaptable learning environments are in demand to house complex, contested and unpredictable practices. Architects are engaged with the task of housing a transformation in the field of education from disciplinary technologies towards student-centred learning where creative and critical capacities rather than social reproduction become key.

There are no easy entry points into *A Thousand Plateaus* or assemblage thinking because one needs to think in a different way in order to understand – it is the deep end wherever you dive in. In the translator's introduction Massumi suggests that one approach the work like music – some parts you will like while others leave you cold. It can also be explored like a strange city or a neighbourhood – almost any chapter can serve as an introduction and you can follow the connections from there: 'The Smooth and Striated', 'Of the Refrain' and 'Micropolitics and Segmentarity' may be the most engaging for architects. Another place to start is the index – find the concepts you are particularly interested in and follow the threads through the text. For Deleuze, philosophy is the invention of concepts as tools for thinking. *A Thousand Plateaus* can be seen as a strange toolbox where the application of the tools is up to us. A tool is something we use to achieve a desired end; it mediates a process of production. What is at stake is not truth but usefulness – how does it enable us to think? The usefulness of some tools and/or concepts will not be apparent as we rummage through the conceptual toolbox; we may also see uses that were never intended. As with any toolkit, the ways we see each concept will depend on our desires. If we are researchers conducting fieldwork, producing papers and concepts, then we will seek analytic, methodological or explanatory tools that help these tasks. If we are designers engaged in transforming the world then we will see and seek our tools in a different way. In either case our goals are practical.

I have argued elsewhere that assemblage can be approached as a theory of 'place' where it can help us engage with the socio-spatiality of the everyday world and therefore with the social dimensions of architecture (Dovey 2010). Assemblage theory offers an approach to theories of place without the reductionism and essentialism that have weighed down such discourse for so long. It is empirical without the reductionism of empirical science; it gives priority to experience and sensation without reduction to essence; and it seeks to understand the social construction of reality without reduction to text.

Assemblage

The concept of 'assemblage' is translated from the French *agencement* meaning 'layout', 'arrangement' or 'alignment' – both a dynamic process and a socio-spatial formation. While there are always debates over translation, this seems the best English word with its mix of noun/verb, stability/change, structure/agency. The French word, however, also connotes the notion of 'alignment' indicating that the various parts of an assemblage are not simply connected but share a certain direction and synergy. Beyond any definition, however, assemblage emerges from the work and is better defined by its use than its meaning – as Deleuze puts it, 'don't ask what it means, ask how it works' (quoted in Buchanan and Marks 2000: 294). The question becomes one of how buildings and places are assembled and how they work.

My interests here also have to do with the larger project of understanding the ways architecture is enmeshed in practices of power. Power is much too large an issue to deal with here in any comprehensive way. It is important, however, to understand and to situate the work of Deleuze and that of Foucault (from which much assemblage thinking is constructed) in relation to the long-standing distinction between power *to* and power *over* – power as the *capacity* to achieve an end (empowerment) and power exercised through *control* of others (authority, force, violence, coercion, manipulation, seduction) (Dovey 2008). The revolution in thinking about power that Foucault initiated can be seen as a rethinking of the ways in which power *to* becomes harnessed to practices of power *over*. With Foucault, however, power retains a bad odour – the critique of the architecture/power nexus remains a critique of the production of discipline and normalised subjectivity; the links with oppression always seems more potent than those with liberation. While Foucault opens up our thinking to ways of understanding power as capacity, as empowerment, it is only to describe our subjection to modern regimes of power *over*.

Architecture is always and everywhere implicated in practices of power; this is the condition of architecture. The desire for an architecture that might escape such practices is often implicated in such practices. The task for architecture is to embrace such an engagement because that is where the emancipatory potential of architecture lies. In everyday life architecture is taken for granted and its potency lies precisely in this capacity to escape contemplation. While the roots of assemblage thinking are in the Foucauldian notion of the 'apparatus' (*dispositif*), assemblage moves beyond instrumentality and pessimism. It enlarges our capacity to understand the implications of Foucault's insight into power as a production of subjectivity and it enables us to understand the key link of power to desire.

For Deleuze, desire is the primary force of life, immanent to everyday life and not limited to the human world. Desire does not exist preformed but is a process of connection and of becoming. Far from thinking of the world as a collection of beings who then have desires, Deleuze insists that life begins from flows of becoming or desire, which then produce relative points of stability (Colebrook 2002: 66). Architecture, as both process and form, can be understood as the result of a multiplicity of desires – for shelter, security, privacy and boundary control; for status, identity and reputation; for profit, authority and political power; for change or stability; for order or chaos. Assemblage is both verb and noun, agency and structure, change and stasis, process and product. Flows of desire are the primary forces of assemblage (as a verb) – the formation of connections that become the assemblage (as a noun).

An assemblage differs from an 'organisation' in that the relations between parts are 'machinic' rather than 'organic'. As Colebrook (2002: xxii) puts it: 'Desire is "machinic" precisely because it does not originate from closed organisms or selves; it is the productive process of life that produces organisms and selves.' From this perspective assemblages of cities and citizens, neighbourhoods and neighbours, houses and homes, schools and classrooms, institutions and states are produced by desires. When used as a noun, assemblages are 'wholes whose properties emerge from the interactions between parts' (DeLanda 2006: 5). But the assemblage is not a thing nor a collection of things. Buildings, rooms, trees, cars, gates, people and signs all connect in certain ways and it is the connections between them that make an assemblage.

Assemblage has a fourfold (or tetravalent) structure formed from the intersections of two primary axes (Deleuze and Guattari 1987: 88–9). The first of these axes opposes and connects materiality to formal expression; it both distinguishes and connects flows and interactions of bodies and things in space to expressions of meaning through language and representation. To see architecture as assemblage is to reconfigure the relation of form to function and avoid a reduction to either text or material conditions. This axis is construed as horizontal – neither side has priority – and is also described as form versus content.

The second axis, construed as vertical, involves an opposition and movement between the formation and erasure of territory – from territorialisation to deterritorialisation and reterritorialisation. This is what we know in everyday terms as the appropriation and/or expropriation of space. In terms of representation it involves the inscription/erasure/reinscription of territorial boundaries and identities; in material terms it involves the construction, penetration and enforcement of material boundary control. While territories are not necessarily spatial, this is what establishes assemblage as the most architectural of concepts in the Deleuzian lexicon.

Territorialisation mediates the degree to which an assemblage is stabilised or destabilised. The concept of territory here is broad enough to encompass everything from the rhythms of the urinating dog to the defence of national boundaries. Territoriality is creative rather than merely defensive, it is a stabilisation of the assemblage, establishing a zone of comfort and order, a sense of home that keeps chaos and difference at bay (Deleuze and Guattari 1987: ch. 11). Deterritorialisation is the process by which territories are eroded or erased, walls are demolished, nations are invaded. Reterritorialisation, in turn, is the formation of new assemblages.

The ways that boundaries are used to construct, perform or inscribe territories is called 'segmentarity':

> We are segmented from all around and in every direction. The human being is a segmentary animal . . . Dwelling, getting around, working, playing: life is spatially and socially segmented. The house is segmented according to its rooms' assigned purposes; streets, according to the order of the city; the factory according to the nature of the work. (Deleuze and Guattari 1987: 208)

Spatial segmentarity is akin to spatial syntax or the use of walls and boundaries to inscribe a social logic of space (Hillier and Hanson 1984). Social segmentarity is in some ways akin to Bourdieu's notion of *habitus* – the set of practical taxonomies, divisions and hierarchies embodied in both habit and habitat (Bourdieu 1990). Segments can divide according to race, class, age and gender with no place for hybridity. Segmented assemblages resonate with other assemblages at similar and different scales. Horizontally, gated enclaves resonate with each other, as do squatter settlements, schools and suburbs. Vertically, the bank branch resonates with the headquarters, as the police station resonates with the state, the classroom with the classifying system and the neighbourhood with the nation. One becomes a bank manager, a cop, a student, an Australian . . . in accordance with different spatial segments.

The vertical dimension of territory and segmentarity marks assemblage thinking as fundamentally multi-scalar. It is impossible to understand the room, building, street, district, city or nation without considering the connections between them. Each segment gains its meanings, functions and capacities from the network of spaces in which it is enmeshed. Crucially, however, there is no privileging of scales – the micro is as important as the macro. A multi-scalar focus will pay attention to both top-down and bottom-up practices, but particularly to the connections between scales and to understanding the flows of desire that are productive of the assemblage in the first place. Assemblage research entails a focus on thick description at every scale and a resistance to any tendency to treat the architectural or the everyday as simply epi-phenomena of larger-scale processes and structures (McFarlane 2011). It opposes the tree-like thinking that privileges change from above and focuses on understanding the relations and dynamics between scales as socio-spatial change spreads up, down and laterally (Dovey 2011). This entails attention to micro-spatialities that may seem like a fetish, but it is here that one finds the micro-practices of power embedded in the mor-phology of the built environment. Multi-scalar thinking is inherently interdisciplinary and requires that we think across the fields of geogra-phy, urban planning, urban design, landscape, architecture, interiors, fashion – overturning any hegemony between fields.

For Deleuze and Guattari there is a distinction between 'supple' and 'rigid' segmentarities. Rigid segmentarities have strong boundaries while supple ones allow a fluidity of lateral connections with potential for old segments to dissolve and new segments to form. This supple segmen-tarity is based on the power of networks and a fundamental distinction between tree-like and rhizomic or networked structures. The tree and the rhizome are metaphors for ways of thinking based on hierarchi-cal control on the one hand and horizontal connectivity on the other. These are part of a set of twofold concepts that can help us analyse the ways buildings work as assemblages: network/hierarchy, supple/rigid, rhizome/tree, smooth/striated, difference/identity, and the more generic becoming/being, potential/actual. Assemblage theory opens up the spatial imaginary in a critical manner, connecting actual with potential.

While there is much more to be said about this, I want to link the idea of assemblage to the concept of place and explore how it might be applied in particular place types. The concept of place is not one that is deployed by Deleuze and Guattari so far as I know, but assemblage thinking is infused with spatiality at every level. The title 'A Thousand Plateaus' is adapted from a concept in Gregory Bateson's book *Steps to an Ecology of Mind* where he described the ways in which dynamic cultural systems can stabilise on a plane or 'plateau' between polarities (Bateson [1972] 2000). The concept of the 'plateau' is central to *A Thousand Plateaus* in the sense of a consistent focus on the spaces between levels and things, and it shares more than etymology with the concept of 'place'. For Bateson, a plateau is a culturally constructed system where the tendency for a system to run out of control – an arms race, crime rates, environ-mental degradation – is countered by a plateau or plane of stability that coexists with constant change. What we sense as the stability of place is often a plateau of development produced by locally sustainable limits.

Yet to perceive place as static is to misrecognise it as a thing rather than an assemblage of differences. As Deleuze (2006: 179) puts it:

> An assemblage is first and foremost what keeps very heterogeneous elements together: [. . .] both natural and artificial elements [. . .] The problem is one of 'consistency' or 'coherence' [. . .] How do things take on consistency? How do they cohere? Even among very different things, an intensive continuity can be found. We have borrowed the word 'plateau' from Bateson precisely to designate these zones of intensive continuity.

Yet assemblage theory is not a theory of place so much as an intellectual toolkit for understanding how places work. To what degree and in what manner is space segmented and territorialised? To what degree and how are material spatial practices and representational narratives deployed in these assemblages and to what ends? What coalitions of desire drive architectural and urban development processes? We need to know a lot more about how architecture is assembled; this is the yawning gap in so much of the research applying Deleuzian theory to built form – the actual mechanisms that operate at and across different scales of room, building, neighbourhood, landscape, city and nation (DeLanda 2006: 31). One of the key tasks here lies in the practice of mapping. For Deleuze and Guattari (1987: 12–13) mapping is a creative act that they distinguish from a simple mimetic tracing: 'What distinguishes the map from the tracing is that it is entirely oriented toward an experimentation in contact with the real.' The map is more than a simple 'tracing' of an existing form because it is infused with a desire to understand how the place might be conceptualised, navigated or changed. Maps reveal the workings of assemblages; they are at once concrete (grounded in a material state of affairs) and abstract (because they cannot show everything, they select and extract layers of data). Maps mediate between the real and the virtual, between past and future, between history and design.

One of the more obscure concepts invented by Deleuze and Guattari is the 'abstract machine' or 'diagram' of the forces comprising an assemblage – at once embodied in the assemblage and productive of it. According to Deleuze (1988: 36), 'the diagram or abstract machine is the map of relations between forces [. . .] that is co-extensive with the whole social field'. One example Deleuze (2006: 123) gives is Foucault's notion of the panopticon – a socio-spatial diagram of one-way visibility wherein practices and subjectivities are produced to meet the anonymous gaze of authority. This diagram of seeing without being seen is evident in the many disciplinary technologies of the prison, factory, school, hospital and CCTV network without being determined in each particular instance. It is an abstraction because an abstract set of relations are evident in all concrete examples, and it is a 'machine' because it is productive of subjectivity. The abstract machine 'is neither an infrastructure that is determining in the last instance nor a transcendental Idea that is determining in the supreme instance. Rather it plays a piloting role' (Deleuze and Guattari 1987: 142).

A diagram is literally a graphic representation of connections between things, a pattern that connects a wide range of assembled outcomes. In many cases the diagram is an image that drives design practices without ever being written down. A stack of serviced floor-plates with a view is a diagram of the immanent forces producing the corporate tower. The flows of desire embodied in this diagram and ultimately this building type include desires for flexibility, the commanding view, corporate identity and profit (Dovey 2008: ch. 8). The diagram of pedestrian paths connecting 'magnet' stores shows how flows of consumer desire are captured in the private shopping mall. Here desires for a safe, clean and cool or warm environment mix with desires for products, for a fantasy world and an anonymous sense of community. The diagram is not a transcendent ideal but a conceptual understanding of the immanent forces of similar place types.

A final word on the rather fundamental connection of design to desire – recall that for Deleuze desire is the primary force of life and of all forms of assemblage. Design is always based in flows of desire. A public transport plan is based on a multiplicity of desires to get to work, to shop and to visit friends. A school design is based on desires for particular modes of teaching and learning, but also often conflicting desires for discipline and liberation. Assemblage thinking enables us to overcome simplistic divisions between materiality and meaning, architecture and planning, form and function, subject and object. It enables us to see buildings and cities as embodying twofold concepts such as rhizome/tree, difference/identity and open/closed. It enables us to break with static, fixed, closed and essentialist notions of place, replacing the Heideggerian notion of being-in-the-world with becoming-in-the-world. It enables a replacement of binary paradigms such as people + environment with the dynamic interconnectivity of the socio-spatial assemblage.

Open Planning

I now want to indicate how assemblage thinking might be applied in a particular research project. As with any toolkit, the ultimate test lies in practice – what new ways of thinking about architecture does it open up? This project, undertaken with educationist Kenn Fisher, is a study of innovative spatial planning in school classrooms. The traditional classroom is a typical case of what Foucault (1979, 1980) terms a disciplinary technology where the gaze of authority works to produce a normalised and disciplined subject. A one-way flow of information is orchestrated from a privileged position that also maintains a controlling gaze over a class of subjects. Classrooms are assembled into schools with corridor access; learning is clearly demarked in space and time from 'play' or 'recess'. Since the early twentieth century we have seen a range of architectural experimentation on the school classroom that has been loosely labelled open planning. Such changes have been generally driven by pedagogical theory sourced to people like Dewey ([1916] 1966), Vygotsky (1978) and others who suggest a multiplicity of ways in which students learn – didactic teaching being just one. There is not scope here to describe this shift in detail but it entails a move from singular and static modes of teaching and learning towards multiple group sizes and activity types over time; from a separation of learning from play to learning through play; from teacher-centred to student-centred with a demand for a range of place types and adaptability.

It has long been clear that student-centred pedagogies are seriously constrained by traditional classrooms. Through the mid-twentieth century there was considerable architectural innovation (Blundell-Jones 1995; Hertzberger 2008) and in the 1970s the so-called 'open plan' school began to proliferate in the developed world, a move that was largely abandoned by the 1980s when many such open plans became re-segmented into traditional classroom cells. There were many reasons for this failure; among them are that designs were often driven by ideology or economy more than pedagogy. In the new century we are seeing a substantial re-emergence of student-centred pedagogy in all educational sectors. So how does architecture respond to such changing pedagogy and how are underlying issues of power, control and discipline played out? Assemblage theory offers a framework for understanding this shift, but also for understanding why it is that so many open plans have failed.

As part of a larger project entitled Smart Green Schools, we analysed a range of award-winning and innovative middle-school plans drawn from organisations promoting new pedagogies and new learning spaces.[1] These plans are replete with spatial categories such as 'general learning area', 'learning commons', 'learning street', 'open learning', 'lounge', 'collaborative learning', 'studio', 'meeting', 'activity area', 'heartspace' and 'breakout'. Each of these can mean many things but our key question is how has space been segmented and assembled? The analysis suggests that there are many different kinds of open planning. When conceived as socio-spatial assemblages of both people and buildings, plans and pedagogies, we begin to expose an extraordinary complexity of activities and spatial types where the potential for any space depends fundamentally on its interconnections with other spaces.

The focus here is on spatial segmentarity with the task to discriminate between different kinds of openness and closure. To understand the emerging plans, a diagrammatic mapping technique has been developed responding to a need to simultaneously represent segmentarity (open vs closed), interpenetration (overlapping), connectivity (adjacency, syntax, through paths) and adaptability (openability, closeability). A typology of five primary plan types emerged ranging from the traditional classroom cluster to the fully open plan. This is illustrated in an indicative manner in Figure 7.1, which shows diagrams of the generic spatial assemblages for each type. Type 1 is essentially a traditional classroom cluster where the inclusion of open learning areas occurs at the level of the school rather than the classroom. Type 2 involves the inclusion of a learning 'street' as the entry space for a cluster of traditional closed classrooms. Type 3 incorporates plans where classrooms within a traditional cluster can be converted through moveable walls to become common learning space and vice versa. Type 4 is where an assemblage of traditional classrooms and learning streets can be converted from closed to open or the reverse. Type 5 is the dedicated open plan that cannot be converted to closed classrooms.

While there are many kinds of adaptability within these assemblages that involve the moving of furniture and changes to governance, pedagogy, spatial practice or timetables, our focus is on the flexibilities enabled by the architectural shell, and it is crucial here to make a distinction between two kinds of flexibility. First there is the reversible convertibility from closed classroom to open learning areas, designed to enable conversion from traditional to student-centred pedagogies and the reverse. Second there is the ways the building enables flexible flows from one activity type to another within a multiplicitous pedagogy. These two kinds of adaptation, that may be termed 'convertibility' and 'fluidity', operate on different time cycles and rhythms, and at different scales of control.

Plan types 1 and 2 are essentially non-convertible; the disciplinary technology of the classroom is maintained and progressive design is contained to a higher level of the spatial assemblage. It is interesting to note that while this is not a quantitative study, almost half of our sample of buildings selected as promoting progressive pedagogies belonged to

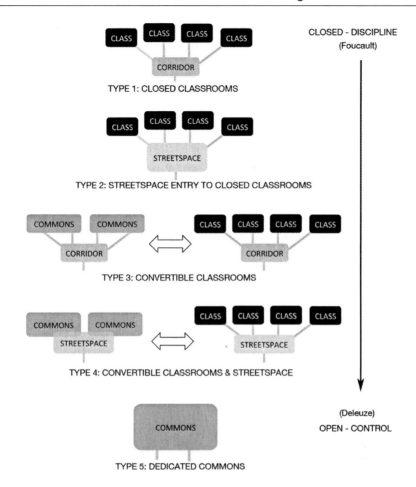

Figure 7.1 Typology of segmentarity.

these types. Analysis needs to pay particular attention to the ways in which the parts are formed from their connections with the whole and to connections between different scales of the spatial assemblage. The distinction between 'streetspace' and 'commons' is based not on size or supposed function but on the existence or absence of through traffic. 'Streetspace' is a thoroughfare that generates social interaction but also loses the acoustic control and privacy necessary for many learning functions; 'commons' is open but not exposed to through traffic. Since it is exposed to prospective parents and visitors, streetspace has become the visible face of new pedagogies – it signifies student-centred learning. Thus we find the emergence of type 2 where streetspace is added to but segmented from traditional classroom space. Traditional pedagogy can proceed under the sign of progressive schooling. From the perspective of assemblage theory this can be understood in terms of 'faciality' – the emergence of an abstract machine or diagram that produces a 'face' of the assemblage – a surface akin to a map which we read as if it were the territory (Deleuze and Guattari 1987: 170–5).

Plan types 3 and 4 are designed with a relatively high level of convertibility between different pedagogies. These plans reflect the tension between pedagogies and the demand for buildings that will satisfy both traditional and student-centred learning. The adaptation from classrooms to commons is not possible during the course of a teaching session and may be controlled by principals rather than teachers or students. These are plan types where pedagogical bets are hedged: both/and solutions popular with funding bodies that seem to embody a resilience that enables pedagogical change without enforcing it. In these plans we can detect a tension between the Foucauldian conception of disciplinary technology and the more positive Deleuzian conception of flows of desire, often evident as tension between teachers wishing to teach in a traditional manner and a principle promoting student-centred learning.

Type 5 incorporates plans that cannot be converted into traditional classrooms, where the commitment to open learning is irreversible. It is important to note here that this does not strictly represent an architectural type; while types 1 and 2 have a very strictly coded spatial structure, types 3 and 4 are less strict and type 5 is an umbrella for a vast range of spatial configurations with considerable scope for architectural experimentation. Some dedicated open plans are highly complex with auxiliary spaces in varying degrees of closure; others are simple barn-like spaces where furniture arrangement and acoustics are left to the occupants. Such open plans are cheaper to construct than segmented plans and can be supported for budgetary or ideological reasons. Just as the classroom reproduces teacher-centred pedagogies, the irreversibility of the open plan can coerce teachers into new pedagogies. As one moves from types 1 to 5 the segmentarity becomes less rigid and more supple. Yet the practices of power also become more subtle; Deleuze describes this as a movement from regimes of *discipline* to those of *control* and warns that these new spaces of openness 'could at first express new freedom, but they could participate as well in mechanisms of control that are equal to the harshest of confinements' (Deleuze 1992: 4).

I earlier suggested two kinds of flexibility or adaptation – convertibility and fluidity. The latter involves the capacity for flow and change between activities within the cluster. This is enabled in part by the scale and openness of the space, yet as the space becomes more exposed and noisy, as the classroom becomes 'streetspace', it can constrain self-directed and reflective activities. In other words the openness also produces a demand for segmentarity, closure or semi-closure. One paradoxical result is that the most open of plans are often not the most fluid because they constrain choice. In this sense fluidity is a condition produced by the conjunction of openness and closure rather than one or other side of this continuum.

The set of twofold concepts sketched earlier are at play in all these plans. As pedagogies move from traditional to progressive the spatial structure moves from the hierarchy of hallway and classrooms to a network of interlinked spaces. The disciplinary striation of types 1 and 2 makes way for the smoothness of open space, singular identity gives way to multiplicity and difference, rigid segmentarity becomes supple – and, potentially, order becomes chaos. Yet this movement is far from simple since the rigidity of segmentarity may be transferred to a higher level of assemblage – the cluster of learning spaces becomes internally open but externally closed with a rigid boundary around the cluster.

Underlying this shift from teacher-centred to student-centred pedagogies is the issue of practices of power and how they are implicated in the architecture. Foucault's work explains a great deal about the traditional classroom, and it also sows the seeds for understanding the architecture of student-centred pedagogies. What he termed the 'apparatus' of power (*dispositif*) (Foucault 1980: 194–228) becomes the assemblage for Deleuze and Guattari (1987) where micro-practices of power are integrated with understandings of the ways productive self-organised wholes emerge from dynamic interactions between parts. In this sense the movement from traditional to constructivist pedagogies and from closed classroom clusters to more open spatial assemblages can be seen to parallel the move from Foucauldian to Deleuzian conceptions and practices of power: from an assemblage of *discipline* to one of *becoming*; top-down practices of power *over* make way for the student-centred power *to*. Again, however, things are not simple. How to stop a student-centred descent into chaos? A significant proportion of the more open classroom clusters incorporate staff areas with a clear surveillance function. On some plans panoptic locations are designed and named as 'resources' or 'coordination'; in others rooms or alcoves are left blank in locations that could be appropriated for staff control. The transformation into an open plan raises concerns about discipline that are addressed by producing new forms of surveillance – one panoptic regime is replaced by another. There is nothing surprising here; micro-practices of power are not eradicated, rather they become more subtle as we move from regimes of *discipline* to those of *control* (Deleuze 1992).

A word is in order about the diagrams in Figure 7.1, which may appear to be reductionist. They are nothing more than conceptual tools, to be judged on their usefulness rather than claims to truth. The diagrams have important precedents in Alexander et al.'s (1977) pattern language and Hillier and Hanson's (1984) spatial syntax. I acknowledge the importance of this work but point out some key differences. Alexander is in many ways an assemblage thinker who wrote the seminal paper 'A City Is Not a Tree' (Alexander 1965) and argued that a building is not a 'thing' but the result of a set of forces (Alexander 1964). A 'pattern' is at once a set of social, spatial, aesthetic and material vectors or forces in a given situation and a diagram that resolves them. The key difference from assemblage theory lies in the essentialism of Alexander's approach, which is organic rather than machinic, transcendent rather than immanent. Hillier and Hanson's (1984) approach, while also demonstrating much in common with assemblage theory, has a positivist and reductionist character that is biased towards the material pole of the assemblage.

The diagrams in Figure 7.1 have two key functions, one practical and one theoretical. The practical function is to identify similarities and differences in plan structure at an abstract level that both designers and educators can understand. The diagrams embody a spatial language that can distinguish, for instance, between 'streetspace' and 'commons', between interpenetration and openability, between 'reversibility' and 'fluidity'. They have the potential to lift the design process out of the simplistic categories of open versus closed and into a discourse of multiple plan types. For architects, who universally loathe being given template plans to comply with, this leaves scope for both creative adaptation within plan types and the invention of new types. The theoretical function of the generic diagrams is that they reveal the immanent productive forces of assemblage, the ways that flows of desire congeal into certain socio-spatial patterns. Each of the cells in the diagrams is a form of territory that may be more or less rigidly inscribed in both material and expressive terms. What I have described as adaptation, reversibility and fluidity can be seen as the processes of deterritorialisation and reterritorialisation where one practice or pedagogy is erased and another is enacted. The current plans mostly reveal contradictory desires for buildings that will support both traditional and student-centred pedagogies – the building is an outcome of the assembled desires of teachers, students, principals, funding agencies, architects and parents.

Open Thinking

The open plan school is just one small example where assemblage thinking might be applied to architecture, and while the focus here has been on spatial segmentarity, there are many dimensions of assemblage.[2] In more general terms assemblage thinking enables a range of approaches to architecture in terms of both theory and practice. It provides a framework within which we might get rigorous about a focus on connectivity and flow rather than object and form. It embodies a focus on between-conditions that privilege the both/and over the either/or. Assemblage theory enables a more rigorous critique of the ways in which architecture works to produce or constrain spatial practices and subjectivities. It enables us to explore the myriad ways in which buildings are produced by flows of desire and are productive of further flows. Assemblage thinking focuses attention on multiple scales of assemblage and on the crucial connections between them.

I argued earlier against any front to back reading of *A Thousand Plateaus* because it is not organised like a tree, and the first chapter 'Rhizome' makes clear the privileging of rhizomic over arborescent thought. This conceptual contrast finds a parallel in the penultimate chapter on striated and smooth space (Deleuze and Guattari 1987). The 'smooth', with its absence of boundaries and slipperiness, is easy to identify with open planning, while 'striated', with its links to 'strict' and 'stringent', is easy to identify with Foucauldian disciplinary technologies. The smooth resonates with the rhizomic and networked while striation resonates with the arborescent and hierarchical (Patton 2000). While the rhizomic and smooth are consistently and implicitly privileged, this priority needs to be read critically as a reversal of traditional forms of thinking that see the world in terms of pre-existing unities. These are not different types of space so much as properties of all spaces; as Deleuze and Guattari put it, 'Nothing is ever done with: smooth space allows itself to be striated, and striated space reimparts a smooth space [. . .] all progress is made by and in striated space, but all becoming occurs in smooth space' (Deleuze and Guattari 1987: 486).

What should we make of the idea that 'all progress is made by and in striated space'? I read this as a recognition that territorialisation, organisation, stabilisations of identities and practices are fundamental to the ways we live. While architects can have a significant impact on the ways in which the smooth/striated twofold plays out, the act of design is primarily one of striation – of stabilising the forms of buildings, the construction of walls, the inscription of meaning – and the idea of designing a smooth space can be a dangerous illusion.

The conceptual opposition between smooth and striated, between lines of flight and points of stability, between 'wings and roots' to add another metaphor, makes it tempting to add the conceptual opposition of space versus place and to identify space with freedom and movement in contrast with the stability and rootedness of place. I think this is a serious mistake and that place is best conceived as the assembled mix. The concept of place has been widely misrecognised as an organic tree-like concept that organises spatial meanings around an essentialised stem. This view of place is understandable since it meets a primary human desire for a sense of home and identity. Place can be identified with the axis of territorialisation along which assemblages become stabilised. Yet the wholesale identification of place with being, stability and striation, with singular modes of rooted sedentary dwelling and stabilised identities, is a narrow, self-deceptive and insular view. Place is an assemblage that stabilises dwelling but also encompasses lines of movement and processes of becoming. The immanence of place is a field of differences within which tree-like stabilised identities are planted.

In all of these senses places can be construed as assemblages in continuous states of change. Such an approach to place runs counter to Heideggerian notions of place as grounded in an ontology of 'being' rather than 'becoming'. Some of those who adopt a Deleuzian approach to built form see the need to overturn the Heideggerian notion of a spatially grounded ontology. For Rajchman (1998: 86) the 'grounding' of dwelling in place is a source of false naturalism and a constraint on freedom: 'we need to get away from the picture [. . .] that the life-world is in the first instance a grounded world.' From this view, the gravitas and heaviness of the earth is to be overcome in a Nietzschean spirit of freedom; place is an anchor which weighs us down. As Rajchman (1998: 88) puts it: 'Once we give up the belief that our life-world is rooted in the ground, we may thus come to a point where ungroundedness is no longer experienced as existential anxiety and despair but as a freedom and lightness that finally allow us to *move*.' There is here a privileging of movement over stasis, of 'wings' over 'roots', which is understandable, but the ideal of severing buildings from the ground on which they stand is wishful thinking that suggests architecture can escape the constraints of dwelling. This involves a denial of the materiality of the assemblage and, ultimately, a reduction of architecture to text. The task is not to decide between an architecture of roots or wings but to understand that it is always both: points of order and lines of flight, smooth and striated, openness and closure.

Notes

The project was undertaken as part of Australian Research Council Linkage Project LP0776850 entitled Smart Green Schools; see <http://www.abp.unimelb.edu.au/research/funded/smart-green-schools/>. I also acknowledge the collaboration of Clare Newton, Sue Wilks, Dominique Hes, Ben Cleveland and Ken Woodman on this project.

1. These organisations were the British Council for School Environments (<http://www.bcse.uk.net>), Design Share (<http://wwwdesignshare.com>) and the Council of Educational Facility Planners International (<http://www.cefpi.org>). The sample included sixty-eight middle-school plans with a global spread but a bias towards the English-speaking world.
2. I have been using the assemblage framework at an urban design scale in the investigation of creative clusters, transit-oriented developments and informal settlements. See Dovey (2010, 2011, 2012) and Dovey et al. (2012).

References

Alexander, C. (1964), *Notes on the Synthesis of Form*, New York: Oxford University Press.

Alexander, C. (1965), 'A City Is Not a Tree', *Architectural Forum*, 122: 1, 58–62, and 122: 2, 58–62.

Alexander, C., S. Ishikawa and M. Silverstein (1977), *A Pattern Language: Towns, Buildings, Construction*, Oxford: Oxford University Press.

Bateson, G. ([1972] 2000), *Steps to an Ecology of Mind*, Chicago: University of Chicago Press.

Blundell Jones, P. (1995), *Hans Scharoun*, London: Phaidon.

Bourdieu, P. (1990), *The Logic of Practice*, Cambridge: Polity.

Buchanan, I. and J. Marks (2000), 'Introduction', in I. Buchanan and J. Marks (eds), *Deleuze and Literature*, Edinburgh: Edinburgh University Press.

Colebrook, C. (2002), *Understanding Deleuze*, Sydney: Allen & Unwin.

DeLanda, M. (2006), *A New Philosophy of Society*, New York: Continuum.

Deleuze, G. (1988), *Foucault*, Minneapolis, MN: University of Minnesota Press.

Deleuze, G. (1992), 'Postscript on the Societies of Control', *Negotiations: 1972–1990*, trans. M. Joughin, New York: Columbia University Press.

Deleuze, G. (2006), *Two Regimes of Madness: Texts and Interviews 1975–1995*, ed. D. Lapoujade, Los Angeles: Semiotext(e).

Deleuze, G. and F. Guattari (1987), *A Thousand Plateaus: Capitalism and Schizophrenia*, trans. B. Massumi, Minneapolis, MN: University of Minnesota Press.

Dewey, J. ([1916] 1966), *Democracy and Education*, New York: Free Press.

Dovey, K. (2008), *Framing Places: Mediating Power in Built Form*, London: Routledge.

Dovey, K. (2010), *Becoming Places*, London: Routledge.

Dovey, K. (2011), 'Uprooting Critical Urbanism', *City*, 15: 3/4, 347–54.

Dovey, K. (2012), 'Informal Settlement and Complex Adaptive Assemblage', *International Development Planning Review* 34 (3), 371–90.

Dovey, K., S. Wollan and I. Woodcock (2012), 'Placing Graffiti', *Journal of Urban Design*, 17: 1, 21–41.

Foucault, M. (1979), *Discipline and Punish: The Birth of the Prison*, trans. A. Sheridan, New York: Vintage.

Foucault, M. (1980), *Power/Knowledge: Selected Interviews and Other Writings, 1972–1977*, ed. C. Gordon, New York: Pantheon.

Hertzberger, H. (2008), *Space and Learning: Lessons in Architecture 3*, trans. J. Kirkpatrick, Rotterdam: 010 Publishers.

Hillier, B. and J. Hanson (1984), *The Social Logic of Space*, Cambridge: Cambridge University Press.

McFarlane, C. (2011), 'Assemblage and critical urbanism', *City*, 15: 2, 204–24.

Patton, P. (2000), *Deleuze and the Political*, London: Routledge.

Rajchman, J. (1998), *Constructions*, Cambridge MA: MIT Press.

Vygotsky, L. S. (1978), *Mind in Society*, Cambridge MA: Harvard University Press.

PART III

GATHERING

Chapter 8
Toward a Theory of the Architectural Subject

Simone Brott

The extraordinary event, for Deleuze, is the object becoming subject – not in the manner of an abstract formulation, such as the substitution of one ideational representation for another but, rather, in the introduction of a vast, new, impersonal plane of subjectivity, populated by object processes and physical phenomena that in Deleuze's discovery will be shown to constitute their own subjectivities. Deleuze's polemic of subjectivity (the refusal of the Cartesian subject and the transcendental ego of Husserl) – long attempted by other thinkers – is unique precisely because it heralds the dawning of a new species of objecthood that will qualify as its own peculiar subjectivity. A survey of Deleuze's early work on subjectivity, *Empirisme et subjectivité* (1953), *Le Bergsonisme* (1968) and *Logique du sens* (1969), brings the architectural reader into a peculiar confrontation with what Deleuze calls the 'new transcendental field', the field of subject-producing effects, which for the philosopher takes the place of both the classical and modern subject. Deleuze's theory of consciousness and perception is premised on the critique of Husserlian phenomenology; and *ipso facto* his question is an *architectural* problematic, even if the name 'architecture' is not invoked. Notwithstanding architecture's vexed history of phenomenology, and its recourse to a Heideggerian reading of being – the belief that architecture's purpose is to stabilise meaning *for the phenomenal subject* – the intention of rewriting the code of subject-object relations for Deleuze and Guattari does not involve the privileging of a seemingly archaic subject (*Dasein*) within a phenomenology of *place* but, instead, demolishing the entire edifying discourse of subjects suspended in signifying chains. Deleuze's critique is as relevant now as it was then, long after the historical revision of postwar phenomenologies, because the phenomenological paradigm persists unconsciously in architectural thought, through the discipline's longer humanist tradition since the dawn of modernity in which architecture has always placed the individual subject at the centre of its formulations, as I will detail. The question asked in this chapter, then, the one never asked, is: how does Deleuze reformulate the problem of subjectivity for architecture? Who or *what* is (or will be) architecture's post-human subject?

Deleuze in fact lets go of the term subjectivity, only ever speaking of 'perceptions', 'singularities' and 'emissions'. Each of these in Deleuze denotes a component 'power' such as a mouth or a breeze, to produce something; not an effect *of* a cause, but an effect as non-sentient, self-mobilising agency, at once producer and produced. Indeed, in *Empiricism and Subjectivity*, 'subjectivity is determined as an effect' (1991: 26), namely the effect of saying 'I',[1] while the term is never formalised into a concept of subjectivity. I use *impersonal effects* to encapsulate Deleuze's shifting terminology on subjectivity; the word *effect*, when its causality is neutralised, perfectly captures Deleuze's productive model of subjectivity in which an architectural work could be considered a veritable subjectivity.[2] For architecture, the *effects* are the indeterminate products (contents) of the architectural encounter, the irreducible moments of a pure visuality prior to unified persons, buildings or any whole whatsoever. While traditionally the personal subject is independent of and, in some senses, antecedent to the architectural encounter, here the encounter has primacy and through it the individual subject is constructed.

Deleuze does not recognise the transcendental ego as a valid paradigm for subjectivity. One cannot forget his response to Jean-Luc Nancy when asked 'Who comes after the subject?' – in short, he responds that there is no subject (Deleuze, in Cadava et al. 1991: 95).[3] There is for Deleuze no constituted subjectivity in the way of an individuated subject with fixed traits. From the earliest schemata there is no 'I', a self-conferred master of a perceptual apparatus or otherwise a receiver, the subject rendered a passive landing site for falling or passing perceptions. Rather, subjectivity is an emergent phenomenon immanent to the production of perception. The 'practical' or affective subjects in the books on Hume and Bergson are figures conceived strictly within Deleuze's critique of phenomenology, in which Husserl's transcendental subject will be systematically denied.

In *Empiricism and Subjectivity*, the 'empirical subjectivity begins from [. . .] an animated succession of distinct perceptions' (Deleuze 1991: 87), and in *Bergsonism* it is not the subject who stands outside perception but perceptions and memories as pure, mobile effects that will constitute subjectivity in and for themselves. Perception for the early Deleuze is autocratic, with its own individuating capacity (temporal agency). Such a peculiar idea of perceptions as detached from their masters can only be made intelligible by observing that perceptions for Deleuze operate at the level of presence, a point belaboured from as early as the 'empirical subject' (1991: 87) in Deleuze's adoption of Hume's term. In *Bergsonism* there is no 'difference in kind' between perception and matter, only a 'difference in degree' (Deleuze 1988: 25) – perceptions do not represent something more original outside themselves but are continuous with matter (Deleuze 1991: 88).[4] Further, 'every perception is a substance, and every distinct part of a perception a distinct substance' (1991: 88); perception 'puts us at once into matter, is impersonal, and coincides with the perceived object' (Deleuze 1988: 25). By extension, an architectural subject can be seen to emerge (freely or otherwise) from this fluid and dynamic field of effects.

It is important to understand that for Deleuze there is no 'container' for subjectivity. Rather, in his colloquy on Hume, the mind is a continuous production of thoughts – there is only the collection and succession of ideas in and for themselves (Deleuze 1991: 87–8).[5] Thought does not mediate between a subject and an object; rather, it takes place in a third register, an absolute outside 'a zone of [. . .] objective indetermination' (Deleuze 1990: 130).[6] This examination of thought and perception in Hume is never developed into an explicit theory of subjectivity; rather, it ramifies into other texts such as *The Logic of Sense*, whose coincident concepts – 'pre-personal singularity' and 'non-personal individuation' – are much more expansive than the terms Deleuze takes from Hume, which still attend to the solitary subject.

'By singularity, we mean [. . .] some element that can be extended close to another, so as to obtain a connection' *in order to engender transformation of a subject*. Examples include the rush of adrenalin, the demolition of a building, the winning of a race, which are all accomplished by a series of critical connections which travel 'in a determined direction over a line of ordinary points' (Deleuze 1990: 109). 'Knowledge and belief' are 'replaced [with] "arrangement" or "contrivance" (*agencement* and *dispositif*) that indicate an emission and a distribution of singularities. Such emissions, of the "cast of the dice" kind, constitute a *transcendental field without subject*' (Deleuze, in Cadava et al. 1991: 95; emphasis added). The world is 'teeming with anonymous and nomadic, impersonal and pre-individual singularities', which constitute the new 'impersonal and pre-individual transcendental field' (Deleuze 1990: 102). Every singularity exists within a series (ibid.: 103) and there is a potential that vibrates across all the series, like a drag race which brings several trajectories, cars and competitors alongside each other, each series bearing a certain potential to crash or to swerve around the other, to be taken over by or to gain on another. Subjectivity is a nomadic field because the potential drives toward any given connection are variable and the singularities mobile.

'Non-personal individuation' means any coherent 'arrangement' (*agencement*) of singularities that may connect with but are irreducible to personhood. A person is only one of many possible individuations such as '*a* life, *a* season, *a* wind, *a* battle, 5 o'clock', each defined by its own self-actuating consistency and distribution. Subjectivity is precisely an effect of processes of individuation; it is 'what makes the individuality of an event' (Deleuze, in Cadava et al. 1991: 95). In this schema, the person (distinct from the I or the ego) is not eradicated, but 'envelop[s] a finite number of the singularities of the system' (Deleuze 1990: 109). A pure outside (the impersonal field) comes, in time, into contact with subjects. The subject yet to come is the subject that has first to be freed from the circular and often malevolent forces that command the dominant chain of signification, that is authorised reality with its manifold illusions, desires, forms of confabulation and discord.

In *Proust et les signes* (1964), Deleuze will compare subjectivity to an 'electromagnetic effect' (Deleuze 2000: 153). Clearly he does not mean semblance or ephemerality. 'Subjectivity is determined as an effect [. . .] the subject is an imprint, or an impression, left by principles that it progressively turns into a machine capable of using this impression' (Deleuze 1991: 113). This elucidates Deleuze's sense of effect as a machinic part that *works*. The personal identity is itself a working effect of repetition: saying 'I' is a machinic part whose 'habit' crystallises personal identity. 'We should not ask what principles [of the mind] are, but rather *what they do*. They are not entities; they are functions. They are defined by their effects' (1991: 132–3). As such, personal identity is *one* set of effects that constitute the new field of subjectivisation. A subject, to a degree, chooses which effects to embody.

In the final scene of David Lynch's *Mulholland Drive*, the primary effect of a character, played by Naomi Watts, *weeping* to the piercing sound of Rebekah Del Rio's detached voice singing Roy Orbison's 'Crying' in Spanish (Lynch 2002), might be called 'an anyone crying'. It is the capacity to cry that persists even when the staged singer collapses onstage, and the voice effect eerily continues, a pure performance detached from any performer. Impersonal effects are thus elaborated doubly: as a power and a partial body. There is not a circularity here in the sense of a linguistic deferral given to classical epistemology, but rather the effect of a recursive *habitus* that propels itself into the future via a series, and which, in turn, presages other events.

What remains to be executed in bringing such ideas to architecture is for impersonal effects and arrangements to be directed toward real ends, versus new fictions and new forms of domination. The visualisation of this new field of effects in architecture involves both the critique of architecture and the renunciation of certain formal procedures that condition architecture for the subject. This latter conditioning is typical of the manner in which architecture is complicit in forming representational orders that seek to control and channel the purely immanent field of its productive agency. The demolition of certain orders seen in various iterations of the architectural avant-garde, historically, is undermined, as processes of reification are always present in the historical process itself – if only in the sense that forms of architecture once considered innovative or new fall again and again to the same forces complicit in defining and categorising architecture (including architectural history itself). It is not accidental, then, that functionalist architecture in its heyday was an authentic attempt to reconfigure the subject, even if the subject was unwilling to attend to this project and rebelled. What Deleuze seems to have in mind, and what Guattari would later explore in 1980s Japan (Guattari 1994, 1996), is a passage out of this historicising game toward the liberation of a new architectural subjectivity.

Surround Effects: Villa Savoye

Stretching from one room to the next, surfaces follow me, approaching and receding, while I attach and detach myself from one effects-series of perceptual and built fragments to the next. But there is only one surface of architectural experience, namely the progressive contact-surface generated via each encounter with built fabric in a series of vivid effects that jump from the visual, haptic and olfactory registers to the mental, affective and psychological registers – and back. Architectural encounter is produced as an abstract surface spanning parallel series of impersonal effects, which places me at once into matter and slowly gives rise to an anonymous subjectivity of architecture.

The surface-effect made with the floor covering, traversing a floor, forms a series (footsteps) that coincides with another, namely the succession of glimpses I extract from the surrounds while walking, scanning a field of vision: a haze of empty rooms passed by quickly while I pursue a particular room; the gleam of a door handle drawn close to the hand that finds it; and, upstairs, a stand of trees suddenly behind the long strips of ribbon-window glass which bring them close to me. What is often described as the subtle ambiguity in modernist architecture between the interior and the exterior is not just an 'effect' of architectural transparency but is germane to a wider effects mechanism in which diverse components from multiple registers cohere. They are effects because they are potent and autonomous, but also transient, disappearing as quickly as they appear – the free facade effect so thin it is forgotten the moment I enter the interior, itself an effect of open space. Modernist space often dissolves and blurs such impressions and distinctions in its attempt to access a real that nonetheless remains elusive.

What initiates this conjoining of the effects into a temporary yet vivid sequence? In every case a catalyst commands a group of effects. The architectural encounter is not random or subjectivistic; rather, there is always an architectural motive in the subjectivisational horizon that we call 'architecture' or 'house'.[7] Here, the classic architectural promenade connects a series of loose effects by a diagonal ramp, the motivating complex or vehicle by which all the effects are given mobility. In this house, the circulation is overdetermined, combining a spiral stair that turns in on itself with a diagonal ramp alongside that disperses everything around it – two circulations, in an effect of compression and doubling, to facilitate not just the literal movement from one level to the next but the sequence which snaps from one effect to the next. What Le Corbusier called the *promenade architecturale* (Le Corbusier 1923),[8] in other words, is a systematic programme of effects, and the house it traverses is a machine for producing and synthesising dissonant effects. The diagonal ramp sets in motion architectural space-time and catalyses the effects cinematically. It is precisely this facility to produce effects that qualifies architecture as a form of subjectivity.

There is, in the architectural encounter, an unmistakable *agencement* that pre-exists all personal agents navigating space; the most apt translation of this Deleuzian term might be 'arrangement'. It is by architecture's 'sheer will of anonymity' that a pure indifference seizes us, and not the reverse, a subjectivising agency prior to the constitution of any building or subject. The selection of effects is accomplished by a certain savagery that transcends personal choice or personality. The glimpse-effect of the roof garden at the top of the ramp causes the spiral stair to vanish, just as a person appearing on the other side of a sheet of glass – transparent or opaque, as recognisable subject or as shadowy form – pulls my gaze through the glass. Every architectural effect produces itself by destroying all the others.

A subjectivity of architecture does not mean the building becomes a person; rather, it confers upon perception, and the accumulation of effects, the sense of individuation and reception of an outside derivative of the entire distribution of effects within my trajectory. The 'I' is an after-effect, something that crystallises through the habit and repetition of walking around a house. The roaming subject fatally links the architectural series to an 'I' (a receiver), mistaking singularism for identity; or, conversely, the series takes the subject in by subterfuge and overturns an 'I' or a 'You'. To be clear, the 'I' itself is not a real illusion but an effect. The illusion lies in philosophy and the metaphysics of agency, in thinking that the 'I' is constitutive, that it precedes the effects. For architecture this would mean that the subject no longer inserts herself into a sign-system in order to establish meaning (phenomenology), but emerges from within the field of architectural effects. An *agencement* (subject-arrangement) ensues, and the interpretive apparatus of subjects under the spell of linguistic or noetic factors is shut down.[9]

In each case, a cloud of architectural effects produces the architectural *real*, the sine qua non for the crystallisation of individuated series. Walls, objects and other components are teeming with loose effects and what emerges is a particular selection or arrangement. If 'I' have a subjectivity, it is a general power to command arrangements, to envelop a series of aesthetic, social and other effects, like anyone else. But it is also the phenomenon of having been selected, of an unconscious desire toward *this* set of effects. The propensity of any set belongs to an architectural subjectivity, which hovers above all such primary locations given to perception and its games of concordance or disequilibrium.

Architecture is exactly the fourth person singular of Deleuze-Ferlinghetti (Deleuze 2004: 118),[10] given by a surface that collapses heterogeneous effects and contrives to produce a feeling of continuity and seamlessness even in the most fragmented and distracted of encounters.[11] When an architecture is truly inhabited, it is as if it begins to inhabit us. Impersonal effects occur without the ego's intervention. When I see a bedroom door, I am by that very event suddenly joined to it, by a line that is invisible but which allows me to see.

An architectural theory of effects rejects gestalt and any overarching syntactic structure in favour of a nomadic distribution of point effects mobilising dynamic events in the real world. A theory of effects is not an abstraction, but real. To state it in the terms of Deleuze's *Bergsonism*, every architectural perception produces a definite substance – and it is this actual presence that is at stake in the surface of an architectural encounter – not a villa, for example, delivered optically or phenomenally as a semiotic object to a subject, but an anonymous Villa Savoye, a series of concrete architectural effects that have no more specific unity than the series itself. This unnameable event erases the name of the object.

It is said that Le Corbusier achieved the *promenade architecturale* by de-emphasising the facade (Sherer 2004). For architecture, this is tantamount to the stripping away of normative identity (removing the mask). Le Corbusier's aestheticised functionalism was a means to effecting the emergence of the modern subject, a subject liberated from the historical detritus of 'traditional' architectures and congested urban orders. His villas were sailing toward the future insofar as they were machines for living or ocean-going vessels headed for tomorrow.

Phenomenology and Architectural History

The theoretical and linguistic treatises of the twentieth century concerned with signs, semiotics and structuralism proper might all broadly be said to have understood perceptual and empirical cognition as the primary field of architecture's subject-production – its site of interpretation as well as its often grotesque ideological instrumentalisation.[12] The figures of phenomenology in architecture begin with the Norwegian theorist Christian Norberg-Schulz (in the 1970s and 1980s) and the French philosopher and historiographer Gaston Bachelard (in the 1930s to the 1950s, and rediscovered in the 1960s and 1970s). There are also the later architectural movements surrounding Aldo Rossi (primarily in the 1970s) and Bernard Tschumi (especially in the 1980s).

In Norberg-Schulz's phenomenological project, *meaning* is what structures the architectural encounter and permits it to be read. There is a self-organising latency that both inhabits and comes to expression in architectural arrangements, including settlements or cities, in built form (Norberg-Schulz 1980: 5).[13] Architecture's purpose is to visualise the distinct character, or what he calls the *genius loci*, of a site, making that esoterics of place evocative and explicit through the manipulation of environmental components, e.g. mountain, river, plain or forest. These primordial impersonal effects come to be expressed via a number of incorporations, many of which remain subliminal, lending a city or town a hidden complicity with that which has often been erased or subsumed over the course of settlement. Architectural form materialises the *genius loci* and converts it into an image to be decoded by the subject.

The *genius loci* is architecture's dialectical *other*; 'it is that "opposite" man has to come to terms with, to be able to dwell' (ibid.: 10–11). In the model of effects, rather than producing meaning for an inert, constituted subject, a Deleuzian architectural subjectivity is immanent in the architectural series. The phenomenological excess of the landscape does not so much figure in the production of that agency as shape it after the fact. Because the idea of *genius loci* has often been criticised as anthropomorphic projection of human agency onto the landscape, it registers as an example of the fantastic elements that circle pure agency (*objet petit a*).[14] If it is truly real (or *of* the real), it is part and parcel of the operation of catalysing impersonal effects and need not be addressed. If, however, it is phantasmatic, it returns only insofar as the subject brings it back to the new subjective field formed by the architectural encounter, effectively re-imagining it as surplus affect.

Yet *genius loci*, infatuated as it is with 'place', is an impersonal power, detached from any particular body or construction, expressed as a singular 'emission' of autonomous elements. Norberg-Schulz describes *genius loci* as the unique 'character', the *Stimmung* (mood) of an environment prior to it being visualised and converted into physical form. Its detached 'characters' (mountain, plain, forest) are clearly effects or *agencements* (arrangements). Character, he argues, 'changes with the seasons, is mutable, is particular to the landscape, etc.' (ibid.). It begins to suggest a conception of architecture as a flexible component within a mobile series. But in terms of impersonal effects, the *Stimmung*, if real, would not form 'a background to acts and occurrences' (ibid.: 8) but rather would be granted the facility to act of its own accord toward whatever end was embedded in its autonomous agency (to enclose, to delimit, to traverse, etc.). *Genius loci* thus remains outside the address of impersonal effects: either before it, as the shadow of a primordial, predetermined whole forming worlds; or in excess of it, as phantasmatic surplus consistent with the remnants of symbolic and discursive orders within the subject's psyche.

For Bachelard, architecture is something that shelters or hides meaning and human values below its surface (within its constructive order). Similarly, in Roland Barthes's *Mythologies* (1957), this hiding confers on cultural systems a fugitive discursive order that improperly informs subjects or *waylays* them en route to integration in a paradigmatic order (Barthes 1979). Here, in many senses, we see the demented side of high structuralist readings of 'place'. However, Bachelard's *La poétique de l'espace* (1957) also hints at a schema of effects in its dialogue with literature and the 'detached image', both of which he endows with an affective power and, in this sense, understands to have the status of free subjectivity. For Bachelard, the aesthetic image, 'the phrase', 'the verse' or 'the stanza' must be 'seized with its unique reality' (Bachelard 1964: xxiv). He implores us to 'take the image in its very being' (ibid.:

xxx). But whereas Bachelard conceives of the image as the product of a consciousness which constitutes it – this being the axiomatic essence of phenomenology – impersonal effects or part-subjects constitute subjectivity directly and not through the circuit of representation.

What Barthes and Bachelard provide, en route to later exiting this very conundrum, is a phenomenology of the image with its constituted consciousness at the centre of an aesthetic system, alien to an impersonal subjectivity. But the consciousness of the image, to use Bachelard's poetic phraseology, 'shimmers' from beneath his phenomenological analysis. What emerges is the thinking toward a potent, autonomous image with its own facility to produce, in other words the beginning of an effects schema.

These earlier phenomenologies of architecture popular in the 1950s, 1960s and 1970s, eventually losing ground in the 1980s, were vindicated by a variety of other new discussions in the 1980s that continued to engage the problem of meaning in architecture, each with their corresponding models of an essentially anarchic architectural subjectivity. In Aldo Rossi's *L'architettura della città* (1966), the defining condition of the city is yet the mysterious agency of *genius loci*.[15] In his version, it is the impersonal spirit inhabiting a place that emerges as witness to the cumulative, historical incisions made in the urban terrain over time – a form of interlocutor for the architectural assemblages and historic monuments that exist as a mnemonic tableau. Each architectural moment – fabric, landscape or monument – is a signifier or point of purchase for this dialogue, which is itself a dialogic encounter that proceeds by fits and starts. Each moment embodies the collective human will or spirit (agency) that produced it, in accord with or in opposition to the *genius loci*, and, when joined together in a series, gives rise to the particular urban character or mnemonic subjectivity that is its 'genius of place'. Cities in this sense collect and synthesise discordant memories, while new architectural subjectivities implanted in their midst have the ability to perform a type of reconciliation, revitalising distressed or discordant assemblages of architectural facts held in tension by virtue of their shared identity and place.

There is also a sense in which the architecture is understood to be properly cognised in the circumambulation between points, in the circuit proper or in the historico-existential function that is perhaps Rossi's real site for architecture. The assimilation of the city by physically traversing it is defined by Rossi as the acknowledgment of something integral to cities that transcends personal journeys or pilgrimages – a process that re-enacts historical processes and, counter-intuitively, contracts this temporal signature into a single present moment or image.

While Rossi's urban *genius loci* is an immanent 'spirit' of architecture, an effects-based impersonal subjectivity of architecture does not valorise human agency, accumulation and cultural memory. Even Rossi's post-modernist depiction of the urban subject remains faithful to a humanist conception of architecture at the service of an ego that is its reason for being. In the case of cultural memory, we may be dealing with a collective ego, even a superego, but we are still in the realm of the cognising subject, and forms of memory are, in part, invented or constructed.

The Elective Élan of Parc de la Villette

A wholly different schema is proposed in Tschumi's Parc de la Villette project, built between 1984 and 1987, a formal grid of follies, plus cultural facilities and thematic gardens built into the serpentine elevated promenade, rising up from a gestalt that generates architecture as a formal series. While in Rossi's schema it is the postmodernist, historical subject who strings together fragments of architectural styles across time and space, in La Villette it is a decentred subject who inhabits the spaces between the points – a dislocated subject untethered from the logic of traditional *or* postmodern architectural composition. No longer at the service of a subliminal *genius loci*, the dehistoricised subject of La Villette (site of former slaughterhouses dating to circa 1867) submits to a formal, modernist grid drained of historical determination. The grid is an abstract machine populated by the fragmentary effects of the follies and gardens. In fact, the most common and generic manoeuvre of this time was to impose a grid and then deform it (or shift it in relation to other forces, which then generated a system of dislocated and often useless parts). Parc de la Villette, like other modernist and postmodernist agitations, is now ineluctably caught up in its own mytho-historical fantasies that fall like a second, invisible grid atop the first. Ironically, Tschumi's most famous project, designed to exclude this historicising process, has suffered the fate of being reabsorbed into the machinery of architectural discourse, with its diachronic bias placing the park within the register of transitional projects permanently suspended between post-modernism and the now.[16] For La Villette, the design of the *point-folies* was based on the erasure of meaning – what is, in Tschumi's discourse, the strident refrain of a formalism lifted away from any programmatic base. This manoeuvre in literature, most famously carried off by Alain Robbe-Grillet, produces the same repetitive and often nonsensical chorus of effects. The erasure of meaning, which was part and parcel of the poststructuralist inquisition of ideation, had direct consequences for the form of subjectivity explored in La Villette, a dislocation and fracturing of semantic and syntactic expression influenced by Tschumi's collaboration with the philosopher of deconstruction, Jacques Derrida, and amplified by the fact that this is a park and not a text. Given the size of La Villette – one of the largest urban parks in Europe – the expansiveness of its somewhat forlorn state further enhances the alienating effects of the regime deployed.[17]

In *La Case Vide*, Derrida famously stated that Tschumi's architecture makes 'a spacing' for the event (Derrida 1986: 5); it enacts the series in order to open a space for something to happen. This performance of architectural spacing or *absence*, he writes, 'leads to a radical questioning of the concept of structure – to its decentering'. This, in essence, is Tschumi-Derrida's conception of the decentred architectural subject – a subject not anchored to structure, to formal 'presence', but one that occurs in the in-between spaces (between subject and object in the representational 'corridors' of a dismantled and defamiliarised grammar).[18] One can *hear* the deinstrumentalisation of formal agency, given to literature, which inflects Tschumi's architecture and Derrida's deconstruction of texts, in the echoing spaces of La Villette. Additionally, one can *see* the cinematic effects of Tschumi's appropriation of montage and *mise en scène* in the subsequent superimpositions of discordant systems over and atop the mostly destitute site in Paris's 19th arrondissement.

The spacing between the follies can be seen as not so much a matter of formal absence as a statement about the desubjectivisation of the urban subject, in Tschumi's non-place where the subject exists only as a projection of *l'absence*. This thinking of a subject that is no longer constituted by instrumentalised processes – no longer phenomenologically conjured by way of representational systems – is, in part, the reason for La Villette's desolate condition.[19] Notwithstanding this progressive shift of subject-forming agencies, the impersonal effects do not leave a blank space, hole or affective void; rather, the desubjectivisation of the subject engages a new primary subjectivity in which individual consciousness becomes a positive, newly freed component or actor in a wider field of production of forces expropriated from signifying chains. What is often missed in the criticism of Tschumi's grid of expansive 'green non-places' is the fact that each one has the potential to be something else from one time to another (Vidler 1986). But what separates Deleuze from Derrida and other theorists of *l'absence*[20] is that there is no need to decentre the subject, because, to reinvoke Deleuze's refrain, there simply is none: no subject, and hence *no* lack or hole to fill with recuperative, therapeutic representations.

Derrida, a contemporary of Deleuze, was of course part of the critique of the constituted subject mobilised by a generation of French thinkers. Derrida's 'Point de folie' already reveals the desubjectivisation of the subject toward the field of impersonal effects prior to the subject:

> And if this happens *to us*, we must be prepared to revive these two words [. . .] It does not happen to a constituted *us*, *to a* human subjectivity whose essence would be arrested and which would *then* find itself affected by the history of this thing called architecture. What happens through architecture both constructs and instructs this *us*. The latter *finds itself* engaged by architecture before it becomes the subject of it: master and possessor. (Derrida 1986: 5)

'Human subjectivity' is then derivative of an architectural historicising process. This retrospective gaze rationalises completely discordant historical singularities or, in Walter Benjamin's sense, it constructs a totally facetious tableau toward present ends – only interrupted in deconstructivist schemas, as the ground for such processes is entirely deformed. Personal identity can only emerge as a subjective product haunted by these effects. One might say that a defective subjective agency is formed in the crucible of the lie. For Derrida, this operative impersonal subjectivity has a circularity that makes architecture part and parcel of the production of meaning and sense; and it is meaning and sense (or nonsense) that is its 'master and possessor'. Architecture remains within the haunted house of representational orders, and exchange value is what holds sway – in other words, the allegiance to Heidegger and Husserl, in which even La Villette remains self-avowedly within a discourse of textuality and hermeneutics.[21]

Derrida emphatically returns to the formulation of meaning via the event of the subject as it cognises all other events from this interior maelstrom of effects, be they distended, attenuated, detached or what have you. For this reason, deconstruction was a fun-house mirror of extended affectivity, in service nonetheless to representational orders but also to the production of a way out of the same.

We can never forget that for Derrida, and the adherents of textuality, architecture was understood to be a kind of text. The follies, he says, 'deconstruct the semantics of architecture' (Derrida 1986: 7), they destabilise meaning. La Villette exists as a discourse or narrative, 'a narrative montage of great complexity' (ibid.: 11) or that great poststructuralist montage called contextualised discursive praxis. Indeed La

Villette catalysed a prolific discourse. After all, what did Tschumi's *The Manhattan Transcripts* (1981) propose other than that architecture is a grand fiction?

La Villette is based, in part, on Tschumi's book, which formed the script for his design. The transcripts are not supposed to represent, 'they are not mimetic' (1981: 8), he said, but 'attempt to play with the fragments of a given reality'. However, such elusive works necessarily remain deconstructive operations. They propose a heterogeneous series, but rather than mobilising the effects as an individuation of material forces, Tschumi is concerned chiefly with a semiological conflict and disintegration embodied by the follies.

This effectively grammatical structuralisation of architectonic form has been demolished with the advent of the *event* as simple subjectivising power given to the real versus the fictitious. Even in Rossi's vision of the positive presence of urban structures, there is a dialectical struggle between the half-real *genius loci* and the historical forms that instantiate it. Impersonal architectural effects operate at the level of presence – not absence or its analogues in distortion and dissonance. Deleuze and Guattari's positive vision of formal *agencement* animates this path toward both heuristic and actually existing forms of impersonal effects. It is the former that inhabit affective territories of subjectivising agency such as literature, art and cinema, while it is architecture that is 'the real thing' and, for this reason, the most highly coveted and contested prize.

The singular motive of impersonal effects is to create something *new*, thus marking a radical shift and wholesale departure from the 1980s theorists of *l'absence*, where architecture's purpose was to reproduce a lack at the centre of the system, calling into doubt figuration itself. This non-productive *agencement* approaches but stops short of engaging existing objects or fields of productive force. There is an entirely compelling, literary quality to this event, while the fact that La Villette is a real park is uniquely unsettling.

The follies are laid out in a strict grid that the subject is asked to traverse, and what is produced and repeated is the formal grid, which re-enacts itself identically with every traversal. Any existential function that might be attributed to such architecture takes place in the phenomenal interior of the solitary subject, whose role it is to fill in the blanks – an automaton or cultural nomad who traces the same semiotic dissimulation ad infinitum, reproducing its irrational desuetude with every journey. Architecture's project of deconstruction argued the self-dismantling nature of structure, revealing a foundational condition (founding crime or act of primary scission) concealed or repressed within the architectural object. What emerged was an eschatological deformation – the inversion of all teleological purposes in favour of absences and echoes, whose irruptive nature was a radical and liberating force in the exegesis of Walter Benjamin (and, today, Giorgio Agamben), forever ploughed back under to generate new deformations, as if it might serve as seed for a new harvest. Deconstruction returns always to an empty origin, a procedure sworn by its progenitors to be its defining creative act.[22] With the release of impersonal effects and the retreat from the poststructuralist project of critique, something new has arrived – the suggestion of something that lies beyond such specular determinations associated with the crisis of the subject.

Such a model of architecture based on wholly free material effects, while not proposing any reductive formalism or specific architectural outcome (utopian or otherwise), nonetheless raises mostly unanswerable questions about architectural ends. These ends, in fact, announce the end of all styles, toward the release of the purely formative 'will to form' secreted in architecture as a form of subjective *agencement* for architecture, and as enemy and nemesis for all manufactured chains of structural and rational aims applied to architecture. These ends come to reside uneasily in the notion of the architectural image, that merely apparent unit in the current discourse surrounding the architectural real.

Notes

This chapter is the development of a previous essay by Brott published as 'Impersonal Effects' in *Architecture for a Free Subjectivity: Deleuze and Guattari at the Horizon of the Real* (Ashgate, 2011). We would like to thank her publisher for granting us copyright permission to reproduce parts of this previous work.

1. In *Empiricism and Subjectivity* personal subjectivity is an effect of habit and repetition.
2. For Deleuze-Hume, causality is itself an effect derived from experience, from the repetition of similar cases. 'The real content of causality – registered by the term "always" – cannot be constituted in experience, because, in a sense, it constitutes experience' (1991: 67).
3. This disavowal, the idea that there is no subject, refers to Deleuze's critique of subjectivity based on the transcendental ego and, for Deleuze, the 'fascinated submission of psychoanalysis to the paradigm of the "subject"' (Deleuze, in Cadava et al. 1991: 94).
4. 'Ideas are not the representations of objects, but rather of impressions; as for the impressions, they are not representative, nor are they adventitious; rather they are innate' (Deleuze 1991: 88).
5. The mind is only *ideas* in the mind: 'we use the terms *imagination* and *mind* not to designate a faculty or a principle of organisation, but rather a particular set or a particular collection' (Deleuze 1991: 87–8).

6. 'A singularity is inseparable from a zone of perfectly objective indetermination which is the open space of its nomadic distribution' (Deleuze 1990: 113). See also Cadava et al. (1991: 95).
7. In Deleuze-Hume there is a precise relation between motive and action inextricably tied to a set of circumstances. Relation, he says, is 'that *particular* circumstance, in which, *even upon the arbitrary union of two ideas in the fancy*, we may think proper to compare them . . . *Circumstance* gives the relation its sufficient reason' (Deleuze 1991: 103).
8. *Promenade architecturale* was Le Corbusier's phrase for the spiral trajectory of the perambulating architectural spectator from the ground floor to the roof-top garden of the Villa Savoye (1931) dictated by the ramp and spiral plan.
9. This does not mean the end of significations or fantasies, only that such spectral images function at the level of a *secondary subjectivity* which adheres to a *subject* who decodes architecture, who forms architectural projections, excuses, hallucinations and so forth. To embrace the real in this manner means to leave behind the pathologies of the subject.
10. Deleuze states, 'Singularities are the true transcendental events, and Ferlinghetti calls them "the fourth person singular". Far from being individual or personal, singularities preside over the genesis of individuals and persons; they are distributed in a "potential" which admits neither Self nor I, but which produces them by actualizing or realizing itself, although the figures of this actualization do not at all resemble the realized potential' (2004: 118).
11. Continuity is really the individuation of effects by sequence and repetition; as Deleuze might say, there are only the detached effects. The dream, for example, while dreamed, is de facto experienced as continuous by the unconscious, whose mechanism is to join the images together; yet upon awakening, one often remembers only a series of disconnected images.
12. Impersonal effects are also phenomenological insofar as they situate the architectural encounter as the locus of subjectivity.
13. 'The purpose of the work of art is to "keep" and transmit meanings' (Norberg-Schulz 1980: 5).
14. Jacques Lacan, 'La séminaire. Livre X. L'angoisse, 1962–3' (unpublished seminar, 16 January 1963). In Lacan's unpublished seminars in 1963, the *objet petit a(utre)* – object small-other or object little-a – is a privileged object, a trace from the *Real*, in the failure of the subject to be incorporated into the *Symbolic*. The Symbolic and the Real are originary states in Lacan's triune schema of the emergence of the subject ('subject' here means an infant in the first eighteen months). Elsewhere I have written about Guattari's use of the Lacanian object a (Brott 2011: ch. 5).
15. See Rossi 1982. Rossi is a central figure in the discipline, in particular for his contribution to postmodern architectural history.
16. I am aware that La Villette is seen as a cardinal point for deconstructivist postmodernism in architecture, but here I am referring to its formal and reductive intent, which remains essentially modernist in spirit.
17. Tschumi's great project, residing at the cusp of the end of the 'reign of the sign', however, discloses more than it intended; it speaks to the long-running novel that is modernist architecture and its troubled relationship to site, especially urban sites.
18. While walking in the park, it becomes clear the architecture lies not in the structures themselves but in the encounter of the gap that arises in walking from one *folie* to the next.
19. La Villette eviscerated such expectations for urban parks and urban subjects programmed by such parks.

20. The decentred subject of immanent materiality clearly transcends the personological subject, but it remains a grammatical elision leading to a type of haunting of texts and architectural forms.
21. Derrida writes: 'If what happens to us thus does not come from outside, or rather, if this outside engages us in the very thing we are, is there a *maintenant* of architecture and in what sense [*sens*]? Everything indeed comes down to the question of meaning [. . .] a question of what happens to meaning [. . .] and so this is the event' (1986: 5). *Hermeneutics* refers to Heidegger's method of 'de-structuring' the language of metaphysics, from which the term *deconstruction* derives.
22. This is intended on the level that structure always pursues its own origin, is self-driven and has a creative movement, however insular or self-referential.

References

Bachelard, G. ([1957] 1964), *The Poetics of Space*, trans. M. Jolas, New York: Orion Press.
Barthes, R. ([1957] 1979), *The Eiffel Tower, and Other Mythologies*, New York: Hill & Wang.
Brott, S. (2011), *Architecture for a Free Subjectivity*, London: Ashgate.
Cadava, E., P. Connor, J.-L. Nancy (eds) (1991), *Who Comes After the Subject?*, New York: Routledge.
Deleuze, G. ([1968] 1988), *Bergsonism*, New York: Zone Books.
Deleuze, G. ([1969] 1990), *The Logic of Sense*, New York: Columbia University Press.
Deleuze, G. [1953] 1991), *Empiricism and subjectivity: An Essay on Hume's Theory of Human Nature*, New York: Columbia University Press.
Deleuze, G. ([1972] 2000), *Proust and Signs*, 2nd exp. edn, Minneapolis, MN: University of Minnesota Press.
Deleuze, G. (2004), *The Logic of Sense*, London: Continuum.
Derrida, J. (1986), 'Point de Folie – Maintenant l'architecture', in *La Case vide: La Villette: 1985 Bernard Tschumi*, London: Architectural Association.
Guattari, F. (1994), 'Les Machines architecturales de Shin Takamatsu', *Chimères*, 21, 127–41.
Guattari, F. (1996), 'The Postmodern Impasse', in G. Genosko (ed.), *A Guattari Reader*, Cambridge, MA: Blackwell Publishers.
Le Corbusier (1923), *Vers une architecture*, Paris: G. Cres.
Lynch, D. ([2001] 2002), *Mulholland Drive*, Universal City, CA: Universal.
Norberg-Schultz, C. (1980), *Genius loci: Towards a Phenomenology of Architecture*, New York: Rizzoli.
Rossi, A. ([1966] 1982), *The Architecture of the City*, Cambridge, MA: MIT Press.
Sherer, D. (2004), 'Le Corbusier's Discovery of Palladio in 1922 and the Modernist Transformation of the Classical Code', *Perspecta 35, Building Codes: The Yale Architectural Journal*, 24–39.
Tschumi, B. (1981), *The Manhattan Transcripts*, London: Academy Editions, St. Martin's Press.
Vidler, A. (1986), 'Trick-Track', in J. Derrida (ed.), *La case vide: la villette 1985*, London: Architectural Association.

Chapter 9

The Holey City: Walking Along Istanbul's Theodosian Land Walls

Catharina Gabrielsson

We trickle down the hill, cats slinking by our feet as we stumble over debris and quickly jump to the side to evade being run over by people and cars, pressing ourselves through the gaps along the facades past the rows of stalls selling oranges and pomegranates until the street suddenly widens and the strait lies before us: the Golden Horn. Stamboul towers up in the haze on the other side of the bridge, its distinctive silhouette of cupolas and minarets emerging from an undergrowth of dilapidated buildings. Here, at the head of the Galata bridge, there is a dizzying sense of arriving at the cardinal point where the world opens up in all directions. It is to experience one's embodied mind as incidental and finally in context, as part of the masses, an ephemeral aspect of the heterogeneous multitude that has lived and died here for millennia. If Istanbul is a materialisation of borders – between East and West, Europe and Asia, Christianity and Islam, History and Modernity – it is also where such borders are exposed for what they are: abstract constructions, artifice. If this is the city of extremes, it is also where extremes converge: the city of translations and transgressions. Istanbul is a place where Western dichotomies are invalidated with such power that we are forced to think and move in other directions.

How is it possible to capture the specificities of Istanbul in terms of contemporary urban conditions? By necessity, it would require a capacity to think diversity, difference and multiplicity. It means to see how processes emerge, break and entwine; how identities shift and change, yet somehow persist with material stubbornness; to detect how mechanisms of power operate spatially and take physical form, but in so doing also give rise to lapses and holes, incessant lines of flight. A postmodern celebration of 'radical indeterminacy' (Dear 2000: 5) will not suffice to explain Istanbul's prolonged existence, serving as capital for three world empires before succumbing to the present one, and currently subjected to perhaps the most violent and austere neo-liberal urban developments in Europe and the Middle East. If Istanbul does hold a promise of reconciliation, it doesn't come from accepting the relativism of knowledge but from the ancient wisdom that everything coexists in a perpetual state of movement and interaction.

Interestingly, Istanbul has recently been adopted as a model for urban resilience within the emerging field of research on cities as complex self-organising systems. Members of the inter-disciplinary research project *Urban Mind* point to how the diversity of 'insurance strategies' of ancient Constantinople – investments not only in military infrastructure, protecting territories and distant trade, but also in systems for supplying, storing and producing food and water – ensured a unique capacity for self-sufficiency during periods of decline and crisis, now seen to hold vital lessons for 'smart cities' and 'sustainable urban growth' (Ljungkvist et al. 2010). Founded on historical ecology and environmental archaeology, this research focuses on the dynamics of urbanism seen as 'constituted on adaptive and interdependent socio-ecological systems, which in turn are linked across temporal and spatial scales in complex and non-linear ways' (Sinclair 2010: 18). Significant for how current climatic concerns generate new disciplinary set-ups and new approaches to urban conditions, the ontology underpinning this project – albeit devoid of philosophical references – clearly runs in parallel to that of Gilles Deleuze and Félix Guattari's *Mille Plateaux*.

'Basically a call to think complexity, and to complex thinking', the 'geophilosophy' of Deleuze and Guattari is becoming increasingly important for advancing our understanding of ecology (Herzogenrath 2009: 4; Tinnell 2011). The validity of rethinking cities has, in particular, been explored by Manuel DeLanda who repeatedly underlines how Deleuze and Guattari's 'realist stance' provides an escape from the oppositional modes of essentialism versus constructivism. But there is a totalising tendency, even a sense of determination, emanating from DeLanda's *A Thousand Years of Nonlinear History* (1997) – one that makes the mid-nineteenth-century planning terminology on 'urban blights' and 'disease', 'healing' and 'surgery' seem comparatively innocent. The shift from using organic *metaphors* to organic *models* seems integral to thinking on cities as complex self-organising systems and involves the risk of obliterating other crucial concerns: questions to do with the political. Set on analysing the 'reciprocal effects of human thought and action on the environment' (Sinclair 2010: 12–13), the *Urban Mind* project deserves a special mention in this respect: it carries an indisputable resemblance to Guattari's insistence that we must change our *minds* before we can save the planet (Guattari 2000). Issues to do with subjectivity, agency and intentionality remain pertinent for our understanding of cities. And analysing the means for escaping, subverting or changing conditions in presumably self-organising urban systems seems more crucial than ever under the threat of climatic collapse, propelled by hegemonic beliefs in global capitalism and the utopia of self-regulated markets.

What follows is an attempt to respond to these concerns, albeit (given the context) in a necessarily incomplete way. Drawing a line of passage along Istanbul's ancient city walls, this chapter is essentially a write-up of a fieldwork operation that (as proposed by Hélène Frichot elsewhere in this book) 'follows the material' under the influence of Deleuze and Guattari. The validity of *Mille Plateaux* in this kind of operation would really need no other explanation than the simple and pragmatic fact that many of the themes explored in the book derive from this part of the world. The rise of the state apparatus, war machines, nomadism, maritime trade, metallurgy, etc. find their empirical sources in early Indo-European civilisations, but are also exemplified in matters closer at hand: the Anatolian rural lands whose deterritorialised population feed the massive immigration that has increased Istanbul's population from 1 to almost 13 million in the last fifty years. So let us proceed, like any other tourist, by going for a walk.

Walking in the City

We are heading towards the city walls to find the place where the Holy Virgin, according to legend, made her first appearance in Byzantine times to muster courage among the city's defenders and fear in her enemies. The sacred spring that burst forth in Blachernae is still in existence and is, for Swedish visitors, strongly associated with another legend, that of the poet Gunnar Ekelöf and his visit to Istanbul in 1965. 'Oh sure – sönderkysst, sönderkysst . . .', the Turkish caretaker of the little chapel responds at my stuttering attempts to explain the *reality* of the icon hung on the wall next to the spring – the blackened Madonna whose features have been wiped out by centuries of devoted kisses.[1] The intensified presence transmitted by this momentary assemblage is a token of how stories in the near and distant past enfold in the mind and programme the subjective experience into something that is only partially exterior or transmitted by the senses.

Walking in the city is thus also practising a discourse. A recurring theme in urban sociology, spanning from Baudelaire's *flâneur* to psycho-geographical drifting to subversive architectural mappings, it is a discourse united by a common practice but with varying implications. Walking serves as a powerful articulation of differences – between object and subject, space and place, experience and intention, representation and reality, normality and deviation – but remains ambiguous: a means for *writing* the city as well as *reading* it, for spatial empowerment as well as for escaping the system of control. De Certeau's understanding of walking as an operative practice, as a production *of* space (rather than something that takes place 'in' it), remains important and transfers effortlessly into a topological understanding (Murdoch 2006). But the dependence on sidewalks implicit in this thinking (Buchanan and Lambert 2005: 3) – as a pre-existent, designated and delimited territory produced by the dominant spatial order – is revealing for the rigid framework of power vis-à-vis resistance underpinning the 'radicalism' of walking. Sidewalks are scarce in Istanbul – there is little provision for making the streets accessible and safe for pedestrians. Walking here means to join in with a movement that has been ongoing among Western intellectuals for more than a century, but also – in distinctive ways – to deviate from it.

After a confusing ride on a commuter train (whose departure is delayed due to a political assembly on the platform) we stand before the city wall at its lowest part, close to the Golden Gate. In Byzantine times, it was a freestanding triumphal arch whose use was reserved for emperors returning victorious to Constantinople after battle. One thousand years later it was walled up by Mehmet II, supposedly to prevent the arrival of a new emperor: that of Christ returning to reclaim the city from the Muslim conquerors. Ever since, it has formed part of Yedikule, a five-sided fortification whose principal use during Ottoman times was as a prison. The obliteration of the gate's original context has been completed by infrastructure – an eight-lane highway obstructs the connection to what was once the road to Rome. But the technology of blocking access integral to war – the apparatus of capture defining the state (Deleuze and Guattari 2009: 468–72) – remains fully legible and indicates clearly the inexorable pincer strategy of the siege. Thus Yedikule shares more than an architectural resemblance with Rumeli Hisarı, the fort along the Bosporus that Mehmet II had built at record speed in order to throttle the provision of grain shipped from the Black Sea. Today Yedikule is a silent, grassy void surrounded by high masonry walls. From the top, precariously balancing on its crest, one is afforded a breathtaking view of the *ecumenopolis* – the city without limits – expanding across two continents.[2] The Sea of Marmara is cluttered with the dark shapes of freight ships resting in the roadstead, awaiting further passage up the strait. We must abandon our search for the display of Ottoman torture tools, the inscriptions of prisoners and the meat hooks fastened into the dungeon walls promised by the guide book. Instead we discover a metal door hanging ajar and manage to creep through to the outside. Hidden from view, against a backdrop of deafening traffic, the Golden Gate is still standing with its Byzantine insignia intact.

The critical implications of walking in the city cannot be sidestepped even when presented in its most practical guise, such as John Freely's *Strolling Through Istanbul: A Guide to the City* (Freely and Sumner-Boyd 1972), whose twenty-or-so itineraries also make up most of the content in *Blue Guide: City Guide to Istanbul* (Freely 2011) (both in numerous reprints). Freely's method of uncovering the city's sights and monuments through a spatial, rather than temporal, linearity can be compared to an earlier example of the same genre, Edwin A. Grosvenor's *Constantinople* from 1895. The simple and direct approach that characterises this literature, one that literally takes the visitor by the hand, suggests that there are even earlier examples, indeed a lineage of writing about Istanbul in this way in line with countless travel accounts and visitors' letters – sources that combine in forming the predominantly Western understanding of the city. Despite their differences, these writings share a similar aim. By establishing a fictitious ground they protect the reader/visitor from deterritorialisation, described by Buchanan as 'a process whereby the very basis of one's identity, the proverbial ground beneath our feet, is eroded, washed away like the bank of a river swollen by floodwater – immersion' (2005: 23). In the labyrinthine streets of Istanbul, one would expect this sense of threat to increase. But Buchanan notes that Flaubert wasn't deterritorialised by the Orient: it confirmed him. He constructed his identity through meeting with the Other, which is also Edward Said's main argument in *Orientalism* (Buchanan 2005: 23). But isn't the concept of the Other always founded on recognition, in that it presupposes proximity and the identification of someone precisely as a 'stranger'? If this state of proximity, at-the-brink, next-to-immersion ultimately serves to *confirm* the modern subject, it shows the tremendous forces at play in maintaining it. The longing to escape is therefore also the longing to undo the boundaries of subjectivity, to dissolve and expand, which serves to explain the power Istanbul has always exerted over the Western imagination. We wander through the city driven by a desire to reconstruct connections that long since have been made estranged, broken and forgotten, to regain our footing in a sense of pre-personal self.

The Theodosian Land Walls

And so we walk from one gate to the next, along the old city walls as informed by Freely's carefully described sequences. Frequently damaged in battles and earthquakes, partly ruined and brutally restored, the Theodosian land walls are still standing along their entire stretch. In combination with the sea-walls along the shores, of which only fragments remain, these walls constituted a near-invincible defence system that protected the heart of the Byzantine empire for more than a thousand years, that is until Mehmet II achieved the break-through 'at their weakest point' on 29 May 1453.[3] The laconic tone of Freely's remark that these walls 'profoundly influenced the history of medieval Europe' (Freely and Sumner-Boyd 1972: 367) differs from that in Grosvenor's description, one that raises the drama considerably:

> Here are combined the stateliness of material power and the grandest works of human achievements, saddening in their overwhelming desolation, and haunted by solemn and undying memories. The walls embrace and centre all the martial past of the capital. The densely peopled triangle they enclose has been more coveted and fought for than any other spot on earth by rival chiefs and empires; but the walls have been the barrier at which the seemingly restless waves of conquest and invasion have been stayed. At their base have fallen in fight a more mixed and more numerous multitude than have died in assault of any other city save Jerusalem or Rome. The fleets and hosts which have besieged the city, following one another like returning tides, have each branded on the wall its fierce autograph in fire and blood. (Grosvenor 1895: 558–9)

Grosvenor's account is literally sublime in conjuring up the incomprehensible depth of time. This sublimity seems to have gone missing today amid the disintegration of the historical context. It is not only due to the traffic or the coarse restoration works that jeopardise the walls' position on the World Heritage list, for the inscriptions remain, and the dust and haze from Grosvenor's photographs still affect one's senses. We climb over piles of debris without knowing if they originate from Byzantine times or from last year's restoration; stumble into dwellings, holdings and haunts only to back out with haste. The 'loss' of sublimity must therefore be related to the transformed position of the viewer, one that, in fact, re-installs the sublime as a challenge to the faculties of reason. What indeed has been lost is the self-assured privileged perspective that characterises Grosvenor's depiction, an 'aesthetical' position in so far as the city stands as a distant motif rather than a compromised and compromising milieu. That is why Grosvenor may give such offhand descriptions of the filthy environment in the walls' proximity and contrast it with the 'delightful and enchanting spectacle' they make when viewed from the sea. But the poverty remains, the barefooted and dispossessed among the dirt and piles of refuse.

The Roman sign for a city, a cross inscribed into a circle, is an apt representation of ancient Constantinople. Surrounded by walls, this was once the centre of a power with global importance, at least as the world was known until the early Middle Ages – a seat for controlling the movements between the Black Sea and the Mediterranean, the land routes towards the East (India and China) and their ramifications into Europe. There is linguistic and iconographic support for the thesis that the idea of the city was once tantamount to the idea of its enclosure, also in alignment with the city founding rituals that were practised in most ancient cultures (Kostof 2004: 11–12; Rykwert 1976). According to Roman tradition, the centre was symbolically marked by a hole (*mundus*) while the border was made by ploughing an insurmountable furrow (*sulcus primigenius*) – both were considered sacred acts. Rykwert retells the story of how Constantine was influenced by a dream when deciding to locate his new Christian capital in what was then the dwindling town of Byzantium (in 326 or 328 AD). He also relates that it was Constantine personally who used his lance to draw the line for Constantinople's city walls. To the great surprise of his entourage, the emperor passed the circumference that had been agreed on and continued walking. When they tried to make him return he replied: 'I shall go on until he who is walking ahead of me stops.' Rykwert writes: 'Whom did Constantine claim to see ahead of him – Christ or an Angel [. . .]? [. . .] or perhaps even Apollo himself, the sun-god, whose incarnation Constantine sometimes thought himself' (1976: 202). A reminder of that episode is the remains of Constantine's statue, the so-called 'burnt column' (Çemberlitaş), believed to hide a wooden fragment of the True Cross in its base.

This hybridisation between Roman mythology and Christianity, fused with pragmatic techniques of domination, is characteristic of Constantinople at its earliest stage. It is made manifest in the procurement of monuments, relics and sculptures fetched from the entire antique world and used to fabricate the legitimacy of the city as centre for the new imperial order. This was a strategy of literally colonising previous meanings, a seizing of symbolical objects whose codes were unhinged, manipulated and reinvented through acts of physical (dis) placement. The de- and re-territorialising of codes tied into Istanbul's history remains a viable strategy, as illustrated by the recently inaugurated tourist attraction *Panorama 1453* located just outside 'the weakest point'. Drawing visitors from across the Middle East, the main attraction of this post-9/11 setting is to be photographed before a coulisse of shattered walls: a theatrical staging complete with cannons, carcasses and screaming soldiers. The militarist and nationalist framework surrounding this spectacle – a mobilisation of former Ottoman glories in support of present-day governmental aspirations – is conveyed by every detail, such as the heroic and personalised depiction of Ottoman troops (in reality a mixed bag of ethnicities, including mercenary Christians) in stark contrast to an anonymous and helplessly flailing Byzantine defence on the crumbling walls. For an aspiring member state of the EU it is a remarkably aggressive manifestation. It differs greatly from how historical sources relate the events in 1453, generally considered as following a prolonged process of internal disintegrations rather than sudden violence exerted from the outside (Crowley 2005; Brownworth 2009). But the distinctive fold between 'fall' and 'conquest' is transmitted by the walls themselves, a material expression of a deep and fundamental ambiguity.

In collecting and allowing for a multitude of heterogeneous practices, the vast expanses produced by the walls were an urban resource. Constantine's limit had been expanded after a mere hundred years and enforced by a state-of-the-art piece of Roman technology named after the emperor Theodosius II (405–50). This unique defence structure with double walls, separated by a terrace and surrounded by a moat, was extremely space-consuming. To ensure manoeuvrability in the event of a siege, it was prohibited to build in its vicinity – an area known in Latin as *pomerium* (Kostof 2004: 14–31; Karlsson 1994). Constantinople thus maintained a broad stretch of unbuilt land along its perimeter, an inner-city rural zone whose main use in Byzantine times was for urban agriculture (Ljungqvist et al. 2010). The implications of the urban fringes go beyond questions of 'urban resilience', however, in involving 'the commons' as well as sprawl, the unregulated expansion of the city. Kostof underlines the importance of the suburbs ('as old as the city itself') in constituting a free zone for trade, free from the oppression of regulations, taxes and tolls within the city proper (Kostof 2004: 47–8). As a catchment area for those refused entry to the *polis*, the areas outside the walls may also be seen as constitutive for the political, essentially linked to the excluded, the non-represented, the silenced and unseen (Rancière 1998). This was where refugees and opportunists gathered, the site of trading for nomadic tradesmen and guild-less artisans. This was also where the dirtiest, lowest and most demeaning city services were located: tanneries, forges, cemeteries – but also hospitals, universities, religious orders, mad- and poorhouses. Yet another quote from Grosvenor serves to illustrate the environment along Constantinople's walls in the late nineteenth century:

> The refugees who swarmed hither from Bulgaria during the Russo-Turkish War in 1877–8 have wedged their miserable shanties close against it, and thereby at many points have concealed the ruins and prevented close approach. Foul odors from these unclean dwellings, and from neighboring heaps of filth of every sort, repel the visitor, and are horribly suggestive of cholera and the plague. (Grosvenor 1895: 562)

The walls collected a world around them: the debris of geopolitical and social transformations as well as the nourishment for development. The *pomerium* was a phenomenon of *transconsistency* (Deleuze and Guattari 2009: 477), a mediator between near and distant forces, formal and informal practices. Even though its military role has long since ceased, this 'geography of defence' continues to be operative. In the summer of 2005, one of the largest black markets in Europe emerged outside the walls along the embankment for the new tramway line then under construction (Mörtenböck and Mooshammer 2007). Swarms of people moved along a stretch of several kilometres lined with piles of things for sale: second-hand clothing, television sets, fridges, computers . . . The self-organised trading in this transitory space was supported by a services system of shuttle buses, street kitchens, middlemen and brokers – much as its informal status was dependent on formal structures, in temporarily occupying the grounds and exploiting the logistics of the construction site. These 'micro-sites of paradoxical and indeterminate cultural production' – the transnationalisation and hybridisation of deregulated flows of people, capital and goods constituting the underbelly of global capitalism – may involve the emergence of migrant and insurgent new political subjectivities (ibid.: 86) but it follows organically from a spatial code established in late antiquity.

The walls have generated more divergent effects but also more continuous ones. The terraces between the walls were used for gardening in Ottoman times, consistent with the Byzantine practice of urban agriculture, a detail telling for the seamless transition between the two empires. The ongoing cultivations along and within the Theodosian land walls give a deceptively informal impression. The land is minutely subdivided by rudimentary fencing that repeatedly forces us to alter our route, making our way past shelters of driftwood, recycled plastics and metal sheeting propped up against the masonry. The ground is populated by people bent over double as they slowly move along the furrows. The plots correspond to a social, economic and spatial system of distribution that cannot be deciphered from the outside. What meets the eye is how the spaces produced by the walls are integrated into the urban economy, allowing for a local production of vegetables sold in the nearby streets.

The Holey City

Distinguishing two discrete forms of central power, both emanating from cities, Deleuze and Guattari refer to the imperial system, where the city extends from the palace, and the town system, that is the correlate of the road (Deleuze and Guattari 2009: 477–9). An ancient metropolis and an imperial capital, Istanbul fuses these systems – one defined by hierarchies, the other by controlling flows – but both depending on techniques for spatial distribution. One is easily led to believe that the town is more egalitarian than the state, but Deleuze and Guattari issue a warning: 'Who can say where the greatest civil violence resides?' (2009: 478). The lure of the metropolis as a vehicle for emancipation and freedom is reflected in the massive waves of urbanisation across the world, but what is rendered clear by the city walls are the intense stratifications that continue to define urban life. No longer machinic in a physical sense, the regulation of entrances and exits is carried out by immaterial means and sets the terms for urban survival. In Istanbul with its extensive realm of informal social networks, livelihoods are to a great extent defined by connections, contacts and channels linked to lineage, birthplace and ethnic and religious origins. This system of strong social ties is said to be typical of non-Western cities and counterproductive for the development of democratic transparency, regulated labour markets, welfare provision, etc. – but it is equally decisive for 'networking societies' in Western democracies, the stuff that makes or breaks careers.

And so the Theodosian walls are not an inside set against an outside, implying a system of power and resistance. Even if reduced to 'form' enveloping a 'content', they aren't a border in a conventional sense but a system of spaces, passages, thresholds and sites with varying degrees of intensity. Deleuze and Guattari's distinction between two predominant spatial modalities – striated and smooth space – is derived from the French anthropologist André Leroi-Gourhan. He suggests that while hunter-and-gatherer societies conceived of space as a territory, defined by crossings and nodes, the transition to agriculture and husbandry generated a different spatial conception manifested by 'the concentric circles around a granary' (Leroi-Gourhan 1993: 327). As the 'primordial repository of nourishment', he compares the granary to the temple, constituting the origin for architecture and (presumably also) for the imperial system (ibid.: 335). The 'humanized cosmos' expressed by the latter (radial space) was thus of much greater interest to Leroi-Gourhan than the 'untamed universe' of the former (itinerant space).

While this distinction is retained by Deleuze and Guattari, the (im) balance is shifted. One is 'striated, by walls, enclosures, and roads between enclosures', a distribution of people in space impregnated with order, language and semiotic codes. The other is 'smooth, marked only by "traits" that are effaced and displaced with the trajectory', an open indefinite space, full of promise and danger (Deleuze and Guattari 2009: 420). Thus striated space is readily identified with confirmed and normative power, while smooth space invites thinking along the lines of escape, freedom and divergence – seemingly holding the promise for another and more liberating architecture. The rich and varied nominations set forth by Deleuze and Guattari, however, suggest the need for a more complex understanding. Rather than dialectical opposites, the smooth and the striated must be seen as dynamically interconnected, as 'two different modes of approaching, understanding and operating in the world' (Hensel et al. 2009: 45). Regarded in terms of power, as systems of distribution, the smooth and the striated are in constant negotiation, generating countless more or less transient intermediary states.

One such state of spatial negotiation is, in fact, named in *Mille Plateaux*: holey space. Deleuze and Guattari bring it up when discussing the evolution of metallurgy and the social transition marked by the stage when people started to 'excavate the land instead of striating it, bore holes in space instead of keeping it smooth' (2009: 458). The importance attributed to material technology for the development of human civilisation (signalled by periodisations based on stone, bronze and iron) is activated by Deleuze and Guattari in specifying the smith as Other, ambulant and itinerant but 'not nomadic among the nomads and sedentary among the sedentaries', belonging neither to the earth nor to the underworld (2009: 457). The holey space that emerges with mining constitutes a radically different kind of spatial production in conformity with the 'vague essence' of the smith whose specificity is that of the hybrid or alloy (ibid.: 458). Elsewhere, holey space is described in a more ephemeral manner, as 'a new smoothness' arising in the striated:

> In contrast to the sea, the city is the striated space par excellence; the sea is the smooth space fundamentally open to striation, and the city is the force of striation that reimparts smooth space, puts it back into operation

everywhere, on earth and in the other elements, outside but also inside itself. The smooth spaces arising from the city are not only those of world-wide organisation, but also of a counterattack combining the smooth and the holey and turning back against the town: sprawling, temporary, shifting shantytowns of nomads and cave dwellers, scrap metal and fabric, patch-work, to which the striations of money, work, or housing are no longer relevant. (Ibid.: 531)

The holeyness of space opens up for different interpretations: lapses and gaps in terms of human cognition and semiotics, deterritorialised codes and identities, disused and slackened spaces. This complexity is rendered concrete by our walk along the land walls, by experiences and uses generated by their material factuality. People gather in cavities and ruins, clotheslines bear witness to inhabitation. Trading occurs along and in between the walls, markets specialising in exquisite doves, second-hand clothes or recycled garbage. We've reached Sulukule, the infamous Roma neighbourhood claimed to have been here since 1045. Despite efforts by the local authorities to cleanse the area, to capitalise on land values and to reprogramme the historic peninsula for the tourist industry, the original inhabitants stay on. Their shacks re-emerge along the walls, even after the extensive demolition that has reduced the neighbourhood to a white patch on Google Earth.

Holey spaces arise and are concretised by the 'creative destruction' of capitalism, through war, disease and natural disasters, by processes of ethnic, political and religious cleansing as well as by fluctuations in the global finance market. The abundance of dilapidated and abandoned buildings in the historic parts of Istanbul stem from all of these factors – a phenomenon that exerts a friction on the aesthetic category of the picturesque. But rather than limited to the effects of violence and decline, holey space offers an opportunity to understand urban dynamics across different temporal and spatial scales. There is evidently a holeyness to the underground cities in Cappadocia (including their complicated causes in religious struggles within the central power) but the informal settlements (*gecekundus*) that make up half of Istanbul's expansion are equally holey, hastily built constructions that over time have been inscribed into such complex legal, political and economical structures that they are impossible to map or define. The concept of holey space – its threats and promises, tactics and strategies – points to the obliquity of rationality and the unforeseeable effects of human constructions, the lines of flight that suddenly emerge embedded in the existing. Istanbul is defined by holeyness. Constituting a point of departure for a generalised theory on contemporary urban conditions, holeyness counteracts dominant cultural readings of Istanbul in terms of loss and nostalgia but also the neo-Ottoman aspirations of the current government set on reinventing the city as a global centre of finance. It is the holeyness of Istanbul that accounts for its resilience, its remarkable ethnic and religious diversity that lasted until the postwar years and the extraordinary biodiversity that characterises it today. In constituting a lapse in the dominant order, it accounts for divergent spatial practices as well as for the shifting of codes and practices – both aspects of profound political and aesthetical importance. This holeyness makes Istanbul prototypical for what would amount to the *post*-postmodern urban condition, were it not for the fact that it is precisely the invalidity of such historical categorisations that is established in Istanbul, once and for all.

Notes

1. The caretaker's reply alludes to the closing words ('kissed to pieces') of Gunnar Ekelöf's poem *ayisma* (nr. 27) in *DIWAN on the Prince of Emgión* (1965), a meditation on the icon guarding the holy spring where the Byzantine emperors are said to have washed their hands from sin. Gunnar Ekelöf's visit to Turkey had a profound influence on his poetry and provided the overarching theme for his final published works, the so-called Diwan trilogy.
2. *Ecumenopolis: City Without Limits* (2011) is a documentary film about Istanbul by Imre Azem (director) and Gaye Gunay (producer). Spun around a narrative of the eviction of migrants and low-income residents victimised by real-estate development, it makes a convincing case for a mega-city set on the course of neo-liberal destruction and ecological disaster.
3. The expression 'the weakest point' recurs in several sources (quoted here from Freely 2011: 48) and refers to the topological conditions where the river Lychos met the city walls at present-day Topkapi.

References

Brownworth, L. (2009), *Lost to the West: The Forgotten Byzantine Empire that Rescued Western Civilisation*, New York: Three Rivers Press.
Buchanan, I. (2005), 'Space in the Age of Non-Place', in I. Buchanan and G. Lambert (eds), *Deleuze and Space*, Toronto: University of Toronto Press, pp. 16–35.
Buchanan, I. and G. Lambert (2005), 'Introduction', in I. Buchanan and G. Lambert (eds), *Deleuze and Space*, Toronto: University of Toronto Press, pp. 1–15.
Crowley, R. (2005), *1453 : The Holy War for Constantinople and the Clash of Islam and the West*, New York: Hyperion.
Dear, M. (2000), *The Postmodern Urban Condition*, Oxford: Blackwell.
DeLanda, M. (1997), *A Thousand Years of Nonlinear History*, New York: Zone Books.
Deleuze G. and F. Guattari, (2009), *A Thousand Plateaus: Capitalism and Schizophrenia*, trans. B. Massumi, New York: Continuum.
Freely, J. (2011), *Blue Guide: City Guide to Istanbul*, 6th edn, London: Blue Guides.
Freely, J. and H. Sumner-Boyd (1972), *Strolling Through Istanbul: A Guide to the City*, Istanbul: Redhouse Press.

Grosvenor, E. A. (1895), *Constantinople*, Vol. II, Boston: Roberts Brothers.

Guattari, F. (2000), *The Three Ecologies*, trans. I. Pindar and P. Sutton, London: Athlone Press.

Hensel, M., C. Hight and A. Menges (eds) (2009), *Space Reader: Heterogenous Space in Architecture*, Chichester: John Wiley/AD.

Herzogenrath, B. (2009), 'Nature/Geophilosophy/Machinics/Ecosophy', in B. Herzogenrath (ed.), *Deleuze/Guattari & Ecology*, Basingstoke: Palgrave Macmillan.

Karlsson, K. (1994), 'Form and Function: A Perfect City Wall', *Cornucopia*, 2: 7, 43–5.

Kostof, S. (2004), *The City Assembled: The Elements of Urban Form Through History*, London: Thames & Hudson.

Leroi-Gourhan, A. (1993), *Gesture and Speech*, trans. A. B. Berger, Cambridge, MA: MIT Press.

Ljungkvist, J., S. Barthel, G. Finnveden and S. Sörlin (2010), 'The Urban Anthropocene: Lessons for Sustainability from the Environmental History of Constantinople', in P. Sinclair, G. Nordquist, F. Herschend and C. Isendahl (eds), *The Urban Mind: Cultural and Environmental Dynamics*, Uppsala: Uppsala Universitet, Studies in Global Archaeology 15.

Mörtenböck, P. and H. Mooshammer (2007), 'Trading Indeterminacy – Informal Markets in Europe', *Field*, 1: 1, 73–87.

Murdoch, J. (2006), *Post-Structuralist Geography*, London: Sage.

Rancière, J. (1998), *Disagreement: Politics and Philosophy*, trans. J. Rose, Minneapolis, MN: University of Minnesota Press.

Rykwert, J. (1976), *The Idea of a Town: The Anthropology of Urban Form in Rome, Italy and the Ancient World*, London: Faber.

Sinclair, P. (2010), 'The Urban Mind: A Thematic Introduction', in P. Sinclair, G. Nordquist, F. Herschend and C. Isendahl (eds), *The Urban Mind: Cultural and Environmental Dynamics*, Uppsala: Uppsala Universitet, Studies in Global Archaeology 15.

Tinnell, J. (2011), 'Transversalising the Ecological Turn: Four Components of Felix Guattari's Ecosophical Perspective', *Fibreculture Journal*, 18, <http://eighteen.fibreculturejournal.org/2011/10/09/fcj-121-transversalising-the-ecological-turn-four-components-of-felix-guattari's-ecosophical-perspective/> (accessed 14 December 2012).

Chapter 10

Deleuze, Architecture and Social Fabrication

Andrew Ballantyne

Buildings are always machines, or – more accurately – parts of machines. In a great variety of ways, they connect with the wider world outside and beyond themselves, in order to produce within and around them the conditions in which life can flourish. Buildings work as technical machines of course, and we notice that fact most often when they break down: when they overheat or when the pipes leak. In ordinary conditions when everything is working properly, the building is the background to life and is not the focus of attention. For most of us most of the time, buildings are part of the unconscious.

We might be inclined to think of a perfect monument as an autonomous form, but buildings are never autonomous. Look at the great pyramids, and imagine them as simple geometric prisms – they are more complicated than that, but let us imagine them that way. They were made from local materials, quarried not far from the site in Egypt, and subject to much less transformation than typical modern building materials. It is possible to imagine how these buildings were built. The stone blocks were piled up to make a very stable structure that has stayed in place for a long time. It is more difficult to imagine why the pyramids seemed to be such a good idea that it was worth spending so much effort in building them. It involved the work of thousands of people over years, and had an impact on the whole structure of the society that produced them. They would not have been possible in a society that was less centralised, concentrating resources from a huge area into the control of a few decision-makers. Without that concentration, the resources might have been dissipated in everyday comfort for a wide range of people. The concentration was possible because of the means of communication made available by the Nile, which was Egypt's great thoroughfare. The pyramids would not have been possible in a society that did not produce a surplus, where all efforts would have instead gone into producing the means of survival. And they would not have been possible without the agriculture that not only produced the food but also a pattern of seasonal working. A large workforce was needed at certain times of the year, but not all through the year, so there were months when the work-force could build. The monuments look like images of geometric purity, but they were thoroughly enmeshed with the society that produced them. They had implications for the lives of everyone who lived in that society – whether or not they actually knew about the pyramids.

It is inevitable that there are interactions between buildings and people. That is the point of building. Sometimes the interactions are immediate, sometimes much less direct. If I think about my own imme-diate surroundings: there are some things here that I have taken trouble with, other things that have just happened without my thinking about them much, but it would be possible very quickly to identify the culture in which I am living – maybe its location on the earth, and certainly its location in time. I am reliant on the know-how of others. I do not have the skill to make the furniture that is in the room. I have not written and printed the books that are on the shelves. I did not find the copper ore, heat and crush it to extract the metal and then pull it into wires for the electrical appliances. All I need to know for my everyday life is that if I am in need of light I can click a switch. The rest of the machine – the nuclear power station, the mining operations, the glass-blowing and skilled workmanship that went into making the light-fitting – all that is part of the social fabric with which I connect and in which I grew up, so it seems for practical purposes to be indistinguishable from nature. It is my environment.

We not only respond in the plane of technical-machines, but also make use of them in other machines that connect with the concepts that are in circulation, in my own mind and in the minds of others. Buildings not only shelter us; we use them in establishing status, and in telling our-selves and others what kind of people we are. This has something to do with the form of a building, in that it is the built form that produces the stimuli to which the concepts connect, but it has just as much to do with the concepts that one uses to deal with those stimuli. The architecture, in other words, is substantially in the mind.

There are some responses to buildings that are clearly personal and specific. The house where I grew up is a particular place that has con-notations for me that it would not have for you. In my imagination I can sense its Oedipalised atmosphere, and remember how – when I visited the place even as an adult – it made me feel like an adolescent again. This had nothing to do with the building's style or expression, but if I were to put in place elements that evoked spaces in that building, they would put me back in that frame of mind. The place would reterritorialise me as adolescent. I could feel it happening when, as a thought-experiment, I tried imagining a cupboard that used to belong to my mother (she was very fond of it) being moved into my house. It was a cupboard that had a strong presence and could have made itself useful, but I could not allow it in. Somehow it would have seemed to be offering my mother's opinions of my decisions taken in its presence, and I do not want to live with that condition. It is perhaps in this relation that the building-as-a-machine has its closest relation to the desiring-machines depicted at the opening of Gilles Deleuze and Félix Guattari's *Anti-Oedipus*, especially the room in which Lenz is questioned by the well-meaning pastor (Deleuze and Guattari 1972: 2; Ballantyne 2007: 61–4).

For as long as Lenz is in the room with the pastor, he is unable to configure his thoughts in a way that seems right. He finds that he has to answer the pastor's questions by situating himself in relation to his parents, when what he longs to do is to situate himself in relation to hills and stars and falling snowflakes – to be absorbed into the landscape. Deleuze and Guattari follow him when he goes out on his walk and leaves the building behind, but I want to draw attention to the role of the buildings there, in enforcing the 'sane' socially endorsed world view (Deleuze and Guattari 1972: 2). Normally this happens without anyone noticing. The rooms would seem to be well arranged, with everything settled and properly ordered. It is Lenz who is breaking down here, and in his schizo-state the room seems coercive. Ordinarily it would not seem coercive because it would be encouraging and helping to hold in place a territorialisation that would already be in place. That territorialisation would be desirable because it would allow one to be 'well adjusted' in the social fabric of which the building is a part. Lenz is of interest because he is not well adjusted in that way. It is because he cannot submit to the building's demands that he is aware of them.

Like Lenz, Georges Bataille had problems in dealing with social norms, but he was more successful in maintaining his intellectual lucidity. He had the same intuition as Lenz when he described architecture as 'the expression of the very being of societies' (Bataille 2005: 16). Where Lenz feels the buildings as a personal problem, Bataille generalises, so that he sees them as problematic for everyone who is excluded from society. This is the inverse way of seeing things from the way the architect normally would. The great commissions of any age come from powerful institutions or individuals. Architects who are ambitious to design great buildings are interested in cultivating links with power.

The way that the architecture-machine works is most clearly under-stood through the use of commonplace examples. Deleuze and Guattari's enthusiasm for creativity and innovation in the production of concepts has made them feel like natural allies for architectural avant-gardists, but to use unfamiliar and outlandish examples here will only make the concept of the architecture-machine sound experimental and exotic, when in fact it is already everywhere in the most ordinary buildings and in ourselves.

In the UK the most-built architectural style during the twentieth century was Tudoresque. Most of the time architects and critics have not approved of it, but nevertheless for the buildings where archi-tects were not in control of the style agenda, especially in suburban houses, Tudoresque has been the 'default' choice for the British masses (Ballantyne and Law 2011). If we try to take these buildings seriously, we need to ask not whether they are good buildings (generally they are the small houses of people of limited means and they are mediocre) but why so many of them were built. What was going on that made them seem to be 'the thing to have'? The answer turns out to be surprisingly varied.

The earliest examples of the Tudoresque appeared in England in the late eighteenth century. It was formulated as an 'Old English' style that could be presented as indigenous and traditional. 'The Tudors' them-selves were an eighteenth-century invention – they never used that name themselves – though they were real enough, and ruled England and Wales through the sixteenth century. In the eighteenth century, the six-teenth century came to be seen as the time when the modern age began and when the nation began to develop its modern character. The build-ings of that age therefore had a particular set of associations that came importantly to the fore in the wake of the French Revolution of 1789. The English landowners then were exhorted to improve the housing stock of rural labourers. Some of the dwellings that were built at that time adopted an Old English style, as a way of giving expression to the fact that these workers were English, not French, and thereby giving emphasis to the fact that they were different from the Revolutionaries.

These are houses with a deliberately counter-revolutionary agenda. They were counter-revolutionary mainly by being decent houses, so that their occupants would have something to lose and would therefore be inclined not to rise up against the current order of things. The stylistic expression was secondary, but it reinforced the message. By being delib-erately old fashioned, the houses suggested continuity with the past and that the care for agricultural workers was a long-established tradition rather than a novelty. The houses were supposed to come with enough land to grow vegetables for subsistence, and were presented as a means to achieve a condition of self-reliance.

By the time that very similar-looking houses were being built in the twentieth century, the tradition of self-reliance was firmly established. It was also an illusion, as the house was actually owned by the bank until its mortgage was paid off. Nevertheless, the affects most frequently generated by these houses when they were built in England were a sense of tradition and self-reliance.

When they were built overseas the building form might be substantially similar, but the affects would be different. Let us imagine that the building form is identical, producing an identical range of sensations and stimuli; the affect could nevertheless be completely different. For example, if the building were constructed as the British Pavilion at the Chicago World's Fair (as happened in 1893) the building would not be 'indigenous' in the same way, but would be representative of a foreign culture. It could be experienced in these circumstances as 'exotic' and 'other'. This effect is most pronounced when the location and climate are at their furthest remove – for example, when they are to be found in Malaysian jungle. The Tudoresque buildings that are to be found in the Cameron Highlands, north of Kuala Lumpur, were originally the buildings that were designed to allow British colonial and postcolonial settlers to feel 'at home' in challenging and unfamiliar territory (Ballantyne and Law 2011: 212–16). However, the Tudoresque is now established in the area as an 'indigenous' style, and it is continued by people who have never been British citizens, for their own reasons. They are mimicking the building-style of a former elite, and for this group the largely unconscious affect is a feeling that the buildings are smart and correct rather than familiar in relation to a now-distant earlier life.

Another set of buildings is represented by a house built in Kota Kinabalu, by a Malaysian doctor who studied medicine in the UK. This house represents a memory of his formative years in England, when he became a doctor and assumed the identity with which he has since lived. His house has validity and authenticity at a personal level (Ballantyne and Law 2011: 235–6). The parallel here is with the Palladian architecture that was built in eighteenth-century England, and which has become so completely representative of that age that it is the first image that comes to mind when the English Country House is evoked. What happened then was that instead of going to university many of the sons of the great landed families would make a tour of continental Europe, passing through France and Switzerland to reach Italy, where they would study Renaissance art and Roman ruins. This 'Grand Tour' would take a year or more, and there would be time for all sorts of diversions and romantic dalliances along the way. They would return home as men of the world, having developed a taste for the Tuscan hills and classical architecture, which they would then try to recapture in their building and landscaping projects back home. Architects' tastes were educated so that they could produce the appropriate effects, whether or not they had the means actually to make a Grand Tour themselves. The point to be made here, though, is to see that as a productive machine, the assemblage of the house and its occupant is producing at a personal level (for the occupant) a feeling of nostalgia for an important part of his youth – along with good living conditions. On a different plane, the assemblage is producing an expression for the elite identity of the doctor in Malaysia. The building is recognisably non-indigenous in that context, so there is a suggestion of cosmopolitanism in it, and the respected figure of the doctor is given an appropriate housing in this cosmopolitan setting.

There is a further complexity, because other people in the neighbourhood have imitated this house, without having any comparable reason in their personal histories to adopt this style of building. Here the elite identity is recognised and 'borrowed', or used at second hand. The buildings could theoretically be identical to and indistinguishable from their model, but in fact the more limited means available tends to mean that the houses are smaller and less well designed. The same thing happened of course with classical architecture in eighteenth-century England, where the owners of many small houses sought to show themselves in a good light by making use of classical columns around the front door or the fireplace. These things happen, and they are not necessarily to be condemned. Contemporary architects are generally more comfortable with the phenomenon when it is a matter of imitating Le Corbusier rather than Palladio, or when the imitation has happened long ago and can be seen as appropriate for eighteenth-century but not twenty-first-century buildings. Nevertheless, it is the same process at work, working sometimes at a popular level on a restricted budget and sometimes with highly educated professionals with a lavish budget.

So, to go back to the idea of the building as part of a machinic assemblage: this conceptualisation of the building leads one to want to understand it in terms of what it produces, and what it produces is not only the building's declared utility (a house, a factory, a theatre), important though that is. It also produces a range of affects that often go undiscussed, but which can be decisive in determining the building's style or form. With a 'traditional' architecture, such as we can take the Tudoresque to be, it can be found in at least four distinct assemblages:

1. Where the tradition is naturalised by being pervasive. Then to build in this way is simply to do what is expected and to behave without eccentricity.
2. Where the tradition is carried into a new zone. For the people building it, it might seem to be identical to (1), but because the surroundings are different there is a sense of the exotic when it is encountered by the local population, and a sense of surreal dislocation when it is encountered for the first time by the builders' compatriots.
3. Where the tradition is adopted for personal reasons by someone who has come to know it. This could happen by dwelling in a building that is constructed within category (1), in which case the adoption would be invisible from outside. It becomes visible when it is adopted and transported elsewhere.
4. Where the tradition is seen to represent the habitat of an actual or former elite, and is adopted in order to give additional status to people who aspire to belong to that elite. They can do this by imitating buildings from categories (2) or (3) and the copies need not be at all accurate, so long as the gesture of association is understood by the anticipated local audience.

Each of these categories suggests a machinic assemblage that could work for any tradition of architectural design, given the necessary conditions. Each of them, however, is driven by a different motive force. The ethos of category (1) is driven by conformity, which might come from the limited materials available in a locality or a limited knowledge about how to use them. It might also come from a conviction that the established way of doing things is the best way to act. In any such case there will be a harmonious building-culture, where each building is much like all the others. Traditional vernacular cultures would fall into this category and their traditions could often be circumscribed by superstition and ignorance, along with pragmatism and the use of local materials. In this category the subject's territorialisation occurs within the tradition and is invisible and natural-seeming. The buildings in category (2) are driven by a desire to maintain the habits naturalised during upbringing, even when the subject is relocated to a place where the tradition is not dominant. It enables the subject to continue in the new place without reterritorialisation. The relation with the building continues in the familiar way, allowing the persistence of a mindset and a modus operandi for 'being-in-the-world' that connects strongly with the place that the building form came from, but is significantly dislocated from the mind-sets and habits around the place where the building actually is. So the driving force could be said to be 'continuity'. The subject continues with the old identity, surrounded now by others who do not share it.

In category (3) there has been a reterritorialisation – inevitably actually more than one – and the subject desires to hold on to the reterritorialisation and make it visible to others. In this case the building announces something like personal development into a more sophisticated adult-hood, comparable to signalling the award of a degree. The driving force might be personal nostalgia, but there is also an overtone of cosmopolitanism and sophistication here. It is nostalgia for a time of development and reterritorialisation, so there is a complex set of affects involved. As a shorthand it can be labelled as driven by sophistication. In category (4) the drive may include an element of feelings of sophistication, but the more powerful drive is something like social aspiration, which we would call 'snobbery' if we were seeing it in a negative light. The people who commission this sort of building believe that they will be able to improve their social standing and keep better company by having the house. If it is not accompanied by some kind of reterritorialisation then it falls back into pretentiousness. The reterritorialisation here is a repositioning in the social fabric, which in polite company is an often-undeclared aim, but the people whose job it is to sell dwellings in cities have a very clear idea of which areas are 'on the right side of the tracks'. A move from one area to another can be not only a relocation but also a reterritorialisation. In London, for example, a move from Brixton to Chelsea would involve crossing a terrain that could be walked over in an afternoon, but the social reterritorialisation involved would be greater than most people can manage in a lifetime (Ballantyne 2007: 9–17).

This gives us four quite distinct architecture-machines with different drives:

1. Conformity
2. Continuity
3. Sophistication
4. Social aspiration.

These are all possibilities for the most traditional kinds of architecture. For a more experimental avant-garde approach to architecture that opens up new possibilities for living, it might seem that we would need another category, but perhaps it comes back into category (3). The drive to reterritorialise and become more sophisticated through living in a new way is already there, and perhaps there is an element of nostalgia in the avant-garde's drive for novelty: a nostalgia to be amazed and have new horizons opened in the way that used to happen in one's youth. It is similarly associated with education and personal development. The important works of the avant-garde are not just novelties – they change the way we see things.[1] Many things that on their first appearance seemed to hold such promise in fact fall away and are forgotten or look merely eccentric with the passage of time. But they were brought into being by the drive to experiment and develop, which puts them into category (3) whether or not they actually succeed.

If we survey the buildings that there are in the world, then buildings in all four categories are well represented:

1. In traditional and vernacular architectures, wherever they are to be found.
2. In places where there has been colonisation or cultural migration, ranging from the Roman buildings across Europe, North Africa and Anatolia to the corporate style of hamburger chains that open up recognisably similar branches in Los Angeles, Moscow and Beijing.
3. Would include the art buildings that figure in conventional architectural history textbooks, along with many other buildings that are excluded from them simply for want of space, by taste or by perceived lack of success.
4. Is composed of buildings that make up most of the fabric of our modern cities, that have no special claim on our attention, but which indicate the aspirations of their inhabitants by making gestures of imitation. They can be large, expensive and skilfully wrought buildings, such as some houses that were built by nineteenth-century industrialists in imitation of the dwellings of eighteenth-century aristocrats. Normally, however, buildings in this category would be seen to be without high-order artistic merit. It was never part of their aim to have it. If they have some artistic merit then it is because (in the social conditions pertaining at the time) that was the means to the desired end of social advancement.

These different types of machines of course play very different roles in the lives and identities of the people and societies with whom they connect. The important thing about them is the use to which they are put, not their particular form. If I have grown up in a traditional community and am faced with the need to build, then if the idea of doing things differently occurs to me (and most likely it does not, not as a practical possibility) then I will feel uneasy about it. To do something that violated the tradition would seem to be bizarre or wrong. In such a case we are all within the chalk circle, all singing the same ritournelle (Deleuze and Guattari 1987: 311). The ritournelle – the little tune – is a world-structuring motif that, through repetition, gives us the feeling of being at-home-in-the-world. Its roots are pre-human, and in Deleuze and Guattari's world it maybe originates in (or perhaps more accurately 'passes through') the world of birdsong. The territorialising effects of birdsong are presented as an early type of architecture, and a child's song as the beginning of an encounter with the universe (Ballantyne 2007: 44–5; Deleuze and Guattari 1987: 311).

Difference in these circumstances is understood as error, not only by others but also, if I have been well-formed in such a society, by me. In such a situation I am hyperterritorialised, with no real sense of there being a real world beyond the chalk circle structured by our song. I see the world as a harmonious place.

In category (2) I move out beyond the circle, into the world, but I take my territorialisation with me. I might look around and notice that the world is polyphonal, but my own ritournelle does not change. I might be deaf to the songs of others, and simply see my project as civilising what was previously barbaric. Or I might hear an unfamiliar harmony as my ritournelle comes into contact with others – maybe making a temporarily productive *agencement* – a little machine that makes something or other happen for a while. But either way, I am territorialised and remain territorialised. I might notice difference, but I do not adopt it, though I might come to notice the contingency of my own culture (Rorty 1989). I might come away from the encounter having realised that my own cultural condition could be different from the way it is – and that it has in fact already become different through this fresh understanding. In the village where I grew up I might think that I am a unique individual, but if I go overseas I suddenly become aware that I am British. If I go to Asia I am suddenly aware that I am European. I might think that I have not been changed by the experiences, but yet I have been: I situate myself differently in the world on account of these encounters, and through the realisation that my own culture is not the whole world.

In category (3) there is change and development. I learn a new ritournelle. I become deterritorialised and disorientated on exposure to the new conditions, and then reterritorialise around a new ethos. Ernest Hemingway described how he was shaped by his formative experiences in Paris, and ever after carried his changed attitudes around with him. Paris, he said, was 'a moveable feast' (Hemingway 2009). It need not have been Paris. For the eighteenth-century Grand Tourists, Rome was equally a moveable feast. One approach here is to reterritorialise in the

new place, and then to go into the future with the new territorialisation
– the new identity – forever changed, but stable and essentially unchanging in the new territorialisation. One could settle permanently in the
new place, and develop by conforming to the newly adopted mores.
Or one could return home, if that still seems possible after the change.
'How ya gonna keep 'em down on the farm, after they've seen Paree?'
(Young and Lewis 1919). Then the culture of the other place is brought
into the chalk circle and becomes a sophisticated cosmopolitan discord
in the harmony, like the trumpet line in Charles Ives' *The Unanswered
Question*, which by itself is unremarkable, but it is set against a calm
continuing sonority that is unperturbed by the trumpet's being in a different key (Ives 1940).

The radical version of this developmental sophistication is to normal-
ise the deterritorialisation and reterritorialisation, so that the absorption
of new ritournelles becomes the way of life. It becomes a continuous
revolution, internalised in the subject or involving the subject in the
changing surroundings. At its most extreme this brings us to the state
of mind demonstrated by Lenz, in which the subject has lost sense of
its 'self' and is uncertain as to the whereabouts of its limits. Inside and
outside no longer have any meaning. Baruch Spinoza pointed out that
'no one has yet determined what the body can do' (Spinoza 1959: 87;
Gregg and Seigworth 2010: 3). This developmental nomadism takes us
wandering in order to explore new possibilities, which are as much possibilities of what one can think as what one can do. Given this essay's
focus, the point here is to reappropriate Spinoza to make the point
that no one has yet determined what buildings can do – or rather, no
one has yet determined the limits of what we can become by engaging with buildings. Deleuze and Guattari's model for the ritournelle
that characterises this kind of development is Schumann, especially his
Etudes Symphoniques of 1837 (to which the chapter heading of '1837:
De la ritournelle' ['1837: Of the Refrain'] alludes) and his late cello
concerto, where the ritournelle wanders away from any 'home' tonality
(Deleuze and Guattari 1980). Exploration and consequent development
can become ends in themselves. For the nomad, it is the journey that
becomes 'home', where one feels that one is most fully oneself. One
takes one's bearings from the present position rather than with reference
to a point of origin.

The problem with this as a continuing practice is that it has no necessary connection back into a social fabric, and the experiments can win
admiration or can be seen as eccentric or mad. Deleuze and Guattari
seem always to encourage the creative and developmental side of things,

but in their descriptions there is always an understanding that these moments of creativity and deterritorialisation are relatively rare. They contrast the 'nomadic war machine' of Genghis Khan with the 'state apparatus' of the Chinese emperors (Deleuze and Guattari 1980). Of course it is the state apparatus – the network of bureaucrats, lawmakers, functionaries and officials – that enables the state to function and that has a need for buildings that help to sustain the relations between the different elements of a society. The nomadic war machine is powerful and effective in its hit-and-run way. The Mongols' great invention was the stirrup, and their skill on horseback was a marvel. They developed to a high pitch of perfection the arts of menace, so that towns surrendered to them as they approached, but when they took over the governance of China, their lack of aptitude for bureaucracy meant that their rule did not last long. It was the state apparatus that produced the Great Wall of China to try to keep the Mongol hordes at bay. The Mongols had huge influence and controlled vast areas of territory, but they did not on the whole commission great buildings. Architecture is the expression of the very being of societies. A sedentary state with a stable apparatus and an effective bureaucracy has more use for architecture than has a nomadic terrorist organisation, and has more certain command of the means to produce it.

The buildings in category (4) are problematic for commentators because they are so easily dismissed. They represent the 'trickle-down' effect of some of the innovations in the experiments of category (3). If the designers of the category (3) buildings were impelled to think for themselves and produced 'art buildings', those in category (4) produce imitations of art buildings which are written off as 'kitsch'. Perhaps that is all one needs to say about them, but such buildings have become the dominant mode of production in the modern world, so they become normative and in such conditions their role as an instrument of social advancement is so readily taken for granted that they have actually – at least for some sections of society – fallen back into category (1) and seem more like a modern vernacular that demands conformity. The particular architectural style hardly matters: the important thing is the aspiration to live in a place with more social prestige. It is that aspiration that has become normalised, so we tend to think that people who do not share the aspiration have 'dropped out' of the mainstream. We might think that they are high-minded and above such things, or we might think that they have failed to meet the threshold conditions for social engagement, but either way they seem to be set apart.

The social connectedness gives the inhabitants and commissioners of category (4) buildings their great strength and resilience. They have merit in one another's eyes, their accomplishments and achievements are validated by one another and can be triangulated to give a sense of objectivity that works with absolute effectiveness within this bubble of relations. In this world the deterritorialisations of category (3) are an irrelevance, and the aspiration is not to be changed by moving into a high-status building, but on the contrary to remain unchanged, but to have one's higher status recognised by others on account of the changed habitation. There is nothing bewildering or disorienting here, no absolutely new ideas or ways of behaving, only the adoption of the social codes of the group to which one aspires to belong.

Wittgenstein said that 'Work on philosophy – like work in architecture in many respects – is really more work on oneself. On one's own conception. On how one sees things. (And what one expects of them.)' (Wittgenstein 1998: 24). This is true of the developmental buildings in category (3) but is less obviously part of the aspiration for the buildings in the other groups. Most buildings most of the time are commissioned with the expectation that one's current needs will be better accommodated than they were before the move into the new building. It is perhaps only in conditions of rare optimism that buildings are commissioned with the expectation that they will bring about changes in their occupants. When the social bonds remain in place, the subject is likely to continue playing the same roles in the same range of networks and to remain the same so far as anyone can tell. The transformations occur when one keeps new company or goes into isolation to work things out for oneself. This happens programmatically in the monastic traditions of various world religions, and with solitary hermits and anchorites meditating or praying. Their cells – or the tops of columns in the case of some desert saints – were designed as places of deterritorialisation, where (isolated from the usual societal claims on one's attention) one could be reterritorialised by the holy spirit.

For us perhaps the most accessible and least alienating account of such work on oneself is Henry David Thoreau's *Walden*. He describes how he set up a minimal dwelling in woods by Walden Pond, which was far enough away from his family's home in Concord, Massachusetts, for him to feel that he was living in isolation (but close enough to be able to walk back to see his siblings and parents). It was an experiment in living as close to nature as he could conceive, but he took books with him and enjoyed company when it came his way, so it was far from being a project of absolute deterritorialisation. Part of Thoreau's account is a reflection on the expense involved in building, and he was at pains that his independence should not be compromised by his little house costing him his freedom. If it entailed the order of cost that normal houses do, then he would have been in a position where for years he would have to earn a wage in order to pay for it. Most people put themselves in such a position without really thinking about it, and then lead lives of quiet desperation in order to hang on to the house and its contents and the social position that might go with them – all things that are not fundamental necessities, just conventional expectations. He went into the woods, he said, 'because I wished to live deliberately, to front only the essential facts of life [. . .] and not, when I came to die, discover that I had not lived' (Thoreau 1897: 143; Ballantyne 2005: 150–6).

The experimentation involved in buildings that matter is experimentation on ourselves. The point is not to find new building forms for the sake of having novel shapes around us, but to find new ways of living that suit us better than the old ways. A large part of what happens to us when we are growing up is an induction into the society in which it is supposed we will be living our lives. The buildings in categories (1), (2) and (4) are all to be identified with common-sense living, where the social fabric is woven and stretched out (Ballantyne 2005: 110–11). The experimental things depart from common sense and produce results that may be no more than outré, but at their most compelling they are individual revolutions that can be taken up more widely to change the way that a whole society thinks of its ways of living. The dwelling is a machine that is involved in the production of a way of life, and in habitual use it is part of the unconscious (Ballantyne 2011: 43–9). Experimenting with the way of life brings the building to the fore as the focus of attention. Even if the way of life does not catch on, to be taken up more widely, at least the subjects who have experimented with their lives know that they have lived.

Note

1. By 'avant-garde' here I mean experimental work that tries out ideas that are new to the architecture world. More precisely one recognises work as avant-garde when it can be seen to have been experimental at one time but which has attracted imitators, so it was 'ahead of the pack'. In the contemporary world it is not always possible to see which ideas will prove to have been fruitful and which are merely 'random' experiments. So for contemporary work anything that is characterised as 'experimental' could be considered to be avant-garde, but when we are looking back at the past we see the avant-garde as 'leading the way' into the future. It is not until after the event that we know what 'the future' might be, but it is made through experimentation of one sort or another.

References

Ballantyne, A. (ed.) (2005), *Architecture Theory*, London: Continuum.

Ballantyne, A. (2007), *Deleuze and Guattari for Architects*, London: Routledge.

Ballantyne, A. (2011), 'Architecture, Life and Habit', *Journal of Aesthetics and Art Criticism*, 69: 1, 43–9.

Ballantyne, A. and A. Law (2011), *Tudoresque: In Pursuit of the Ideal Home*, London: Reaktion.

Bataille, G. (2005), 'Architecture', in A. Ballantyne (ed.), *Architecture Theory*, London: Continuum, pp. 16–25.

Deleuze, G. and F. Guattari (1972), *Anti-Oedipus: Capitalism and Schizophrenia*, trans. R. Hurley, M. Seem and H. R. Lane, New York: Viking.

Deleuze, G. and F. Guattari (1980), *Capitalism and Schizophrenia 2: A Thousand Plateaus*, trans. B. Massumi, London: Athlone.

Deleuze, G. and F. Guattari (1987), *A Thousand Plateaus: Capitalism and Schizophrenia*, trans. B. Massumi, Minneapolis, MN: University of Minnesota Press.

Gregg, M. and G. J. Seigworth (eds) (2010), *The Affect Theory Reader*, Durham, NC: Duke University Press.

Hemingway, E. (2009), *A Moveable Feast*, New York: Scribner's.

Ives, C. (1940), *The Unanswered Question*, composed *c.*1906. Privately published.

Rorty, R. (1989), *Contingency, Irony and Solidarity*, Cambridge: Cambridge University Press.

Spinoza, B. (1959), *Ethics: On the Correction of Understanding*, trans. A. Boyle, London: Dent.

Thoreau, H. D. ([1854] 1897), *Walden: or, Life In The Woods*, Vol. I, Boston: Houghton, Mifflin.

Wittgenstein, L. (1998), *Culture and Value*, Oxford: Blackwell.

Young, J. and S. M. Lewis (1919), *How Ya Gonna Keep 'Em Down on the Farm (After They've Seen Paree)?*, music by Walter Donaldson, New York: Waterson, Berlin & Snyder.

Chapter 11

Politics + Deleuze + Guattari + Architecture

Adrian Parr

This chapter raises red flags over the use of Deleuze and Guattari's concepts in architectural thinking and praxis. I propose that by focusing too closely on the formal elements of architecture, all the while developing an architectural strategy based on enfolding, the encounter between architecture and Deleuze and his collaborations with Guattari has had the unfortunate consequence of not fully engaging with the transformative impulse of their work. Although the encounter between architectural practice, Deleuze, and Deleuze and Guattari has dislodged the dualisms that traditional architecture is premised upon, a largely formalist attitude has remained intact. This compromises the political commitment of Deleuze and Guattari. The more pertinent question that needs to be posed in response to the voracious appetite architectural practice and theory has had for Deleuze and Guattari's conceptual apparatus is: what kinds of affects does this formal exercise in enfolding create?

When Deleuze entered architectural discourse and practice, a shift toward experimentalism and the logic of conjunction and connection that typifies a Deleuzian ontology pushed architecture in exciting new directions. Architecture was no longer viewed as an entity that frames space, or is itself enclosed by a frame; instead it was transformed into an event: a temporal modality that could strive to enfold the stabilising relationship between figure/ground, plan/section and frame/structure. This move generated a series of twisting shapes, warped surfaces, differentiating environments, vertiginous experiences and undulating forms. As I will describe in more detail further on with reference to Peter Eisenman and Greg Lynn's work, one concept that became especially popular in architectural circles was that of the fold, along with the related concepts of becoming and force (see Eisenman et al. 1991; Lynn 1993).

Deleuze mobilises the concept of the fold as he develops his broader philosophical project of univocal being and an ontology of becoming.

He revokes common dualisms, such as inside/outside, figure/ground and organic/inorganic that define the manner in which thought operates and life is apprehended. As Deleuze insists, 'The outside is not a fixed limit but a moving matter animated by peristaltic movements, folds and foldings that together make up an inside: they are not something other than the outside, but precisely the inside *of* the outside' (Deleuze 2000: 96–7). Through folding, boundaries are perforated and smudged, they excessively proliferate, swell and release a complex array of movements that augment and affirm a creative process of difference and change, or what Deleuze elsewhere describes as 'becoming'.[1]

In Deleuze's view there isn't a being that changes, nor one that is folded. Instead, 'the relation to oneself is the affect of self by self, or folded force', or what Deleuze describes as Memory and forgetting (unfolding) (Deleuze 2000: 104, 107). As folding and the related concept of becoming attest, the process of differentiation intrinsic to mutation and change does not come about by activating individual differences or stable entities. Rather, change as Deleuze describes it operates by opening an inside up to its outside, such that other processes of differentiation and transformation inflect and destabilise the interiority of the inside. In this context the concepts of folding and becoming prompt us to move beyond representational thinking and structures – identity, being, subject, reason – for the simple reason that these are limited to framing the dynamic flow of life with codes, rules and orders. As such they only serve to inhibit creative change.

Instead of asking 'What is folded?', perhaps the more pertinent question might be: 'What can folding *do*?' To answer this it might be helpful to look to Deleuze's work on Nietzsche, and in particular his use of Nietzsche's ideas concerning reactive and active forces, for both folding and becoming characterise one kind of relation between forces: they are productive of and produced through active forces. Reactive forces like representational thinking confine difference to identity and they impose a goal on movement. Deleuze defines these forces by the 'mechanical and utilitarian accommodations' they make (Deleuze 1986: 41). Reactive forces hamper creative and dynamic change by systematising and regulating the direction movement takes, subordinating the openness and unpredictability of transformation to the logic of identity or mimesis. Meanwhile, active forces generate connections and affects. Put differently, they are purely and simply affirmative (ibid.: 186).

Within architectural circles these concepts – folding, becoming and force – gained traction through the latter part of the twentieth century coinciding with an influx of English translations of Deleuze's, and

Deleuze and Guattari's, work. Theorists who are popular in architectural circles such as Elizabeth Grosz, John Rajchman, Manuel DeLanda, Jonathan Crary, Sanford Kwinter and Andrew Ballantyne all use Deleuze in sophisticated and intriguing ways throughout their own work.[2] Furthermore, there is a whole gamut of architects who directly lean upon Deleuze as integral to their design thinking, including Eisenman, Lynn and Philippe Rahm (to name a few). Indeed Eisenman wrote the Foreword to Elizabeth Grosz's *Architecture from the Outside* in which she approaches the study of architecture through an analysis of the creative inflection and production of time, space, matter and the body (Grosz 2001: xi–xiii).

Building upon his earlier interest in Derrida, Eisenman uses the Deleuzian fold as a strategy to interject the discursive function of the fully coherent finite subject who enters the world, experiences and then interprets it, to produce spaces that present an alternative order to the usual hierarchies established by separating interiority from exteriority.[3] In this context, the profile that elevates and separates architecture from its ground undergoes a procedure of blurring, 'where not only the profile but the entire organisation is blurred conceptually so that it is no longer seen as merely fulfilling a function embodying its interior form' (Eisenman 2007: 61). The idea is to move away from forming space to an architecture of spacing. One of the ways Eisenman has done this is by producing conditions of interstitiality. He is interested in questioning the hierarchical order that informs the design process, whereby the production of form (such as the walls, floors and roofs used to enclose a space) precedes spatial conditions, the latter being the effect of form production. Eisenman exposes how spacing takes place within the process of forming. Instead of approaching presence as the opposite of absence, he activates the presence within absence, articulating the architectural problem as a 'state of becoming' such that in its repetition it is always undergoing change (2007: 57). He summarises his understanding of this in the following way: 'Thus in architecture such a process might be iterative, might have directions and energy, and might deal with forces and flows which could be multiple, reversible, and deformative rather than linear and transformative' (ibid.). At the time this was an atypical approach to design thinking and practice, as his design for the Bibliothèque de l'Huei in Geneva, Switzerland (1997) amply demonstrates.

Eisenman's Bibliothèque de l'Huei went through three key phases. With the first phase Eisenman follows the common iterative approach to diagramming. He combines the organisation of functions, function types and site analysis. From this initial diagram a container with the most appropriate entry point and circulation paths is produced, the form of which is determined by its primary function – to provide shelter. It is with the second, more arbitrary diagram that Eisenman puts Deleuze and Guattari to work, setting out to 'include function and image without having the container be seen as a result of their intervention' (Eisenman 2007: 59). The second diagram is not simply one that is immanent to the first, but is chosen on the basis that it has within it a process with the potential to transform the first diagram. Some of the secondary diagrams he uses include: 'soliton waves, neural functioning, DNA structures, liquid crystals . . . sine waves, fractals, and morphing' (ibid.). Eisenman's aim is to modify traditional architectural tropes and create new ones, all the while creating affective interstitial spaces (ibid.: 63). As such, the first two diagramming processes proved insufficient for creating architectural tropes, prompting a third design phase that he describes as more 'arbitrary and aleatory in nature' (ibid.: 66). He adds:

> Here there is a necessary back and forth which comes between a physical, three-dimensional model and the composite diagram. Ultimately the intention is to make corrections in the diagram to incorporate the figural tropes so that the diagram can then run by itself . . . This running by itself would give further small-scale articulations – windows, rooms, and corridors – which, because of the diagram, are no longer legitimized by function, aesthetics, or meaning. (Ibid.)

It is worth pointing out that for centuries architectural thinking and praxis have been committed to a metaphysics of presence, where even in virtual reality, as Eisenman explains, 'architecture is still imagined as a physical body' (ibid.: 46). Consequently the fundamental architectural spatial condition has been one of extension: the subject enters and moves about space by either running into or avoiding the objects that fill space or the boundaries often used to define it. This extensive approach to space is one that Eisenman has consistently challenged (ibid.: 41).[4] In his hands Deleuze and Guattari's conceptual apparatus facilitates the creation of affective spaces. And one way he does this is by working with multiple temporalities.

In the Rebstock project Eisenman smudges the figure/ground and plan/section dualism, injecting uncertainty into the 'boundaries of the Rebstock site as well as within the spaces defined by individual buildings' (Williams 2000: 206). He introduces the idea of the fold into the design process, as a third condition, one that operates in between the figure and ground, plan and section dualism, refashioning these in the process.[5]

Working with different temporalities he rejects the common view of urbanism, one that focuses on the objects that fill an area, insisting that the urban landscape is constituted by events. In James Williams's assessment this approach affirms the 'differential quality of existence'; it is inherently transformative without reducing design to the hellhole of relativism, undifferentiated problems and useless chaos (as Manfredo Tafuri and his criticism of architecture's encounter with Deleuze might have us believe) (Tafuri 1990: 11; Williams 2000: 211). In his analysis of Eisenman's Rebstockpark competition Williams provides a cogent argument against Tafuri's criticism that Deleuze suffers from an absence of 'critical effectivity', by closely scrutinising Deleuze's understanding of the problematic (Williams 2000: 202). Williams makes an important clarification, stating that innovation is conditioned by the problematic, and this condition affirms criticality without reducing the critical to a reactionary stance or useless relativity. In other words, the problematic ensures we 'grasp the significant aspects of our worlds by expressing them in new ways, ways which will inevitably change them' (ibid.).

Like Eisenman, Greg Lynn, who worked in Eisenman's office before going out on his own to create an architectural studio called Form, has experimented with the process of enfolding in an effort to complicate the ways in which architecture deals with gravity (see Greg Lynn's website <http://glform.com/>). Leaning upon an array of Deleuzian influences from Gottfried Wilhelm Leibniz to Henri Bergson's *Matter and Memory*, he injected an open-ended approach into the design process aspiring to 'animate form', as he describes it in a book of the same title (Lynn 1999). What resulted was a fascinating array of warped, mutating, voluptuous and undulating forms. This was achieved by stretching the limits of computer software, critically engaging with the hidden potential of geometry as the basis of architecture, and by fine-tuning his appreciation for materials and the techniques of construction. For instance, Lynn uses calculus in his design of form, where previously this had been restricted to the design of mechanical and acoustic systems. Unsurprisingly, his primary design tool is the computer; it allows him to embrace the organisational properties of topology, time and parameters in a way that he felt 'inert mediums such as paper and pencil' could not (1999: 20). In this way, Lynn turned his back on the static model of architecture, in particular the Cartesian view of gravity as defined in isolation from the dynamism of force and time. Going on to position himself against the concept of 'stasis' as it dominated architectural practice and discourse, Lynn argued that by defining gravity as the 'unchanging constant force of a ground point' architects turned gravity into an 'ordering system'. On the other hand, he was more interested in investigating a 'more complex concept of gravity' whereby 'mutual attraction generates motion' (ibid.: 14). To summarise, Lynn uses animation software to generate and transform form instead of as a representational device.

Like Eisenman, Lynn transformed the vertical premise at the core of architectural practice. The verticality that characterises many urban skylines such as New York, Sydney or Chicago is a case in point. They exemplify the ways in which architecture has tended to reduce the dynamic connection between force and gravity to a simple problem of gravity transferral to the ground through the vertical organisation of a building's structure. In response, Lynn begins his project by reconceptualising the 'ground and vertical in light of complex vectors and movement'; then from here he reorients buildings beyond the simple vertical (1999: 14).

For instance, Lynn began his House Prototype design for a small family summer house in Long Island (the clients had requested the house follow an 'H' plan organisation) by studying the forces of the site. He did this by attending to the site's features of attraction and repulsion. From here he produced a series of maps that diagrammed how these forces behaved, all of which he discovered moved in a variety of ways (linear, radial, vortex). From this initial exercise five areas of focus emerged: '1) the location of a neighboring house, blocking the view of the Atlantic Ocean, 2) a large tree also located in the line of sight to the ocean, 3) an existing foundation from the previous house, 4) an existing driveway, 5) an existing orchard on the site' (1999: 144). Before incorporating dimensional volume into the analysis, Lynn and his team adopted a massing strategy; the outcome was an 'accordion-like' surface. Then the surface was placed in a field of forces, and despite the surface having a disorderly behaviour to it, its overall pattern curiously overlapped with the previous studies conducted (ibid.: 146). Through computer modelling Lynn and his team were able to develop a series of prototypes, inflecting the house's conditions to produce different skeleton options, tensile structures and the connection between structure and site forces. I mention the Long Island House Prototypes because they point to an underlying fascination Lynn has for Deleuze's concepts of becoming and the fold as these play out in architectural thinking and practice.

In the context of Lynn's work, the processes of enfolding and creative change endemic to Deleuze's thinking have allowed him to activate space: structural rhythms, architectural surfaces and planes, and orientation set each other in motion through a process of dynamic differentiation. Out of this wild concoction playful forms appear. By folding the inside out and the outside in, Lynn develops new ways of massing that are not restricted to the external building shape; instead they are 'porous and elastic', such that the outward shape also projects the 'shape, plan organization, spatial and section type, and façade' (Lynn 2008: 40).

All in all, regardless of the intellectual and creative curiosity Deleuze has sparked in Eisenman and Lynn, both continue to follow a formalist template. It is formalist in so far as their approach to design thinking and practice is primarily concerned with the development of new architectural tropes and languages. Their encounter with Deleuze and architecture does not engage with socio-political phenomena outside of such architectural tropes and language, such as neo-liberal forces of privatisation, consumption, competition and commodification, despite the fact that these are what inscribe, shape and inform life in the contemporary world of the late twentieth and early twenty-first centuries. In this way only architectural values are used, and although design becomes an end in itself it retains the self-referentiality of a formalist attitude.

Admittedly Eisenman has recognised in his writings the radical potential inherent in the differential and repetitive production of Deleuze in the context of architectural praxis, arguing it creates spaces of excess, which he says 'requires a radical change in the existing modes of production and consumption'. In this way architecture 'becomes a political act', which he clarifies in the following way:

> To produce a condition of spacing, of interstitiality, of something which cannot be consumed because it is no longer legitimated by utility and significance, is not merely an aesthetic argument, it is a political argument; it is speaking of a different kind of excess. Thus processes which produce difference can be seen to be resistant to the existing spaces of power. (2007: 71)

Although Eisenman's work has a stronger political charge to it than Lynn's, because of his use of interstitial conditions and his honest engagement with the tensions history produces, this being an argument I present in *Deleuze and Memorial Culture* in my discussion of Eisenman's *Memorial to the Murdered Jews of Europe* (2005), I am not convinced that refusing to 'provide a secure and final experience', as Williams notes he does in the Rebstock Project and its use of historical forces, is political enough (Parr 2008: 143–65; Williams 2000: 218).

It is not Deleuze's thinking that is at fault, as Tafuri would claim; rather architects have chosen to turn a blind eye to the politics underpinning Deleuze's work, preferring instead to isolate the scientific models that Deleuze leans on as the primary space in which the encounter between architecture and Deleuze takes place.[6] There is a whole body of thinking on Deleuze and Guattari that focuses on the political potential of their work – Michael Hardt and Antonio Negri, Ian Buchanan, Rosi Braidotti, Todd May, Eugene Holland, Paul Patton and Nick Thoburn to cite just a few examples. And I clearly share sympathies with this camp. The political charge offered by Deleuze and Guattari to present itself throughout design thinking and practice cannot stop with design being an end in itself. I remain struck by how little this rocks the architectural establishment. Let's face it: building is first and foremost a political practice. There is a site that is shaped by conflicting vested interests and histories, issues of proprietary ownership, capital investment and expenditure, along with labour relations and resources that are consumed.

It is not just the concepts architects have chosen from the Deleuzian menu that determine the institutionalisation of hybrid and undulating architectural forms, it is the priorities that determine how these concepts are put to work that neutralises the political condition of design thinking and practice. If concepts such as the fold, force and becoming are not connected to the larger political impulse driving Deleuze and his collaborations with Guattari, the concepts are no longer tools in the way that Deleuze insisted they need to be treated, rather they become so profoundly un-Deleuzian as to be a political distraction. The practical inconsistency arises from choosing to use the concepts solely as a way to generate and transform form and architectural tropes. Ironically this is in itself a truth production, hereby turning design thinking and practice into a prescriptive exercise. It also has the unfortunate consequence of diverting attention away from how the profession of architecture affirms the neo-liberalisation of life, which I understand to be the intertwined forces of privatisation, competition, individualism and consumption.[7] The point is that choosing a depoliticised use of the concept of forces over and above the more political experience and movement of forces that align themselves with the axiomatic of capital in the late twentieth and early twenty-first centuries is not a value-free exercise. Indeed, it keeps architectural praxis and theory focused on the production of forms that work in the interests of neo-liberalism; meanwhile, larger social issues of equality and environmental degradation are played down.

In 1990 Derrida sent Eisenman a letter in which the philosopher points to a metaphysical presupposition at the heart of Eisenman's fascination for the presence of absence. Derrida presents an important problem at the core of Eisenman's work. He does this by posing the following series of questions to the architect: 'In what terms does one discuss glass? In terms of technology and materials? Economic terms? Urbanism? Social relations? In terms of transparency and immediacy, of love or supervision, of the potentially effaced boundary between public and private, etc.?' (Derrida 2007: 163). The concern Derrida raises here ultimately points to the creation of 'spaces in which it is difficult to leave traces' (ibid.: 164). This is a political problem of forgetting. Citing Walter Benjamin Derrida illuminates the problem in terms of a '"new poverty" ([. . .] an errant mass of poor, indeed of the "homeless", irreducible to categorisation or classification and to long-standing marginality or of the social ladder: the low income, the proletarian class, the unemployed, etc.)' (ibid.). Intriguingly in his response to Derrida Eisenman is willing to acknowledge neither the ethical problem 'new poverty' poses in relation to forgetting, nor the broader political implications Derrida's critique has for design thinking and practice. Actually Eisenman's retort exposes the formalism of his approach: 'My architecture asks, Can there be an *other* in the condition of aura in architecture, an aura that both is secret and contains its own secret, the mark of its absent openness? This may involve the difference between the thing as word and the thing as object, between language and architecture' (Eisenman 2007: 4). Therein lies the limitation of the interstitial condition and the spaces of excess this produces; this approach never fully recognises that design is a collaborative and critical process and as a service it only serves a fraction of the world's population and even less of the world's ecosystems and population of other-than-human species. Paul Polak starkly puts the situation into perspective: 'Ninety-five percent of the world's designers focus all of their efforts on developing products and services exclusively for the richest ten percent of the world's customers. Nothing less than a revolution in design is needed to reach the other ninety percent' (Polak 2007: 19).

I prefer to start not by asking what architecture has built but to investigate what architecture has taken away. Who has been denied a place? Who cannot access a healthcare facility? Who can't go to school because a school building is unsafe? What places have been assigned to whom and who is marginalised by this distribution of power throughout the social field? If there is a myriad of intersecting forces and energies travelling throughout the built environment, how might architects affirm the common spaces embedded in these connections to create a better world for all life on earth? And 'better' in what sense? That is, how might the concept of 'better' be used without creating a value judgement, or fabricating a universal condition that dominates difference? Deleuze and his work with Guattari provide some useful intellectual tools to respond to these questions because for them the movement of forces and energies making up the social field are pre-personal singularities, and as such they are neutral until they are given a particular investment that either obstructs change or facilitates a creative process of transformation. This means it is not simply that an architect (and his/her team) designs a better world. Such an approach would simply invoke a masculinist paradigm all the while replicating some of the worst forms of androcentric culture, whereby the architect is understood as speaking on behalf of all life on earth. Life cannot be positioned inside the halo of the Architect-Creator in this way. Rather the politics arising from the encounter between architectural discourse and Deleuze and Guattari comes from how architecture can effectively activate avenues through which common life might be rendered visible and audible once more (to borrow from Jacques Rancière) and this requires a more collaborative paradigm (Rancière 2010; Parr and Zaretsky 2010: 6–12).

Although the contemporary architect's interest in Deleuze has pushed the profession in new directions, a conundrum has emerged: despite the destruction of Cartesian space and the break with the modernist focus on form, architecture as primarily a form-producing exercise has not waned – if anything it has strengthened. Problematising the figure/ground dialectic in the way that Eisenman and Lynn have done continues to leave the broader democratic question of the commons, capital and community unaddressed.

The encounter between architecture and Deleuze has resulted in outside forces – such as history, landscape patterns, scientific models, computer software programming and the patterns arising from natural systems – entering design thinking and practice. This has led to new massing strategies (Lynn, for instance, has used Blob – Binary Large OBject – modelling software as a tool) such that architectural surfaces are no longer restricted to the definition of being an exterior structural covering; landscape surface pattern and form now transform into the building surface; biological patterns become the basis for architectural structure or spatial organisation; the dynamic forms arising out of moving particles have animated the form and texture of building surfaces; and the active memory of the virtual has led to the view that architecture not only contains the traces of the past but even informs the process of design thinking and practice. These are all instances of architects innovatively engaging with the 'outside' forces in the development of architectural form and the organisation of space. Oddly enough those same outside forces that architects have been prompted to engage with as a result of their encounter with Deleuze include neither the forces of capital accumulation that striate space and territorialise the built environment, nor the fascistic energies that find investment in the social field making it an unfriendly place for immigrants, the poor, homeless, the sick or other-than-human species.

One reason for this bias might be that the materialist dimension of the outside forces in question are sanitised and neutralised when reformed as abstract forces that are placed in the service of formal problems such as structure, massing, site organisation, volume production, surface modelling, principles for plan organisation and new architectural geometries. As abstractions, outside forces are emptied of their materiality and the struggles that inform them. Instead of the condition of the outside and the manner in which this folds into the inside to politicise design problems, this potentially political condition of exteriority is dissipated when it functions self-referentially.

If we return to the old Nietzschean problem of reactive and active forces, one that Deleuze himself was intrigued by, surely the question of what kinds of forces architecture activates and is activated by is the political architectural problem par excellence.[8] What conditions of change can architecture facilitate and promote? For Deleuze and Guattari this question is not defined by a subject or the state, it is pre-personal. Indeed, politics as such is a pre-personal condition of transformation. The politics of the concept of becoming is therefore a movement between states or situations or even architectural tropes (the latter being a movement that Eisenman fully recognises). But the movement itself is not reducible to one system, structure or situation of architectural tropes, grammar or language. By limiting the movement to that of architectural tropes and language, the deterritorialising lines of flight that unpredictably traverse other lines of flight – such as capital, community or ecosystems – are submitted to the reterritorialising order of dominant socio-political arrangements. The character of this dominant socio-political arrangement is a free-market credit-based economy that is supported by the political forces of neo-liberal restructuring and privatisation and the overall plunder of the world's commons and natural resources (water, atmosphere, forests, local communities and indigenous knowledge). The process of folding architecture therefore has to become something other than merely parroting, or worse still promoting, the dominant forces that shape our current socio-political situation.

As Sergio Palleroni (2008) has so fittingly noted, 'One thing that happens to the poor is that they are marginalised to the point where they become noncitizens, nonmembers of the economic community. They are excluded from all the decision-making processes that affect their lives.'

From here he poses the following question: 'How do you bring people back into decision-making?' For Palleroni this is inherently a design problem. He responds, 'Our answer is through the act of building, the act of design, the act of creating' (Palleroni 2008: 275). In a similar vein, Bryan Bell asks: 'How can we expand the practice of design to provide for the rest, the great number currently underserved, and to play an active role in responding to the social challenges we face in the world?' (Bell 2008: 15).

Neither Palleroni nor Bell cite Deleuze, Guattari or even Derrida for that matter when describing their approach to design. They do not refer to the concepts of folding, becoming or forces when they write about architecture, or collaborate with communities to build elegant low-income housing that addresses social and economic disparities, or when they work with culturally and economically appropriate technologies, or as they strive to be ecologically sensitive, or even as educators teaching students the importance of learning experiences in real-world, real-life situations. So why even bother talking about their work in a volume dedicated to Deleuze and architecture? The answer is simple. For Deleuze and Guattari politics entails experimenting with contemporary forces and situations. In a world where the outlook for climate change is bleak indeed, where 1.37 billion people live under the international poverty line of $1.25 a day and where global poverty drops as inequity rises, the 'contemporary' situation design thinking and practice responds to must be: poverty, disease, illiteracy, the free-market and ecosystem collapse. As architects set out to engage with the forces and energies of the contemporary world, they need to become more sensitive to these forces of marginalisation and moreover be more willing and committed to effectively dealing with them.[9] Or as Deleuze and Guattari write: 'Creations are like mutant abstract lines that have detached themselves from the task of representing a world, precisely because they assemble a new type of reality . . .' (1988: 296).

In other words, design thinking and practice need to become less abstract and more affective: more open to being messed up by the struggles and tensions of poverty, homelessness, dispossession, pollution, disease, illiteracy, thirst, starvation, ecosystem collapse, climate change and species extinction. This involves a serious move away from construing the social field as an 'object', one from which through a subsequent process of abstraction architecture is born. How might design thinking and practice dust off the cobwebs of a formalist attitude in all its interiority and engage with the outside energies and forces shaping life in the contemporary world?

Politics involves challenging pre-given structures and rules through a creative re-examination of the social conditions that inscribe majoritarian organisations, which I should add minoritarian political forces interrupt and transform. So while there is an absence of Deleuzian lingo in the Bell and Palleroni camp of architecture, we would be hard pressed to deny that the activist impulse Deleuze advocated for throughout his life and work animates their approach to design thinking and practice. This is because Bell and Palleroni work with local initiatives and collective energies to radically change the investment of social energies that result in the vast majority of life on earth remaining invisible and inaudible. And they are not alone in this venture. There is a growing number of architects and architecture programmes dedicated to broadening the scope of architecture so as to create structures for inclusion which bring 'design of very high quality to bear on critical social, economic, and environmental issues' (Bell 2008: 15).

In light of this, how might architecture activate the politics of outside forces more in design thinking and practice? How might the practice of design thinking be part of the process of training architects to become more socially, environmentally and economically agile? In posing these questions I am consciously not appropriating the conceptual apparatus developed by Deleuze and Guattari as the basis for design, one that I have argued above has led to a more prescriptive design outcome; I am far more interested in investigating how design thinking and practice massages forth the activist impulse at the heart of Deleuzian philosophy.

In his architecture of the borderlands, which is also the title of a book by Teddy Cruz, Estudio Cruz engages with the forces of control and the politics of land use as it shapes the US/Mexico border and the surrounding neighbourhoods. He transforms the notion of a 'boundary' as the line where a space ends into an action out of which space is activated. He basically deterritorialises the boundary and transforms it into a line of flight as he investigates neighbourhoods on both sides of the border and uses these studies to inform his work. His approach to design begins with conflict and social relations (ecological, economic, cultural, linguistic), such as in his entry portal to the US neoclassical pavilion for the 11th Architecture Biennale in Venice that presented the US/Mexico border conditions and life along the border and which visitors to the exhibition had to 'cross'. Cruz expands architecture beyond the confines of built form to include workshops, seminars, walking tours of the border and exhibitions.

Continuing on, Michael Zaretsky in the design of the Roche Health Center in Roche, Tanzania, began his design thinking with the specificity of the local situation – investigating the skill-set of the community, indigenous materials, oral histories and economic activities. The goals were to 'provide quality health care services to the Roche community and outlying areas, to serve as a center for community collaboration, meetings, and education, and to educate community members on health issues so that Roche may become a healthier society' (Lucker 2011: 2). The project involved training and employment initiatives for the unemployed, as well as a process of knowledge sharing between the US students and local Tanzanian populations. The collaborative design process involved meeting the village elders, holding community meetings, visiting informal women's groups and holding discussions with local health professionals. The building of the Medical Center not only provided the community with a new building, it also improved the economic vitality of the village as locals were provided with paid employment and training in new culturally appropriate technologies that could be used for other building projects and to generate income in a community with high rates of unemployment, along with facilitating a collaborative learning context between locals, US students and teachers, and Tanzanian health professionals. When taken together these elements produced a series of complex connections between the locals, history, the medical community, the design team and local ecologies. Zaretsky used the specificities of the site to passively cool the building, all the while carefully selecting appropriate technologies (interlocking stabilised soil bricks or ISSB) with the majority of the building materials being locally sourced. Meanwhile the oral histories inscribing the site were treated as a differential relation in the present, giving consistency to the project, yet all the while shifting the ground of that memory in new directions. The Health Center was strategically located so that it would not only serve the local Roche community but the surrounding community as well. It was reported by Spencer Lucker of the Clinton School of Public Service that 'Of the 274 patients of RHC, 159 are residents of Roche village, making up 58% of the patient pool. However, RHC has seen patients from 19 other villages in the surrounding areas, some travelling across the border from Kenya' (2011: 7).

In these few examples cited above, architecture becomes a mode of political activism in that it does not follow conventional routes of dissent and as such the activities it generates and inserts into the social sphere are more resilient against appropriation by the state or the corporate sector. The internal and external relations that condition design thinking and practice are massaged to produce affective capacities. In this way, design as activism is as much a matter of designing affective relations as it is the effect of those selfsame affective relations. I couldn't think of a more transformative and joyful approach to design thinking and practice than that!

Notes

1. In particular refer to Chapter 10 (on 'Becoming-Intense, Becoming-Animal, Becoming Imperceptible . . .') in *A Thousand Plateaus* (Deleuze and Guattari 1988: 232–309).
2. Rajchman was responsible for providing the English-speaking world with the first translations of Deleuze and Guattari with his publication of *Rhizome* and *Nomadology* with Semiotext(e). He also participated with Deleuze in the 1975 Columbia University conference on schizophrenia. Examples of the use of Deleuze include: Elizabeth Grosz, *Architecture from the Outside* (2001); John Rajchman, *Constructions* (1998); Manuel DeLanda, *A Thousand Years of Non Linear History* (1997) and 'The Nonlinear Development of Cities' (1999); Sanford Kwinter, *Architectures of Time: Toward a Theory of the Event in Modernist Culture* (2001); Andrew Ballantyne, *Deleuze and Guattari for Architects* (2007).
3. Heavily influenced by Derrida during his early years as an architect and in particular the theory of deconstruction, Eisenman's work exposed how architecture is always already a priori textual. Two notable projects that spring to mind are the Aronoff Center at the University of Cincinnati (1988–96) and his House projects beginning with House I in 1967 and ending with House XI in 1975, all of which made important contributions to the deconstructive move in architectural thinking and praxis.
4. I speak from experience here because I spend a great deal of time in Eisenman's Aronoff Center at the University of Cincinnati, this being a building I have taught in for six years now. The DAAP building, as it is otherwise referred to by faculty and students, deliberately disorients the subject through a playful arrangement of circulating paths and skewed walls set at angles. After six years I am only now beginning to figure out how I can navigate the building without getting too lost. I admit the journey has been frustrating at times (especially when I am running late for class or a meeting), but overall the ways in which the architecture confounds the clarity of the relationship of form to function, and of signification to aesthetics, have been a stimulating encounter.
5. In Eisenman's thought-provoking essay on the Rebstock project he acknowledges that Deleuze was a key influence in his thinking (see Eisenman 2007: 12–18).
6. Tafuri writes: 'By no means do we intend to sing hymns to the irrational or interpret the ideological groups in their complex interaction as "rhizomes" *à la* Deleuze and Guattari. We firmly believe it is necessary "not to make rhizomes" of those groups. Implicated though it may be in the objects and phenomena it analyses, historical criticism must know how to balance on the razor's edge that separates detachment and participation' (1990: 11).
7. For a powerful analysis of neo-liberalism see David Harvey, *A Brief History of Neoliberalism* (2005).
8. Deleuze dedicates the whole of Chapter 2, 'Active and Reactive', to the analysis of Nietzsche's concepts of force, will to power and the eternal return. See Deleuze, *Nietzsche and Philosophy* (1986).
9. What they don't point out in their analysis is that poverty may have declined but inequity rose. See Chandy and Gertz (2011), 'With Little Notice Globalization Reduced Poverty'.

References

Ballantyne, A. (2007), *Deleuze and Guattari for Architects*, London: Routledge.

Bell, B. (2008), 'Preface: Expanding Design Toward Greater Relevance', in B. Bell and K. Wakeford (eds), *Expanding Architecture: Design as Activism*, New York: Metropolis Books, pp. 14–17.

Chandy, L. and G. Gertz (2011), 'With Little Notice Globalization Reduced Poverty', in *Yale Global*, 5 July, <http://yaleglobal.yale.edu/content/little-notice-globalization-reduced-poverty> (accessed 18 October 2011).

DeLanda, M. (1997), *A Thousand Years of Non Linear History*, New York: Zone.

DeLanda, M. (1999), 'The Nonlinear Development of Cities', in A. Marras (ed.), *Eco-Tec: The Architecture of the In Between*, New York: Princeton Architectural Press, pp. 22–31.

Deleuze, G. (1986), *Nietzsche and Philosophy*, trans. H. Tomlinson, New York: Columbia University Press.

Deleuze, G. (2000), *Foucault*, trans. S. Hand, Minneapolis, MN: University of Minnesota Press.

Deleuze, G., and F. Guattari (1988), *Capitalism and Schizophrenia: A Thousand Plateaus*, trans. B. Massumi, London: Athlone.

Derrida, J. (2007), 'Appendix: Letter from Jacques Derrida to Peter Eisenman', in P. Eisenman, *Written into the Void: Selected Writings 1990–2004*, New Haven, CT: Yale University Press, pp. 160–8.

Eisenman, P. (2007), *Written into the Void: Selected Writings 1990–2004*, New Haven, CT: Yale University Press.

Eisenman, P., J. Rajchman and Galerie Aedes (1991), *Unfolding Frankfurt*, Berlin: Ernst & Sohn.

Grosz, E. (2001), *Architecture from the Outside*, Cambridge, MA: MIT Press.

Harvey, D. (2005), *A Brief History of Neoliberalism*, Oxford: Oxford University Press.

Kwinter, S. (2001), *Architectures of Time: Toward a Theory of the Event in Modernist Culture*, Cambridge, MA: MIT Press.

Lucker, F. S. (2011), 'Roche Health Center Evaluation Report', *Clinton School of Public Service*, June–August.

Lynn, G. (ed.) (1993), *AD: Folding in Architecture*, London: Wiley Academy.

Lynn, G. (1999), *Animate Form*, New York: Princeton Architectural Press.

Palleroni, S. (2008), 'Building Sustainable Communities and Building Citizens', in B. Bell and K. Wakeford (eds), *Expanding Architecture: Design as Activism*, New York: Metropolis Books, pp. 274–9.

Parr, A. (2008), *Deleuze and Memorial Culture: Desire, Singular Memory and the Politics of Trauma*, Edinburgh: Edinburgh University Press.

Parr, A. (2013), *The Wrath of Capital: Neoliberalism and Climate Change Politics*, New York: Columbia University Press.

Parr, A. and M. Zaretsky (eds) (2010), *New Directions in Sustainable Design*, London: Routledge.

Polak, P. (2007), 'Design for Other Ninety Percent' in C. Smith et al. (eds), *Design for the Other Ninety Percent*, New York: Cooper-Hewitt National Design Museum, 19–25

Rajchman, J. (1998), *Constructions*, Cambridge, MA: MIT Press.

Rancière, J. (2010), *Dissensus: On Politics and Aesthetics*, trans. S. Corcoran, London: Continuum.

Rappolt, M. (ed.) (2008), *Greg Lynn FORM*, New York: Rizzoli.

Tafuri, M. (1990), *The Sphere and the Labyrinth*, Cambridge, MA: MIT Press.

Williams, J. (2000), 'Deleuze's Ontology and Creativity: Becoming in Architecture', *Pli*, 9, 200–19.

PART IV

CARING

Chapter 12

The Ethological City

Cameron Duff

First, the feet settle, a slight flexing of the ankles, toes exploring the surface of the ground for the purchase of a secure foundation. Breathe, look down, move. Balancing, tilting, the ground approaches, hands outstretched. Fingers probe the pavement, the feel of diverse sensations: the coarseness of the cement, fine differences in textures, the pressure of the body's impending weight in the pads of the fingertips. Head down. Weight shifting to the hands, space inverting with the transition in orientation. Pause, breathe, look down once more, think of the movement to come. Kick (right foot). This is the point of the handstand; balance to motion to rest. Hands still, wrists strong, hips affecting gravity's force in their alignment above the head, knees and ankles touching, stillness comes fleetingly. The body rests for a moment with the concrete; the spine like the wall it may yet need to touch against. Bodies moving and resting together, each involved. There is no handstand without the cement, the wall, gravity's pull and sway, without the city, without the body. Hands and pavement, weight and movement, motion and rest. An ethology of bodies, cities, affects, relations, encounters and events. A handstand.

In this handstand, there is the body, there is the city and there is (*a*) life (Deleuze 2001: 27–32). Yet, there is also a call to abandon the convenience of a subject and its objects; the familiar taxonomy of a body willing its movements in the midst of passive objects, surfaces and contexts. Such conventions inevitably ignore most of the bodies assembled in the event of the handstand (Bennett 2010: 4–6). So, how might the body-becoming-city-becoming-body instantiated in this event be observed, theorised, cared for? How should the movements implicated in these bodies be identified and attributed? The movement and rest inaugurated in the event of the handstand describe a nexus of intensive and extensive forces, a society of bodies resonating together in the

Figure 12.1 Placement. Photograph by anon.

Figure 12.2 On the corner. Photograph by anon.

transience of balance. Balance is a capacity, established and enacted in the meeting of bodies, in their becoming active. The resulting handstand is ethological – a function of bodies acting together, insinuating themselves into the muscle-bone-concrete-gravity-belief-desire-motion of the inverted body – an instance of the environment entering 'into the nature of things' (Whitehead 1968: 138). Such is the life of the modern city, of bodies and assemblages. This chapter investigates this life, drawing insights from the writings of Gilles Deleuze and inspiration from the reports of urban inhabitants collected in ethnographic studies conducted in Melbourne, Australia (see Duff 2010, 2011 for details). The figure of ethology emerged as the primary object of this ethnography, revealing the force of the assembled city. Deleuze's ethology (1988: 123) describes the assembling of bodies (both human and non-human) in permutations of subjectivity, materiality and corporeality, in 'relations of motion and rest, slowness and speed between particles'. Taken together, the ethology and the ethnography essayed in this chapter highlight the felt sensation, the feel and emotional resonance of place, unfolding the life of the city in its 'free and wild state' (Deleuze 1994: xx).

Steps to an Ethology of Place

The urban environments of the modern West inspire a range of affective encounters, shaping the dynamic experience of place while adding to the tenor of a city's myriad identities. This imbrication of place, matter, affect and subjectivity is suggestive of Gilles Deleuze's idiosyncratic cartography of lines, movements, speeds and slownesses (1988, 1992, 1994). These lines and speeds describe the 'latitude' and 'longitude' of complex bodies and the variable relations and affects that compose them. The subject as it is traditionally understood disappears from this account, replaced by an ethological body of events, affects and relations. This figure stands in contrast to the 'molar' forms of identity and subjectivity typically associated with the study of cities, urban planning, architecture and place (Thrift 1999; Brott 2011). Ethology calls attention to the composition of complex bodies; human and non-human bodies, materialities, bodies of ideas, sound, infrastructure, crowds and forms; and as architects have long attested, the bodies of the built environment itself (see Dovey 2010: 13–20). Ethology speaks to this assembling, the drawing together of diverse forms in the collocations of the assemblage (human and non-human). Departing somewhat from more familiar Deleuzian themes of the smooth and the striated, of territories and territorialisation, this chapter explores Deleuze's major writings in an effort to describe an *ethological* city and the diverse assemblages and subjectivities such a city supports. The goal is to outline a practical and experimental ethics of urban life equal to the social, political and aesthetic becomings that transform this life. This should yield a novel diagram of the city's movements and a means of harnessing these movements in the generation of new aesthetic and political expressions. It should also extend the use of Deleuze's work in architectural theory and practice beyond the 'exhausted' notions of space and territory to embrace a new set of ethological resources useful for the analysis of urban 'life'.

Central to this ethology are the inventive conceptualisations of affect, multiplicity and relationality that Deleuze (1988, 1992) proposes, and the novel accounts of subjectivity and embodiment that these concepts support. Deleuze's ethology highlights the mutually reinforcing and recursive connections that enmesh bodies in diverse territories, places or milieus. This work draws attention to the individuation of bodies without presupposing a stable subject of this individuation (Brott 2011). Individuation ought here to be understood as something akin to an event, or the means by which diverse elements are composed and affected in the creation of new assemblages. Drawing together material and corporeal elements, the human and the non-human, objects and spaces, signs and values, organs and functions, assemblages define what an ethological body 'can do'. A body's affects, capacities, functions and relations are not fixed in this sense, but rather are forever becoming according to the specific assemblages a body is capable of entering into (see Deleuze and Guattari 1987: 260–3). Applied to the study of the 'modern' city, Deleuze's ethology highlights the body-becoming-city, becoming-place, becoming-collective characteristic of the everyday experience of urban life. This logic applies as much to the body of the (post)human subject as it does to the bodies (material, relational and affective) of the built environment (Dovey 2010). The *quality of urban life*, its concrete richness, is enhanced in the provision of new affective sensitivities and new relational capacities, which extend the spatial and temporal range of the body-becoming-city-becoming-subject (Awan et al. 2011). Such an ethology has important implications for the ongoing development of a participatory architectural theory and practice, more alert to questions of sustainability, health, well-being and democracy in urban settings (Blundell-Jones et al. 2005; Brott 2011).

Ethology and the Subject of Becoming

The ethological account of encounters, affects and relations that Deleuze derives from the early modern Dutch philosopher Baruch Spinoza provides a unique model of the immanent constitution of subjectivity, the body and ethics (Gatens 2000: 60–2). This account establishes a new method for philosophy: *a philosophy of the body*, of encounters and relations, ideas and affects (Deleuze 1988: 17). Deleuze (1992: 257) notes that Spinoza utterly transforms this philosophy in asking not what a body is, but rather 'what can a body do?' This empirical question holds the key to the development of an ethological account of the city and its diverse architectures, introducing new ways of conceiving of place and place-making while highlighting the co-constitution of subjects and cities in assemblages of human, non-human, organic and material bodies, actors, objects and entities (Dovey 2010; Grosz 2001). Deleuze's ethology emphasises the composition – the assembling or 'acting together' – inherent in city life, including the organisation of infrastructure, the assembling of bodies and the modulations of movement and rest typical of these bodies. This analysis hinges on the novel characterisations of the 'individual' contained in Spinoza's ethics and developed in Deleuze's subsequent readings.

Spinoza's ethics are concerned with the distinctiveness of individual bodies and the manifold affects and relations that comprise their characteristic structure. To ask what a body can do is to ask what particular relations a body (whether human or non-human) is capable of 'composing' with other bodies (Deleuze 1988: 127). It is to ask what particular affects determine that body in its capacity to affect and be affected by other bodies, both organic and material (Deleuze and Guattari 1987: 260–3). This approach defines individual bodies in terms of their 'capacities' rather than their 'functions' (Buchanan 1997: 75), while drawing attention to the differences that distinguish one body from another. Ethology, as such, concerns the 'study of the relations of speed and slowness, of the capacities for affecting and being affected that characterise each thing [. . .] and the variations or transformations that are peculiar to them' (Deleuze 1988: 125). This study involves two methods: one kinetic, the other dynamic. Following Spinoza, Deleuze (1992: 201) observes that individual bodies are composed of an 'indefinite' number of 'simple bodies' connected via 'characteristic relations'. This body is 'permanently open to its surroundings' (Gatens 2000: 61) in that the simple or 'extensive parts' that make up the complex body are constantly entering into differential relations with other 'external' bodies (see Deleuze 1992: 191–2). All bodies necessarily enter into relations with varied simple bodies in order to preserve those associations which 'maintain the individual in its existence' (Gatens 2000: 62). This logic is as true of the relations required to maintain 'organic' bodies as it is of the relations subtending material, non-human or 'built' bodies (Grosz 2001: 48–9).

The extensive parts that make up the complex body routinely pass through relations of 'composition' and 'decomposition' as certain parts of the complex body are lost while others are added. These parts are themselves organised in kinetic relations of 'motion and rest' (Deleuze 1988: 123), which determine the manner in which the complex body's extensive parts are connected or composed, so defining its 'individuality' or identity. Yet this individuality also extends to the unique combination of affects and sensations that express individual bodies. Spinoza argued that all bodies are characterised by dynamic capacities to affect and be affected by other bodies, both complex and simple. Affects are an emergent effect of a body's encounters, with each encounter transforming the nature of that body's relations and hence its manifest capacities. Given the heterogeneity of these relations, and the encounters that sustain them, a body's 'capacity to be affected does not remain fixed at all times and from all viewpoints' (Deleuze 1992: 222). Determined in each instance anew by their affects and relations, all bodies are defined by 'continuous variation', by their becomings rather than their continuities (Deleuze 1988: 123–7).

It is for this reason that Deleuze insists that we do not know what a body can do, because we cannot know in advance what distinctive affects and relations a complex body might become capable of. The range of affective capacities that determine the individuality of the body is itself the product of the 'very great number' of relations that compose that body (Deleuze 1992: 218). It follows that all complex bodies differ from one another by a matter of degree according to their capacities to affect and be affected, and by their capacities to enter into new relations with other bodies. This produces a 'new conception of the embodied individual' in which the analysis of affects and relations replaces the study of structure and functions (Deleuze 1992: 257). This new conception requires that one consider individual bodies in terms of their 'power of acting', where this power stands as an index of a body's capacity to enter into diverse relations and experience diverse affects. This power grows as a body becomes more capable of entering into novel relations with other bodies, and thus more capable of affecting and being affected by these bodies. The powers of all bodies grow in this way, from organic, 'living' bodies (Grosz 2011: 33–9) to the bodies of works of art like a painting or a novel (Deleuze 1998: 1–3), or indeed to the powers of the built environment, and the structures and enclosures that relationally and affectively activate the life or 'passions' of 'lived place' (Thrift 1999: 302–10).

This finally reveals something of the nature of affect in terms of its transitions and effects. Drawing on distinctions available in Latin – *affectio* and *affectus* – Spinoza notes that affect describes both the particular state of a body at any specific moment, and its transition from one affective state to another, and thus from one quantum of power to another. Hence, 'affectio refers to a state of the affected body and implies the presence of the affecting body, whereas the affectus refers to the passage from one state to another, taking into account the correlative variations of the affecting bodies' (Deleuze 1988: 49). In each instance, affect constitutes a modulation of a body's power of action, or its capacity to affect the diverse bodies, both human and non-human, that it encounters. All affects are a product of encounters in the world, in that every encounter subtly transforms a body's affective capacities. Spinoza argues that two kinds of encounters – and the affects they give rise to – must be distinguished (Deleuze 1992: 239). First, Spinoza describes encounters in which diverse bodies meet in such a way that the characteristic relations of each body combine to augment or facilitate the power of acting of each body. These encounters are good for each body in that they 'agree' with each body's essence or nature, thus producing the affects of joy. In experiencing joy, a body quite literally takes on new extensive parts that enhance its power or range of actions in the world. Naturally, bodies also experience encounters that involve a diminution in their power of acting and so produce the affects of sadness. These encounters involve combinations of bodies and their attendant parts and relations that serve to undermine, decompose or even destroy one or several of the constituent relations that define each body. This is the reason why Spinoza argues that all encounters involve a shift in a body's perfection or 'force of existing', in that good encounters involve the transfer of power from the affecting body to the affected body and so invest that body with joy and an increase in its power of acting, while bad encounters involve a decrease in the power of the affected body and so invest that body with sadness (Deleuze 1988: 50). The effort to increase one's 'good encounters' and the joyful affects that attend them, while also attempting to minimise one's 'bad encounters' and their debilitating restrictions, should be understood as the pragmatic, empirical foundation of Spinoza's practical ethics (Deleuze 1988: 17–29).

The individual that emerges in such an ethics is an assemblage of diverse simple bodies connected in extensive parts and composed in recursive encounters. *Human bodies* attain in this assembling an individuality that is also a characteristic subjectivity (Deleuze 1988: 76–7). This is an embodied subjectivity, a situated *or spatialised* subjectivity that is always, already a multiplicity. It is a subject of connections and relations in the mind and of affects and relations in the flesh, all constituted in the manifold encounters of immanent experience. In proffering such a model of subjectivity, Deleuze's reading of Spinoza facilitates the development of an ethological account of urban life. Rather than distinguish bodies from the complex places they construct – subjects from their contexts – Deleuze's ethology offers a processual vision of city life, highlighting events and encounters and the affects and relations by which these events compose or construct the city. Ethology suggests that subjectivity emerges in the city-becoming-subject of bodies in their assembling.

Fragments of Subjectivity

Ethology spatialises subjectivity. It distributes it among and between the diverse objects, encounters and bodies that characterise everyday life. Ethology discovers an ontological place for all bodies, the sentient and the inert, considering the affective and relational significance of their encounters in producing the effects of subjectivity, those 'drops of experience, complex and interdependent' (Whitehead 1978: 18). Subjectivity should not in this respect be understood as an emergent effect of mind, of a bounded psychology, any more than it should be regarded as a trick of 'our' unique physiology or biology. Without denying the importance of these categories – mind, psychology, physiology, biology and so on – subjectivity can't be reduced to them in any simple ontological calculus (Grosz 2011). Subjectivity is the achievement of bodies acting together. Remove one or another of these bodies and the subject so constituted changes also, sometimes profoundly, other times imperceptibly. Subjectivity inheres in the assembling of bodies, in their affects and relations, and in the ways these relations transform the capacities to affect and be affected immanent to the assemblage itself (Latour 2004; Rölli 2009). Bodies and parts, encountering one another in the event of their mutual affective and relational constitution, 'express' subjectivity in their concrescence. Subjectivity, in other words, lies in the hand meeting the concrete, palms pressing into the textures of haptic sensation, where each (hand and concrete) composes a subject. The subject is *expressed in the assembling of these bodies* and not only in the flesh and brain of the human body rearranging its spatial orientations in preparation for the handstand.

It is for these reasons that Deleuze adopts the language of cartography, of charts, maps and lines, to develop the idea of a spatialised subject in his unique ethology (West-Pavlov 2009: 223–7). Tracing lines of latitude and longitude, the charts and maps that are the product of cartography become for Deleuze (1988) a means of 'diagramming' the particular conjunction of affects and relations that compose subjectivity on a given 'plane of consistency'. Distributed in space (and time) subjectivity is composed of pre-individual, asubjective singularities or 'haecceities' that combine in the course of their individuation, their subjectivisation (Deleuze and Guattari 1987: 260–3). The combination of these singularities, these affects, events, relations and haecceities, each time produces a new individual, a new subject, differing by a matter of degree from the individuations that precede it. This is not to suggest that there is no relation of continuity between the moments of this individuation – that the subject differs unrecognisably from itself from one event to the next; only that subjectivity is defined by the 'elements belonging to it under given relations of movement and rest, speed and slowness (longitude); the sum total of the intensive affects it is capable of at a given power (latitude)' (ibid.: 260). Subjectivity should in this respect be understood as a multiplicity of diverse elements assembled in distinctive relations that are themselves 'mobile, spread out across a surface, topographical' (West-Pavlov 2009: 226). There is not a subject and its objects, but rather events of subjectivisation, of individuation, effectuated in the meeting of elements in space and time, of space and time. Subjectivity is ethological, combinatorial, an assembling of elements acting together, resonating in their affects. Deleuze's ethology provides a means of mapping the spatial distribution of these elements – these fragments of subjectivity – and the events of their becoming.

Recently, critics of this conception of subjectivity have objected to its apparent 'flattening' of all ontological distinctions between subjects and objects (Harman 2009: 221–3). Often targeting the renderings of subjectivity presented in actor-network theory (and Bruno Latour's writings more narrowly), rather than Deleuze's ethology per se, it is nonetheless contended that the 'symmetrisation' of subjects and objects enacted in this ethology reduces all bodies to inert matter, removing the means of distinguishing the discrete capacities that characterise individual bodies, the human and the non-human in particular (see Sismondo 2010: 89–90 for a review). It follows that the human actor is characterised in the same way, and according to the same ontological assessments, as the material objects that he or she daily encounters (see also Fallan 2008: 81–7). There is no difference, in other words, between the hand and the concrete, to return to the leitmotif that has animated so much of the discussion in this chapter thus far. While there are certainly passages in Deleuze's writings that when taken in isolation do little to refute such ontological propositions, it is clear that Deleuze's mature philosophy is concerned with the *imbrications* of matter and force, of human and non-humans, the extensive and the intensive (Rölli 2009). Deleuze (1988: 125–7) is interested in tracing the becoming subject of bodies and forces encountering one another in assemblages, and the differential relations that give rise to the effects of subjectivity in these assemblages. Far from according all entities, all forces, the same finite measure of reality, Deleuze is concerned with tracing the processes by which 'life' is organised in new individuals; with the ways 'experience in the making' gives rise to new subjects (Robinson 2010: 128). All kinds of entities, forces, signs and processes participate in this subjectivisation, which is not to say that they are all equal, just that each is indispensable to the subject so assembled. Indeed, it might be preferable to describe the subject as a kind of *dense point* radiating out through a series of intensive and extensive relations in and with the world. Such a subject describes a 'segment of the world [. . .] a zone of intensity' (West-Pavlov 2009: 231) that differs from other such zones only to the extent that it expresses different kinds of relations with the world.

The handstand instantiates one such 'zone of intensity', drawing together myriad forces in the expression of subjectivity; an inverted body-becoming-city-becoming-still. According to Deleuze's ethology, the handstand is not merely the artful, athletic expression of an intentional agent, for the concrete is also active, as are the wall, gravity, the weather and the distractions of passing traffic, among other assembled forces (see also Deleuze 1998: 1–3). As a participant in one of the ethnographic event–assemblages (see also Duff 2010) alluded to above observed:

> The wall is very important when you are learning handstands. The wall takes away the fear of falling, so it kind of soaks up your anxiety. I've started seeing more walls now and going, just trying them out, that feeling. I see a wall that looks right and I feel like being upside down, just to see how things look.

The handstand is perhaps a trivial example with which to draw so radical a picture of city life, yet it dramatises what is at stake in any ethological account of cities, bodies and subjects. As much as it solicits the expressive force of muscle, bone and desire, this handstand also relies on the reassuring stability of the city's streetscapes: a wall, a locked door, a flat expanse of concrete, children's playground equipment. While not every body assembled in this event is capable of the intentionality required to initiate it, the event is nonetheless impossible without these bodies. As Bruno Latour notes in another context, 'there might exist many metaphysical shades between full causality and sheer inexistence' (2005: 72). Perhaps the world should not be organised so neatly into intentional subjects and passive objects. In spatialising subjectivity, Deleuze's ethology draws attention to the array of bodies at work in the everyday construction of the city. This is a relational city, an ethological city, an ethical city. It is surely a city that is familiar to architects, despite the novelty of some of its terms. So how, in the service of a participatory city, may architects incorporate more of these intensive and extensive forces in the mobilisation of an expanded design theory and practice? Who, what else might be made to *participate* in the city?

A Participatory City: Bodies, Concrete and Things

The idea of participation, of 'user' involvement in design practice, has become an important feature of architectural debates in numerous contexts (Jenkins and Forsyth 2010: x–xiii). While the goals of participation vary – from an interest in the ways architecture may promote 'active citizenship' to a more mundane interest in incorporating the perspectives of 'end users' within the design/build process – each seeks to expand architecture's public franchise by shifting the practice of architecture from a narrow technical specialism to a more inclusive, empowering and/or publicly engaged activity (Blundell-Jones et al. 2005: xii–xv). Oftentimes, the shift towards a participatory architecture is presented as part of a broader historical and political movement for democracy, empowerment and enfranchisement, particularly among social groups typically excluded from everyday architectural praxis (see Blundell-Jones et al. 2005: 138–40; Awan et al. 2011: 37–9). A significant feature of this move has been the idea of 'people determining their own environment' in the context of a broader assertion of the public's 'right to the city' (Harvey 2008: 23). As David Harvey has observed, such a right 'cannot be divorced' from a discussion about 'what kind of social ties, relationship to nature, lifestyles, technologies and aesthetic values we desire' (ibid.). As such, the discussion of access and participation in the city is less concerned with the distribution of social, economic and material resources than with the 'right to change ourselves by changing the city' (ibid.). Participation in architecture thus assumes a broad remit, concerning both the 'use value' of individual buildings and the proper place of architecture within the broader web of social, economic and political governance in the city (see also Awan et al. 2011; also Jenkins and Forsyth 2010).

Existing discussions of participation in architecture have, however, largely confined themselves to the consideration of *human participation* in the design and construction of public buildings. The problem of 'use value' for example, has largely concerned consultation with a public identified as the likely end-users of a piece of architecture, and the attempt to incorporate their needs and preferences within the design process. Architecture in this way is positioned as an object of human fascination, of human occupation and human needs. Notwithstanding the emergence of a more 'ecological' architecture concerned with questions of climate change and sustainability, architecture defines the *umwelt* of the human animal and few others (Grosz 2001; Buchanan 1997). In keeping with the ethological analysis offered throughout this chapter, it is reasonable to ask what an expanded 'right to the city' *more cognisant of the interests of non-human forces* may consist of. What might a participatory architecture alert to the intensive and extensive forces that compose bodies and assemblages and cities actually look like? To ask such questions is to begin to explore the ethical, pragmatic, aesthetic and political implications of Deleuze's ethology for thinking about cities, public space and design. It is to imagine a society of concrete, bodies and things active in the everyday making of the city, their rights assured in the care one takes to preserve this city. The first step towards such a praxis is arguably to make room for the array of ethological processes at work in the making of the city, including the production of subjectivities and the transformations of place described above. The buildings, objects and things that comprise the material city don't merely have a functional, aesthetic or heritage value. They are also active in the living modulations of the city and their force must be preserved if the ethological city is to become the object of a participatory architecture. So how might these forces come to participate in such an architecture?

Concrete cannot be made to speak in a public meeting, but its resonances can be transmitted in other ways (Latour 2005). The photographs reproduced in this chapter capture something of the affective and relational involvement of walls, concrete and matter in the ethological modulation of city life; their lingering haptic presence in the hands that press against them bear the traces of this modulation. Just as these traces have become the object of an expanded 'sensory ethnography' (Pink 2009), it is possible that they may also inveigle their way into the deliberations of a public and participatory architecture. Research innovations emerging in ethnography, the visual arts and architecture itself provide important inspiration for such a practice. Each suggests a further intervention in the 'thinking-doing' relay that sustains the design/practice of contemporary architecture (Jenkins and Forsyth 2010: x). Perhaps this relational diptych may yet acquire a third term in the expression of a thinking-affecting-doing. So how might one affect affect?

In much recent visual ethnography the body has been repositioned as a dynamic research instrument in an attempt to find new ways of registering the affective and sensory traces of everyday life (Hesse-Biber and Leavy 2010). This has included the use of various emerging information and communication technologies which provide a basis for recording a broader array of sensory data (Pink 2009: 97–100). Drawing on memory, perception, whimsy, imagination, fantasy, reason and observation, the use of film and photography, auto-ethnography, creative writing, interviews and walking tours, among more conventional observational techniques, provide a basis for documenting more of the affective transitions typical of the ethology described above (Hesse-Biber and Leavy 2010). This kind of ethnography takes seriously Deleuze's insights into the production and reproduction of subjectivity in assemblages of diverse human and non-human actors. It invites one to record the trace of concrete and grit on the hands of the city's inhabitants; the feeling of spine becoming wall, becoming still of the inverted body of the handstand; the warmth of the sun resonating in the walls of buildings on a quiet suburban street. This ethnography cares for the assembled society of bodies active in the handstand and it is why this motif has featured so prominently throughout this chapter. Sensory ethnography in the social sciences, along with performative research methods in the visual arts, seeks to document in varying ways the acting-together of bodies in their ethological and affective assembling, and to make these documents available for yet more thinking-doing (see Pink 2009: 8–20). Each suggests a basis for including a wider array of forces in the deliberations that inform participatory architecture, in that each furnishes various means of registering the trace of these forces in everyday life.

If such methods are to be useful to architects it may well be that the idea of participation needs to take on a more performative and affective hue. Such an architecture will concern itself with research as much as practice, with affect as much as physics and with things as much as people. In developing a more performative and affective participatory praxis, architects and designers will need to find new ways of becoming sensitive to the ethological modulations of the city. The dividend to be gleaned from such innovation is surely the opportunity to nurture the divergent subjectivities that thrive in our cities (Brott 2011). If Whitehead (1968: 138) was right about the ingressions of context into the nature of all things, then it is plain that architects (among other custodians of the city's infrastructure) must care for these contexts as much as their human inhabitants. To do so is to protect the range of non-human actors – the concrete and walls, the breezes created in the gaps between office towers, the noise and bustle of the machinic street – that participate in the becoming-subject of the city assemblage. A participatory architecture more sensitive to the forces that produce subjectivity in the city will be more concerned to protect these forces through a form-making-design-praxis that fosters rather than silences them. It will create a place for handstands. It will cherish the feeling of the hand meeting the concrete, the tactile sensation of grit beneath one's fingernails and the press of the surface into the palms of one's hands. It will find ways to protect these affects in public places because it will be concerned with ethology as much as economics or even ecology. Above all, it will welcome 'life' back into the city.

References

Awan, N., T. Schneider and J. Till (2011), *Spatial Agency: Other Ways of Doing Architecture*, London: Routledge.

Bennett, J. (2010), *Vibrant Matter: A Political Ecology of Things*, Durham, NC: Duke University Press.

Blundell-Jones, P., D. Petrescu and J. Till (eds) (2005), *Architecture and Participation*, London: Spon Press.

Brott, S. (2011), *Architecture for a Free Subjectivity: Deleuze and Guattari at the Horizon of the Real*, London: Ashgate.

Buchanan, I. (1997), 'The Problem of the Body in Deleuze and Guattari, Or, What Can a Body Do?', *Body & Society*, 3: 3, 73–91.

Deleuze, G. (1988), *Spinoza: Practical Philosophy*, trans. R. Hurley, San Francisco: City Lights.

Deleuze, G. (1992), *Expressionism in Philosophy: Spinoza*, trans. M. Joughin, New York: Zone Books.

Deleuze, G. (1994), *Difference and Repetition*, trans. P. Patton, London: Athlone Press.

Deleuze, G. (1998), *Essays Critical and Clinical*, trans. D. W. Smith and M. Greco, London: Verso.

Deleuze, G. (2001), *Pure Immanence: Essays on a Life*, New York: Zone Books.

Deleuze, G. and F. Guattari (1987), *A Thousand Plateaus: Capitalism and Schizophrenia*, trans. B. Massumi, Minnesota, MN: University of Minnesota Press.

Dovey, K. (2010), *Becoming Places: Urbanism/Architecture/Identity/Power*, London: Routledge.

Duff, C. (2010), 'On the Role of Affect and Practice in the Production of Place', *Environment and Planning D: Space and Society*, 28: 5, 881–95.

Duff, C. (2011), 'Networks, Resources and Agencies: On the Character and Production of Enabling Places', *Health and Place*, 17: 1, 149–56.

Fallan, K. (2008), 'Architecture in Action: Traveling with ANT in the Land of Architectural Research', *Architectural Theory Review*, 13: 1, 80–96.

Gatens, M. (2000), 'Feminism as "Password": Re-Thinking the "Possible" with Spinoza and Deleuze', *Hypatia*, 15: 2, 59–75.

Grosz, E. (2001), *Architecture from the Outside: Essays on Virtual and Real Space*, Cambridge, MA: MIT Press.

Grosz, E. (2011), *Becoming Undone: Darwinian Reflections on Life, Politics and Art*, Durham, NC: Duke University Press.

Harman, G. (2009), *Prince of Networks: Bruno Latour and Metaphysics*, Melbourne: re.press.

Harvey, D. (2008), 'The Right to the City', *New Left Review*, 53, 23–40.

Hesse-Biber, S. and P. Leavy (eds) (2010), *Handbook of Emergent Methods*, London: Guildford Press.

Jenkins, P. and L. Forsyth (2010), *Architecture, Participation and Society*, London: Routledge.

Latour, B. (2004), 'How to Talk About the Body? The Normative Dimension of Science Studies', *Body & Society*, 10: 2–3, 205–29.

Latour, B. (2005), *Reassembling the Social: An Introduction to Actor-Network Theory*, Cambridge: Cambridge University Press.

Pink, S. (2009), *Doing Sensory Ethnography*, London: Sage.

Robinson, K. (2010), 'Back to Life: Deleuze, Whitehead and Process', *Deleuze Studies*, 4: 1, 120–33.

Rölli, M. (2009), 'Deleuze on Intensity Differentials and the Being of the Sensible', *Deleuze Studies*, 3: 1, 26–53.

Sismondo, S. (2010), *An Introduction to Science and Technology Studies*, 2nd edn, Oxford: Wiley Blackwell.

Thrift, N. (1999), 'Steps to an Ecology of Place', in D. Massey, J. Allen and P. Sarre (eds), *Human Geography Today*, Cambridge: Polity Press, pp. 295–323.

West-Pavlov, R. (2009), *Space in Theory: Kristeva, Foucault, Deleuze*, New York: Rodopi.

Whitehead, A. N. ([1938] 1968), *Modes of Thought*, New York: Free Press.

Whitehead, A. N. ([1929] 1978), *Process and Reality*, New York: Free Press.

Chapter 13

Architectures, Critical and Clinical

Chris L. Smith

In *Essays Critical and Clinical* (1993) Gilles Deleuze suggests that medicine (the clinical) might distil from literature (the critical) a symptomatology. And it is this symptomatology that I am interested in *for* architecture. For when Deleuze speaks of the 'writer', I cannot but help think that he might have also easily spoken of the *architect*, and when Deleuze speaks of literature (of text, of style, of its 'revolutionary force') I cannot but help think he could almost as easily have spoken of *architecture* (Deleuze and Guattari 1972: 106). Deleuze writes: 'The writer as such is not a patient but a physician, the physician of himself and of the world. The world is a set of symptoms whose illness merges with man. Literature then appears as the enterprise of health' (Deleuze 1997: 3). In this chapter I will suggest that under the same terms architecture also might appear as the enterprise of health.

However, I start this chapter not with architecture as such, nor with Deleuze's notions of the critical and the clinical, but rather with a Victorian recollection. It is the recollection of someone who had taken flight from two surgical operations in his time as a medical student in Edinburgh, before taking flight from a career in medicine itself. It is the recollection of the naturalist Charles Darwin. In his autobiography Darwin writes:

> I once saw [. . .] in the streets of Cambridge almost as horrid a scene as could have been witnessed during the French Revolution. Two body-snatchers had been arrested, and whilst being taken to prison had been torn from the constable by a crowd of the roughest men, who dragged them by their legs along the muddy and stony road. They were covered from head to foot with mud, and their faces were bleeding either from having been kicked or from the stones; they looked like corpses, but the crowd was so dense that I got only a few momentary glimpses of the wretched creatures. (Darwin 1958: 23)

For a 'body-snatcher' the corpse is a commodity in that it is able to be sold to medical schools as a training device for the development of skills that may subsequently be applied to the bodies of the living, albeit ailing. For a 'crowd of the roughest men' the deep reverence for the corpse can well be enacted on the living body as an act of violence that seeks to rid the living body, albeit morally ailing, of that which dissociates it from the dead. I would suggest that the early contemporary preoccupations of architectural discourse relating to the *body* can, on multiple counts, be distinguished as the discursive methodology of either 'body snatcher' or 'crowd of roughest men', replacing the corpse with the ailing body and the ailing body with the corpse, respectively.

It can be imagined that Darwin hid himself in the Cambridge crowd and removed himself from a medical career for fear of the noise of violence which characterises both 'bad operations [. . .] before the blessed days of chloroform' (Darwin 1958: 12) and the harsh on-street urban management of social and moral illnesses of the time.

The Therapeutic and the Diagnostic

The architectural response to the problem of the 'body-snatchers' was at once simple and direct. The graves of individual bodies came to be protected by heavy table tombstones, mortsafes and vaults (Holder 2010). Those without the economic means for such protections placed pebbles and flowers on the graves as a way to detect disturbances. In Edinburgh and the areas around the Scottish medical schools, watchtowers were constructed in cemeteries so that the graves of the newly buried might be watched over for a few days till their flesh had decomposed to the point where they were no longer valuable to the medical educators.[1] Many cemeteries of urban Britain had large fences and walls erected to protect the bodies of the newly dead from the medical establishment. In this regard architecture is therapy. A solution to a problem. An answer to a pathology (in this case a social more than individual pathology). And architecture has a long history of positing itself as therapeutic, as solution, as answer.

There is a sense, however, in which architecture is not therapeutic after-the-fact but indeed diagnostic. One could argue that had the cemeteries of Edinburgh already been designed with tall walls and with watchtowers to accommodate relatives of the newly deceased then the body snatching would not have occurred. This would be something like architecture as preventative medicine: diagnosing a possible social ill, striking before symptoms manifest. And architecture also has a long history of posing itself as diagnostic, as mitigating problems before they occur. Indeed watchtowers were also constructed in cemeteries in Northumberland, in the north of England, where there is no recorded history of body-snatching. The placing of pebbles and flowers on graves and the construction of walls around cemeteries today might be one such odd diagnostics – protecting against an ill, independent of its occurrence, posing an answer independent of any particularly poignant question.

The therapeutic and diagnostic positioning of architecture persists. Modernism reignited the Enlightenment fascination with forms of knowledge that went back to 'first principles' and a belief that uncovering a cause would allow a better articulation of an effect. In modernist architectural manifestos this position is often posed as a questioning of architectural traditions and conventions. Traditional forms of architecture were presented as belonging to realms of faulty logic. They were not necessarily presented as bad solutions per se but rather as solutions that failed to address real problems, largely because the problems themselves were not well articulated. Le Corbusier states the position in Darwinian terms in his text of 1923 *Toward a New Architecture*:

> Architecture is governed by standards. Standards are a matter of logic, analysis and precise study. Standards are based on a problem which has been well stated. Architecture means plastic invention, intellectual speculation, higher mathematics. Architecture is a very noble art. Standardization is imposed by the law of selection and is an economic and social necessity. Harmony is a state of agreement with the norms of our universe. Beauty governs all; she is a purely human creation; she is the overplus necessary only to men of the highest type. (Le Corbusier 1927: 135–8)

Le Corbusier's text, replete with late Victorian humanisms and fixations with the problem/solution dualism, is still a standard on the reading lists of architecture schools internationally and its version of causality is still prominent in architectural pedagogy today.[2] The 'problem-based learning' of most architecture schools relies on the premise that in a question lies a solution, if only the diagnostic skill of the student might uncover it.

What I am interested in here is not this play between questions and solutions nor the dualisms of therapy and diagnosis but rather the sense whereby architecture might constitute a symptomatology. Symptomatology is not concerned with origination, nor with 'giving a reason', nor with causation (as with etiology). Symptomatology is the study of signs – full stop. Daniel W. Smith, the Deleuzian scholar and one of the translators of Deleuze's *Essays Critical and Clinical*, suggests that:

> What a doctor confronts in an individual case is a symptom or group of symptoms and his [*sic*] diagnostic task is to discover the corresponding concept (the concept of the disease). No doctor would treat a fever or headache as a definite symptom of a specific illness; they are rather indeterminate symptoms common to a number of diseases, and the doctor must interpret and decipher the symptoms in order to arrive at the correct diagnosis. (Smith 2005: 183)

Symptomatology as such is an implicating, an infolding and a concern with what constitutes, constructs and accompanies a particular condition or life event. Daniel Smith suggests that for Deleuze, 'while etiology and therapeutics are integral parts of medicine, symptomatology appeals to a kind of limit-point, premedical or submedical, that belongs as much to art as to medicine' (Smith 1997: xvi). Deleuze turns to literature (the critical) as a means of investigating this medical (clinical) notion. He suggests that writers do not account for, or necessarily represent, the world but rather construct or compose worlds from indeterminate symptoms. Writers compose the terrains, interactions, inversions: the sense of alternate worlds which constitute modes of existence. There is in symptomatology an infolding of contexts and selves and a constructing, a configuring, of both. A delirium. For Deleuze, 'the ultimate aim of literature is to set free, in the delirium, this creation of a health or this invention of a people, that is a possibility of life. To write for this people who are missing . . . ("for" means less "in the place of" than "for the benefit of")' (1997: 4).

Defining Symptomatology

Distilling a history *for* architecture that posits itself symptomatologically is (in one sense) far more difficult than isolating the therapeutic and diagnostic positioning of architecture. Such an architecture would concern itself neither with uncovering underlying or foundational logical structures nor with posing solutions to commonly stated problems. This is because symptomatology is at once more concrete-real and more abstract-real. It is concrete-real in its attention to the actualities of material existence and the temporality of events. It is abstract-real in that any attention paid to the concrete-reality of the world necessarily involves an indulgence in the rich complexities, intensities and contingencies of life. An architecture posited as symptomatology might engage with the immediacy of the present by exploring and experimenting within the world and its 'symptoms'. This architecture would express new ways of thinking about life and experiment with novel ways of living. Such an architecture might operate not as a backdrop or stage-set to life but rather would be *implicated* in life itself, in a manner that resonates with what Roland Barthes describes as a 'theatricalisation'.

In his book *Sade, Fourier, Loyola* (1971) Barthes suggests that theatricalisation is not simply 'designing a setting for representation, but unlimiting the language' (Barthes 1997: 5–6). When he turns to the literary work of the Marquis de Sade Barthes exchanges the word 'writer' for the word 'formulator' and he suggests that Sade 'always sides with *semiosis* rather than *mimesis*' (ibid.: 37). That is, for Barthes, Sade is not an author who *refers* to things, who answers questions or *represents* events or situations, but rather Sade *constitutes* a new world of elaborate spaces and machines and populates that world with a new people – for new and intense acts of love and violence. In this way Sade is a symptomatologist.

The medical condition *sadomasochism*, defined by Krafft-Ebing some fifty-five years after the death of Sade, but during the lifetime of the writer Baron von Sacher Masoch (from which the term masochism is drawn), is a key example engaged by Deleuze to explore the connection of the critical (in a literary sense) and the clinical (in a medical sense). In Deleuze's extended essay 'Coldness and Cruelty' (1989) he turns to the 'differential mechanisms' of literature and medicine in the construction of the medicalised condition of 'sadomasochism'. There is a very tight logic to the essay (Smith 2009: 45–57). The clinical aspect of Deleuze's argument in 'Coldness and Cruelty' is explicit: it is foremost a critique of Freud's formulation of sadomasochism and the reiterated aim of the essay is to establish 'irreducible causal chains' for sadism and masochism (as separate mechanisms) (Deleuze 1989: 14). Deleuze's argument is that the relationship between sadism and masochism is one of analogy only and that 'in place of a dialectic which all too readily perceives the link between opposites, we should aim for a critical and clinical appraisal able to reveal the truly differential mechanisms' (ibid.: 14). This impulse to isolate causes is not, however, one that pervades 'Coldness and Cruelty' where 'the clinical specification of sadism and masochism are not separable from the literary values particular to Sade and Masoch' (ibid.: 14).

In Daniel Smith's introduction to Deleuze's *Essays Critical and Clinical*, the question of this link between literature and medicalised life is raised and Smith suggests it is the 'symptomatological method' that makes the link possible. For Smith:

The fundamental idea behind Deleuze's 'critique et clinique' project is that authors and artists, like doctors and clinicians, can themselves be seen as profound symptomatologists. Sadism and masochism are clearly not diseases on a par with Parkinson's disease or Alzheimer's disease. Yet if Krafft-Ebing, in 1869, was able to use Masoch's name to designate a fundamental perversion (much to Masoch's own consternation), it was not because Masoch 'suffered' from it as a patient, but rather because his literary works isolated a particular way of existing and set forth a novel symptomatology of it. (Smith 1997: xvii)

In *The Logic of Sense* (1969) Deleuze describes artists as 'clinicians of civilization' (1990: 273) and notes that as with the literary origins of masochism and sadism 'from the perspective of Freud's genius it is not the complex which provides us with information about Oedipus and Hamlet, but rather Oedipus and Hamlet who provide us with information about the complex' (ibid.: 237).[3] In these cases it is art and literature – the critical – that precedes the clinical.

Just as the literary precedes the medical in these cases, it may be argued that the architectural and urban also precede medicalisations of the body. This is both in the sense that urban settlements and the architectures of civilisations predate much of which we would recognise as medical practices, and in the sense that architecture housed (constructed) the bodies that came to be dissected and diagnosed.[4] The experimental collecting of, assembling of, differential, incompossible elements into a concept or an event that is characteristic of symptomatology is a method that those working in the areas of tectonic culture, such as architects and urban designers, well recognise. Architecture, or at least a particular experimental edge of architecture, infolds and implicates materials, geometries, sites, scales, labour, movement, etc. in generating a kind of event we do not have or cannot as yet have, a future for a people who are not yet. In this sense architecture operates as a collective enunciation (or utterance): speaking at once for and in place of a people.

But the relay between philosophical notions and architecture flows both ways: Deleuze also plays with architectural and urban spaces. There is a spatial indulgence in *Essays Critical and Clinical* that makes that work at once alluring and complex for the architect, for those engaged in a building and a constructing of the world. It should be noted that the phrase 'spatial indulgence' might not, however, be so apt for describing the spatial engagement of Deleuze. It is not space *in* or *of* itself that Deleuze fixates upon, but rather it is the implicating, the milieus and the trajectories, that are entailed in the life of space that are the philosopher's investment. For Deleuze is interested in the

Figure 13.1 Brion-Vega Cemetery, San Vito d'Altivole, Carlo Scarpa (architect). Photograph by Amy DeDonato, 2 July 2009. Reproduced with the permission of Amy DeDonato.

spatial in as much as life is spatial. All of life. And all of life a milieu. For Deleuze:

> A milieu is made up of qualities, substances, powers, and events: the street, for example. With its materials (paving stones), its noises (the cries of merchants), its animals (harnessed horses) or its dramas (a horse slips, a horse falls down. A horse is beaten . . .). The trajectory merges not only with the subjectivity of those who travel through a milieu, but also with the subjectivity of the milieu itself, insofar as it is reflected in those who travel through it. (1997: 61)

And even the architectures and the cities of the dead – cemeteries – are places of qualities, substances, powers and events: milieu, subjectivities and trajectories. It is to one such instance of a city of the dead – one particular architectural edge – that I wish to momentarily turn: Carlo Scarpa's Brion-Vega Cemetery of 1968–78 (see Figure 13.1).

Delirious Architecture

The work of the Italian architect Scarpa was known to Deleuze. Not, of course, by travel, more by visitation than visit. In *What Is Philosophy?* (1991) Deleuze and Guattari refer to the 'thickness' (*épaisseur*) that Hubert Damisch, the philosopher of aesthetics and art history, identifies in his theoretical excavations of the 'underside' of painting (Damisch 1984: 99–120). Deleuze and Guattari suggest that such thickness is identified by Damisch 'at the level of the architectural plane when Scarpa, for example, suppresses the movement of projection and the mechanisms of perspective so as to inscribe volumes in the thickness of the plane itself' (Deleuze and Guattari 1994: 195). For Damisch all art is a theoretical object. He points out, in a project not dissimilar to that of the critical and clinical, that techniques and perceptual qualities often precede scientific explanation and categorisation.[5]

Scarpa's Brion-Vega Cemetery is located in San Vito d'Altivole, north of Bologna (where in 1319 the recorded history of the body-snatchers began).[6] The Brion-Vega Cemetery is a monumental tomb cum landscape designed for the Brion family, founders of Brionvega (the Italian electronics group). The architect, Scarpa, is himself buried in this cemetery in the interstitial space, the thickness, created by the walls of the old and new cemeteries. He fell down a concrete stair – not here in a cemetery full of concrete steps, but in Japan in 1978. Scarpa had spent the last ten years of his life realising this incredible cemetery and described the work in literary (critical) terms:

> I have tried to put some poetic imagination into it, though not in order to create poetic architecture but to make a certain kind of architecture that could emanate a sense of formal poetry [...]. The place for the dead is a garden [...]. I wanted to show some ways in which you could approach death in a social and civic way; and further what meaning there was in death, in the ephemerality of life – other than these shoe-boxes. (Scarpa 1989: 17–18)

There is, in the Brion-Vega Cemetery, the studied and technical configuring of geometries, scales, compositions, perspectives, fragments and trajectories. These incompossible elements are examined and arranged as independent signs or symptoms. Critics of Scarpa's work often describe these elements in terms of the 'fragment'. I would argue that Scarpa assembles fragments as 'dissociated' symptoms. For Marco Frascari, the mobile hectic, hypnotic drawings of Scarpa – of all elements at all scales

Figure 13.2 Concrete gate, Brion-Vega Cemetery, San Vito d'Altivole, Carlo Scarpa (architect). Photograph by Amy DeDonato, 2 July 2009. Reproduced with the permission of Amy DeDonato.

and all at once – are emblematic of the fragmentation of Scarpa's work as a whole (see Figure 13.2). In 1984 Frascari wrote:

> Scarpa is a *Magister Ludi*, and his buildings are texts wherein the details are the minimal unit of signification. The joints between different materials and shapes and spaces are pretexts for generating texts. The interfacing of commentaries with preceding texts in the architecture of Scarpa is always a problem of joints, and in the joints he achieves the change of conventions. (Frascari 1984: 31)

By 1991 Frascari had refined this idea, suggesting that it is not by analogy or 'the change of conventions' that the drawing practice of Scarpa relates to the built work. In his text *Monsters of Architecture* Frascari turns to the literary trope of *metonym* to describe a type of consistency of incompatible elements and scales that an architecture like Scarpa's generates.

Scarpa also knew his materials. He knew how to work them, how to push them. He could make the heavy hover. In *Essays Critical and Clinical* Deleuze describes Masoch's use of words as transforming suspense into suspension. Scarpa achieves something similar. The most seemingly weighty and stable of elements is made mobile when part of a trajectory: the concrete gate (Figure 13.3) is poised and requires the lightest of pressure to open. Scarpa pushes matter (and not words) to the 'point of suspension, a song, a cry or silence – a song of the woods, a cry of the village, the silence of the steppe', as Deleuze writes of Masoch (1997: 55). For beyond the geometry of the Brion-Vega Cemetery, beyond the signs, elements and fragments, beyond the concrete, beyond the concrete steps, there is a style or a concept, or a milieu.[7] A milieu that moans. A distinct deep moan.

Deleuze writes in *Critical and Clinical*, 'to exhaust space is to extenuate its potentiality by making any encounter impossible' (1997: 160 and 163). The experience of the Brion-Vega Cemetery is exhausting. It is not that you cover too much distance here and it is not that you move at too great a pace. The exhaustion is mellower than this. It is the exhaustion of all that moves. All Scarpa's incompatible fragments, elements, symbols and signs are mobile. They articulate trajectories, always taking you somewhere else: the wall beyond the corn; the corn and the village beyond the wall; the bridge, the island, the waters and the tomb beyond the stair. It is an exhaustion of a journey without end.

For Deleuze, 'when sculpture ceases to be monumental in order to become hodological: it is not enough to say that it is a landscape and that it lays out a place or territory. What it lays out are paths – it is itself a voyage' (1997: 66). The voyages of the Brion-Vega Cemetery are not, however, voyages taken. They are like Deleuze's own travels, 'intensive' rather than in extensity, visitations rather than a visiting. The cemetery is exhausting as a replete experience. No. It is beyond replete and rather an exhaustion like an excess. There is here a weightiness, a momentum generated by a thickness, a mobility yet to be excavated. That which Le Corbusier might have been referring to as an 'overplus'. An overflow or a heaving sigh, a voice given to forces and movements.

The Brion-Vega Cemetery is consistently incomplete. Incompletion is

Figure 13.3 Composition and hodology, Brion-Vega Cemetery, San Vito d'Altivole, Carlo Scarpa (architect). Photograph by Amy DeDonato, 2 July 2009. Reproduced with the permission of Amy DeDonato.

the device, the dispositif, the structuring principle. The wilful incompletion of the cemetery generates openings, leaves it open. The cemetery is full of empty and open spaces, niches and voids that the living cannot occupy, and paths and stairs that they cannot traverse (see Figure 13.4). It is, in this sense, open for imaginings, dreamings and projections. These incompletions would seem to be openings for those that rest in tombs. In this sense Scarpa designed, as Deleuze might suggest, 'for this people who are missing' where '"for" means less "in the place of" than "for the benefit of"' (Deleuze 1997: 4). I like to imagine that Deleuze

Figure 13.4 Concrete stairs, Brion-Vega Cemetery, San Vito d'Altivole, Carlo Scarpa (architect). Photograph by Amy DeDonato, 2 July 2009. Reproduced with the permission of Amy DeDonato.

was speaking of Scarpa and the Brion-Vega Cemetery when he wrote in critique of Freud

> the unconscious no longer deals with persons and objects, but with trajectories and becomings; it is no longer an unconscious of commemoration but one of mobilization, an unconscious whose objects take flight rather than remaining buried in the ground. (Ibid.: 63)

Incompletions

Scarpa's elements take you, as you take them. A thick delirium of selves and spaces. Scarpa's concrete stairs lead you around the cemetery but also run you up walls; close in upon themselves, upon you; take you below water lines; have you enter the sky; have you fly. You cannot walk these steps. Or at least you cannot walk the steps as one might usually walk a step. The steps abstract your movement in concrete. Such an architecture plays with the laws by which a stair might operate or be operational (symptomatology is abstract-real). At the same time Scarpa constructs a subjectivity of death and departure and articulates it as an actual problem (symptomatology is concrete-real). Scarpa's work engages with the present by reinterpreting the world and its 'symptoms'. Opening up new ways of thinking about life and death and in so doing creating new ways of living. The elements both 'bear' and give birth to new peoples. In this sense Scarpa's Brion-Vega Cemetery is posited as a profound symptomatology.

Indeed the Edinburgh cemetery constructed in the nineteenth century also might be posited as a symptomatology, its walls and watchtowers inextricably implicated in the medicalisation of the body and the experimental construction of life. The walls and the watchtowers exist today (and are reconstructed in new cemeteries); they exist beyond the therapeutic (there are no more body-snatchers) and beyond the diagnostic (the crowd of roughest men has surely dispersed). The architecture of the Edinburgh cemetery, in the here and now, as with the architecture of Scarpa's Brion-Vega Cemetery, operates as a set of 'indeterminate symptoms common to a number of diseases' and the pebbles, flowers, walls, steps and watchtowers an intervening, an experimenting, in the changing new worlds architecture constructs in concert with the corpse.

Notes

1. Holder suggests that all communities in proximity to the schools of medicine in Edinburgh, Glasgow and Aberdeen engaged means of protecting the dead. Mortsafes and watching were the key measures taken. Watch-houses were also constructed in remoter Scottish areas and in Northumberland. Extant examples include Dalkeith Cemetery, near Edinburgh, and the New Calton Burying Ground, Edinburgh. In Udny Green, in Aberdeenshire, there is a unique rotating morthouse (Holder 2010).
2. Le Corbusier, *Toward a New Architecture*, 10 and 102 for example: 'Standards are a matter of logic, analysis and minute study; they are based on a problem which has been well "stated"' (10); 'The lesson of the airplane lies in the logic which governed the enunciation of the problem and which led to the successful

realization. When a problem is properly stated, in our epoch, it inevitably finds its solution' (102).

3. This of course follows Nietzsche's description of the philosopher as the 'physician of culture' (Nietzsche 1979: 175).

4. Architecture and urban settlement were also important in the locating of anatomical dissections. One of the distinctive features of the images of the sixteenth-century Flemish anatomist, Andreas Vesalius, was the relationships established between the corpse and urban settlement.

5. *L'Origine de la perspective* (1987) would be a good example. Damisch points out that perspective in art preceded its formalisation in science.

6. Body-snatching co-evolved with the study of human anatomy at the University of Bologna and the first recorded body-snatchers were (not surprisingly) medical students (Frank 1976: 399–400).

7. It is worth noting that this milieu was broader than architecture and included literature and art. According to George Dodds: 'In commenting on the design process and the locale, he [Scarpa] cited a number of key works of literature upon which he reflected while designing the project. These include the garden landscapes of Francesco Colonna's *Hypernotomachia Poliphili*, where the chaste body of Polia is pursued in the dream of Poliphilo; the garden of Professor Canteral in Raymond Roussel's *Locus Solus*, where preserved bodies float in a strange and magical watery substance called *acqua micans*; and the funereal landscapes of Edmondo De Amicis whose picturesque cemeteries are inhabited by young maidens eating and drinking [. . .]. In all of these visual and textual narratives the body – typically the female body situated in a landscape or garden – figures prominently. This may help explain why the design drawings for the Brion sanctuary, more than any of Scarpa's other projects, abound with images of nude females. Although these images often appear somewhat ghostlike, they reflect the manner in which Scarpa imagined the living body physically engaging the Brion sanctuary, both directly and as a site from which to view a distant idealized landscape' (Dodds 2002: 247).

References

Barthes, R. (1997), *Sade, Fourier, Loyola*, trans. R. Miller, Baltimore, MD: Johns Hopkins University Press; original French edition published 1971.

Damisch, H. (1984), *Fenêtre jaune cadmium, ou les dessous de la peinture*, Paris: Seuil.

Darwin, C. (1958), *The Autobiography of Charles Darwin and Selected Letters*, ed. F. Darwin, New York: Dover Publications.

Deleuze, G. (1989), 'Coldness and Cruelty', in *Masochism*, trans. J. McNeil, New York: Zone; original French edition published 1967. This essay is an expansion of ideas first developed in "De Sacher-Masoch au masochisme", in *Arguments*, 5: 21 (January–April 1961), 40–6.

Deleuze, G. (1990), *The Logic of Sense*, ed. C. V. Boundas, trans. M. Lester and C. Stivale, New York: Columbia University Press; original French edition published 1969.

Deleuze, G. (1997), *Essays Critical and Clinical.*, trans. D. W. Smith and M. Greco, Minneapolis, MN: University of Minnesota Press, 1997; original French edition published 1993.

Deleuze, G. and F. Guattari (1983), *Anti-Oedipus*, trans. R. Hurley, M. Seem and H. R. Lane, Minneapolis, MN: University of Minnesota Press; original French edition published 1972.

Deleuze, G. and F. Guattari (1994), *What Is Philosophy?*, trans. H. Tomlinson and

G. Burchell, New York: Columbia University Press; original French edition published 1991.

Dodds, G. (2002), 'Desiring Landscapes/Landscapes of Desire', in G. Dodds and R. Tavernor (eds), *Body and Building: Essays on the Changing Relation of Body and Architecture*, Cambridge, MA: MIT Press, pp. 238–57.

Frank, J. B. (1976), 'Body Snatching: A Grave Medical Problem', *Yale Journal of Biology and Medicine*, 49: 4, 399–410.

Frascari, Marco (1984), 'The Tell-the-Tale Detail', *VIA*, 7, 23–7.

Frascari, Marco (1991), *Monsters of Architecture: Anthropomorphism in Architectural Theory*, Lanham, MD: Rowman & Littlefield.

Holder, G. (2010), *Scottish Bodysnatchers*, Port Stroud: History Press.

Le Corbusier (1927), *Towards a New Architecture*, trans. F. Etchells, London: Architectural Press; original French edition published 1923.

Nietzsche, F. (1979), *Philosophy and Truth: Selections from Nietzsche's Notebooks of the Early 1870s*, trans. D. Breazeale, Atlantic Highlands, NJ: Humanities International Press.

Scarpa, C. (1989), 'Can Architecture be Poetry', in P. Nover (ed.), *The Other City: 'Carlo Scarpa: The Architect's Working Method as Shown by the Brion Cemetery in San Vito D'Altivole'*, Berlin: Ernst & Sohn, pp. 17–18.

Smith, C. L. (2009), 'Text and Deployment of the Masochist', *Angelaki: Journal of Theoretical Humanities*, 14: 3, 45–57.

Smith, D. W. (1997), 'Introduction: "A Life of Pure Immanence": Deleuze's "Critique et Clinique" Project', in G. Deleuze, *Essays Critical and Clinical*, Minneapolis, MN: University of Minnesota Press, pp. xi–lvi.

Smith, D. W. (2005), 'Critical, Clinical', in C. Stivale (ed.), *Gilles Deleuze: Key Concepts*, Chesham: Acumen, pp. 182–93.

Chapter 14

Abstract Care

Stephen Loo

Contemporary digital architecture has long been accused of emphasising the abstract over the real and material. The abstract in digital architecture is commonly conceptualised as reductions of formal and behavioural patterns into codes and algorithms distilled from the real, and put to scientific use as the genetic instructions of future formal, spatial and material configurations. Abstractions become the exchange mechanism required to enact genealogical lines between a set of qualia – predetermined values – and the family of coming forms, if not the space of possibilities for these forms, governed by resemblance and/or representation.

As the practices in digital architecture progress through the 1990s and into the turn of the new millennium, and with the arrival of new software and increasing computational power, as well as new friendships between architecture and the fields of philosophy, neuroscience, psychology, biology, environmental science, cultural studies and so forth, the use of codes as abstractions has moved from a predictive model for the design of objects and spaces to one which emphasises the processual and the performative. Rather than thinking and practice led by linear correspondences and governed by Euclidean geometrical fidelity between mathematical equations representing abstractions and fixed outputs of architectural objects, digital architecture is now predisposed to speculations about the process of 'designing' itself, taking leave of the imperative of form of designed objects per se. Rather than stable forms, architecture seeks the architectonics of continuous variation and movement. The mathematics here moves from the classical principles of geometry to the differentials of modern calculus. And the aesthetic is one based on ongoing variations of curvilinearity rather than the fixity of linearity.

Recent theorisations of digital architecture go something like this. Architecture in the flows of information, capital and ecologies – which to Guattari is tripartite: environmental, social and mental-subjective – starts to display an extraterritoriality; it is dispersed and without the imprimatur of fixed identities. These contemporary flows arguably suspend or make unavailable the possibility for autonomy of architectural form and sovereignty of the designer as the normative centres for creativity, command and production. The architectural entities that form, deform and reform in flows interact in a molecular realm of becoming, in abstract diagrams on an immanent plane of existence. Therefore the 'space' of digital architecture, whether this is the space of possibilities that emerge from the interaction of digital code and material flows or actualised spaces and places that are the result of digital interactivity, loses its geographical and functional coordinates, and can no longer fully mediate the extant life within them if mediation proceeds from an ontology defined by functionality, economics and expediency.

Abstract Intensities

'Life' in contemporary digital architecture seems to come from within: it is the intensive force internal to the assemblage or system that gives it its constituent self-transforming power. Abstractions in the form of mathematically based genetic codes and computational algorithms in this scenario are activators in horizontal relationality, i.e. an informational milieu without a predetermined plan, but whose interactions provide an organismic vitalism and the grounds for emergence.

Manuel DeLanda's seminal essay 'Deleuze and the Use of the Genetic Algorithm in Architecture' in 1992 lays the theoretical groundwork for the use of the genetic model in digital design. Drawing from Deleuzian philosophy, DeLanda frames the morphological evolution of digital forms away from thinking based on linear or metricised space, towards population, intensive and topological thinking (2002: 118). DeLanda's aim is to enrich the search space of design from predictable genetico-mathematical models by presaging the idea of intensive qualities and the infinite field of design possibilities that cannot be closed down by code. He believes there is no comparison between the current abstract possibilities, generated by the human practices of computationally driven digital architecture and the abundant and unimaginable combinatorial productivity of natural forms. Natural processes seem to be governed by 'body plans' which are what Deleuze calls 'abstract diagrams' (DeLanda 2002: 119). Abstractions here are not limiting or restraining, but are diagrams of nature that move towards the infinite and do not exhaust their possibilities. They are abstractions that contain within them 'virtual multiplicities'; they are the source of potentiality, an intensive condition which puts in place a constant outward movement of newness.

So, in DeLanda's model, abstractions are not reductive but performative: they generate new and novel diagrams of movement that lead to new associations and collectivities. The tendency to emphasise intensive process over outward forms is therefore also a move towards a relational aesthetics within an ecological mode of design, that is ecology as relations between the subject and its environment, between the inside and the outside. In this model for ecology, the human being is not the sole creative source. Instead, the biological paradigm promulgated in contemporary digital architecture instates the non-human world with an interior creative force given by a certain consistency or organisation of the beings within it. These projects enact a discursive continuity and perhaps an ontological consistency between organismic behaviour and that of technologically mediated productions.

Exhausted Geometries

Have we reached a point of exhaustion from the contingency that arrives with total serialism in digital architecture? Has architectural form in the digital domain exhausted its aesthetics, as its process-oriented and relationally based outputs are starting to show a highly familiar resemblance: their surface appearance multi-celled, their volumes blobby or their shape formless? Many argue that these digitally derived and mediated forms are irrational abstractions because they conform less to conventional ideas of functionality or humanism and are relatively unbuildable (although this is not necessarily accurate, as there is a greater likelihood that parametrically derived designs are geometrically and structurally resolved, possess material economies and as such are more constructible, because the limits of these multiple parameters are already built into digital models, generating outputs that are within a range of solutions with best fitness for purpose or context).

Geometric and algorithmic abstractions operating upon discrete cellular entities produce forms that tend to curve. The continuous movement of topological transformations related to the curve of quantum mechanics, while resisting the unidimensional transformation along a linear (causal) trajectory of Newtonian physics, tends to produce architecture which is inevitably self similar in form. Variations of curvilinear forms are more curves. In comparison to the assemblage of discrete and discontinuous geometrical forms, the 'continuous' topology of self-varying forms can be argued to contain a built-in aesthetic exhaustion of sorts, at least when considered superficially or at a macro scale.

Digital architecture, in this state of exhaustion, remains unqualified and undifferentiated, withholding its actualisation into specific identifications, whether in a formal, functional, ideological, aesthetic, social, cultural or individual sense. Through Aristotelian philosophy, it can be argued that the very characteristic to *not be* (one thing, and perhaps also some-thing) is the constitutive power of digital architecture. Can it be argued that this undifferentiated, uninscribed vitality is the manifestation of pure potentiality which to Agamben (1998: 45), following Aristotle, is the absolute biopolitical material?

The realm of abstraction in genetic algorithms and parametrics, as it presages the production of continuous movement with emergentist tendencies, is therefore an indistinct threshold zone where life is placed both inside and outside of the code. In this zone of indistinction, design is arguably positioned outside the possibility of resistance, owing to the smooth flow between external and internal milieus, between abstract code and the experiential dimension of perception and existence. And space becomes unqualifiable by geometry as an ambivalence exists between it being an extensive attribute in epistemological exteriority to the entities in relation, and ontologically univocal and therefore intensive to the individual entities continuously in the process of becoming-collective, becoming-other.

Flat Relations

This impersonality of digital architecture has been used to eschew the authorial intention of architects, allowing instead, as Jane Bennett would say, for matter to be vibrant (2010) and for entities that make matter up to be seen as self-organising in their relationality. We do not speak of the human creator, but that the entities and objects within this field have their own agencies, within which the human designer is but one, and the human is itself made up of multiple relational bodies and their own agencies. As Bruno Latour postulates in his actor-network theory, the relations between entities are inseparable from their individualities. That is, actors are constantly individuating, undergoing transformations, as they interact at various levels with each other, whether literally or in abstraction, in mind or reality. And there is no hierarchy between actors.

The ontology of the milieu digital architecture would be, to Levi Bryant, a 'flat ontology', where being is composed entirely of objects and entities (2011: 3–4) in which there is an '"equality of being" [. . .]

not only is being equal in itself, but it is seen to be equally present in all beings' (Deleuze 1992: 173). To Bryant,

> while an ontology based on relations between general types and particular instances is *hierarchical*, each level representing a different ontological category (organism, species, genera), an approach in terms of interacting parts and emergent wholes leads to a *flat ontology*, one made exclusively of unique, singular individuals, differing in spatio-temporal scale but not in ontological status. (2011: 9)

Deleuze's position is appropriated by proponents of a current 'movement' called 'object-oriented ontology', whose philosophical approach is in turn consistent with many parts of contemporary digital architecture and supports the possibility of architecture being released from humanist determinants. Object-oriented ontology speculates on a radically materialist or realist approach to the world as completely made up of objects, where objects have ontologies independent from those defined by human beings. The actual material outputs of digital architecture, whether they are cellular structures organised in involuted volumes or blobs with reactive surfaces and so forth, are characterised by immanence in which 'there are only assemblages composed of heterogeneous terms on equal ontological footing' (Bryant 2011: 10).

Owing to what Quentin Meillassoux sees as the inescapable correlationism between thinking and being (2008: 5), philosophical speculations surrounding what it is to consider the facticity of objects in their own ontology are therefore a vehement critique of anthropocentric thinking, in the service of dethroning the rational human being as the source of philosophical and scientific thought. This is an important observation in the rise of mathematically based abstract production in digital architecture, where mathematics is purportedly the purest and most impersonal of all thinking.

However, while object-oriented ontology may be a version of Deleuze's immanence of entities in 'ontological equality', the status of relations between entities must be clarified. It is this relationality – described and enacted by abstract codes in digital architecture expressed, and expressible, as mathematics, and whose terms have their own ontology and can exist outside of the rationality of human beings – that is of concern to this chapter.

What then is the connection between the material abstraction and the immaterial mathematics that relate them? Deleuze in *Dialogues* states that 'relations are external to their terms' (Deleuze and Parnet 1987: 55). The exteriority of relations means that the entities are not the direct result of their relationship with others, and that entities survive in their own modalities outside of the relations they have with others. Like Latour's actor-objects that remain separate from their participation in assemblages, entities themselves transform being in relation, but there is no linear connection between relations and transformations. What exists here is something like a phase-shift, a relatedness by virtue of a non-relationality between relations and their terms. It is also part of a Whiteheadian extensivity of relations, a reaching out by entities in a network which infects other relations and their entities (Whitehead 2004: 185). Relations are therefore able to jump states or modalities, capturing their transitions and their effects. Luciana Parisi, using the metaphor of a virus in connection to digital architecture, states that

> the metaphysical dimension of relationality attributed to network and viral architectures needs to include the abstract capacities of experiencing change by capturing the transition from one state to another or registering the algorithmic passing between distinct blocs of space-time. In other words, such relationality needs to be implicated in the process of infection that makes networks more than a formal organization of parallel viral programs. (2009: 351)

The relations between abstract material entities are themselves abstractions by virtue of being transitions or changes that can be apprehended. However, as the following arguments will demonstrate, abstract relations can only be apprehended experientially, as affect, and thus in excess of formal mathematical relatedness. To say it otherwise, mathematics as the abstraction of the movement of change has an affectual ontology, not just a materialist one. The suggestion here is that we need to account for the experiential dimension of abstract extensiveness without relying on the terms in relation (Parisi 2009: 351). How then can we reconcile an affectual ontology at the heart of mathematical abstraction within digital architecture's predisposition to the antihumanism of object-oriented ontology, when all relations to be relations need to be (humanly) sensed and experienced as such?

Plane Love

Computationally based digital architecture – invoking a milieu of interactivity and transformation driven by a radical open-ended relationality, where heterogeneous terms or entities in relation swirl among and extend to each other, organised by internal forces of networked associations and geometries, and creating image forms that emerge as fast as they dissipate – has developed a love affair with Deleuzian immanence. This is paradoxical given that architecture's disciplinarity has historically been founded on discrete concrete effectuations prepositioned on identity and clarity. The mathematicisation of associations and the geometrification of form require an immanent milieu that supports an emergentist paradigm for a new speculative approach to materialism.

So why the love affair? Perhaps it is because Deleuze's immanence has itself a geometry and an architecture: it is a plane. Deleuze's plane of immanence is aporetic and its geometry is appropriated by architecture, whether consciously or otherwise, as the logical and material instantiation of its often unquestioned ontology. As an aporia, the thinkability of the plane of immanence – which is on all counts formal, consistent and real – is at the limit of human attention. The existence of the plane would be something that enacts what Bernard Stiegler sees as an irreducible inadequacy between knowledge and the knowable object of knowledge, one that creates a *desire* for human understanding of the object of knowledge (2010: 111).

So, how can digital architecture apprehend Deleuze's plane of immanence as a concept, with its totally immersed, embedded and flattened consistency, with radical differen*ciation* at its very heart? How can the plane of immanence be the representation, metaphor, metonymy, expression and so on of digital architecture, when every (architectural) description of the plane reliant on geometry and founded on mathematics always already defaults into a transcendental metaphysics that is ontologically inconsistent with immanence itself? What is the geometry, or in fact mathematics, of this 'desire for human understanding' that Stiegler mentions in the aporetic experience of the plane that is nothing more than pure relationality?

I would argue that architecture's love affair with immanence is exhausted by its relegation of the affectual dimension of its geometrical and mathematical grounds as phenomenologically transcendental. What I mean here is that the ontological equality of the computational milieu ends up being interpreted as a transcendental domain of non-differentiation, and more disturbingly as neutral, autonomous, ubiquitous and perhaps non-identifiable and therefore an uncritical and apolitical acceptance of difference. Digital architecture needs to take seriously the geometry that it invokes, and the mathematics that shapes it. Although architecture strives, it cannot really reach the plane of immanence through further abstraction and geometrification in the rationalist tradition which instates a neutrality or a mentalist design that arrives from a disembodiment. The geometry of the plane needs to be reconceptualised as an abstract design that *is* virtual (potential) and performative in terms of its qualitative self-differentiation.

Being a Spinozist

What is it to *be* (human) on the plane of immanence in the context of digital architecture? On one hand, the process of actualisation of the virtual being on the plane of immanence, while reliant on necessary, qualified and singular entities, can never be predetermined owing to the radical multiplicity and unforeseeable organisation of the entities. On the other, the ontogenetic processes on the plane have mechanisms that are able to set immanent forces loose from the strictures of predetermined forms, for entities or bodies to discover their own ends and invent their own constitution. Any abstraction, as an event of actualisation, on the plane is a new creation immanent to the movement of being itself. There is no separation between being and its actualisations, as the latter as extensions of being are already within the ontological register. Being is always already actual, fully expressed in body and thought (Hardt 1993: 115). What is essential to note here is that the expression of attributes as extensions of being – abstractions in mathematics and geometry are a case in point – *affirms* being. In a Spinozist ontology, the expression of being, which is the expression of difference that makes clear its internal structure, is precisely the movement of being (Hardt 1993: 113–14).

The mechanism that operates the Deleuzian ontological movement is *affect*. Following Spinoza, a body is not a fixed entity but a dynamic relationship, whose limits are subject to change depending on what it encounters affectually. When two bodies meet, they are either compatible or incompatible, they either compose a new relationship or decompose each other. Compossibility represents what is common to the bodies in relation, an *epistemological* connectivity which Spinoza calls 'common notions' (Spinoza 1996: 37–40). Common notions are specific performative or active agreements between local bodies which, in possessing an internal logic, envelop and explain their cause: they become 'adequate ideas' (as opposed to true ideas).

Spinoza leverages an epistemological parallelism between the idea of being and the object of being.[1] Empirical ideas and the power to think are equated to the power to be and act. The ontogeneses of ideas and matter cross; they make each other up and compose a universe together. So abstractions, as empirical, divide the virtual field up into laws and fields of actual entities, manifesting the plane with relations. And mathematics as a language of abstraction will always be incomplete as it is itself always in the process of individuation. The creativity of the incomplete language of abstract entities on the plane of immanence that participates in the creation of the new order of language doubles back to affect the primary laws of that plane (Canning 2001: 66–7). To be human is to belong to this empirical creative plane.

From this the epistemological idea of being (through abstractions as language, machines, geometry and mathematics, etc.), insofar as it envelops and expresses its own cause, is therefore singular like being, and takes on an ontological character as it is expressed as an adequate idea. The conception of adequateness of truth of an idea is thus what Michael Hardt calls an ontologisation of epistemology (1993: 88–90).

The central mechanism of Spinozist philosophy, the 'common notion' as the epistemological relations between composable bodies, is a flow of information between one body and the next, governed by an adequacy of ideas and our emotions or affections. Arriving at adequate causes of our affects (internal or external) entails an increase in productive capacities. Common notions as abstractions between bodies entail 'keeping form' in the process of individuation. The specific form of every entity at one moment is in*form*ation that augurs the next relational movement it makes and so forth.

Far from cutting off the potential for becoming, information is, in Gilbert Simondon's account of the entropy of individuation, precisely what preserves the metastability that is generative of the new. The body is not reduced to a pre-individual singularity, it is a living being transacted by common notions and epistemologies that plays a necessary role in individuation, acting as 'a node of information, transmitted inside itself' (Simondon 1992: 306) And the individuation of a body instigated by information is always only 'temporary resolutions taking place in the heart of a *metastable* system rich in potential' (ibid.: 300).[2] Individuation is therefore inseparable from the abstract empirical order to which it gives rise. The empirical field of human abstraction is where complexity emerges, and the production of intensity is as a result of, and within, extensive processes of, in the present case, geometry and mathematics.

Different Maths

At this point I need to track back to the computational digital architecture with which the discussion began. Deleuze's philosophy of immanence provides the plane as an abstract geometry to express the process of individuation as the ontological condition of digital architecture.

Reflecting upon the generative potential of digital architecture as a system of individuation whose vital processes lie on the actual material plane transducted by the flow of information, it can be said that its power of effectuation, and its efficacy of resistance to a reductive model of mathematisation of design, are made clearer if we can identify logically and corporeally (as adequate ideas) the compossible relations on the plane of immanence that increase the power of entities to act. This means identifying, in geometry and its associated mathematics, the strategies and systems (epistemologies) in play when the pre-individual becomes individuated.

Peg Rawes argues, through Antoine Picon's work on geometric production in architectural design since the eighteenth century, that mathematics, the most universal of ontological fields, somewhat counterintuitively provides the restraint to the viral molecularity in contemporary digital architecture (Rawes 2012). The mathematics of the non-differentiated milieu that is the plane of immanence is calculus, differential calculus to be precise. Calculus allows an abstraction of the plane made up of infinite and infinitesimal entities, each with an 'equality of being' (Deleuze 1992: 173) and whose agencies are impersonal and whose inventiveness is unfettered with a loss of restraint (Rawes 2012).

Calculus is the mathematics of the infinitesimal. In the history of mathematics, there are various ways in which to apprehend the infinitely small. Leibniz developed a method to investigate the infinitesimal as it applied to curves, through the idea that a curve is made up of a continuity of polygons whose lengths become infinitely small, regressing towards points, as the number of polygons used to describe the curve increases. Allow me a more detailed description of Leibniz's geometrical method of infinitesimal calculus to demonstrate the affectual ontology implicit within mathematics. The length of the secant, a line that connects two points on a curve, diminishes as the points draw closer. The limit point of the relations between two points on the curve is when these points meet, when the secant resolves itself to be the tangent to the curve at a single point. The relative rate of change of the x and y dimensions between the secant and the limit condition of the tangent is the *differential* – dy/dx – one of the two fundamental concepts in Leibnizian infinitesimal calculus (the other is integration).

The geometry of the relationality between two points, as an abstraction of the relation, can be apprehended as real, that is until we reach the milieu of the infinitely small, 'just' before the two points meet and the polygon becomes a curve. Simon Duffy, in investigating how Deleuze uses Leibniz's differential logic to construct a philosophy of difference, posits how differentials actually exist beyond the quantities (points on the curve) existing, or already having vanished:

> Differentials do actually exist. They exist as vanishing quantities in so far as they continue to vanish as quantities rather than having already vanished as quantities. Therefore despite the fact that, strictly speaking, they equal zero, they are still not yet, or not quite equal to zero. (Duffy 2004: 200)

That is, the differential relation itself, dy/dx, subsists as a relation, and the relation no longer depends on their terms (ibid.). So, how is this abstraction in mathematics, which describes the pure relationality in the infinitesimal construction of the plane of immanence at its every 'becoming-point', to be apprehended, when the plane is a horizontal network of forces, bodies, connections, relations, affects and becomings, ontologically flattened, with no beginning or end? To geometrically understand how this relationality between infinitesimal points on the plane of immanence as an abstraction can be apprehended by implicating an affectual dimension in mathematics would re-characterise humanism in digital architecture and its mathematical ontology to resist immediately flipping the argument into a transcendental phenomenological domain. The human is always already implicated in the self-differentiation of the plane of immanence in relation to the affectual dimension of mathematics expressing the geometry of the plane, whose limits of differentiation can only be apprehended in a mode that Rawes calls 'sense-reason' (Rawes forthcoming).

This is an argument for why abstractions that humans produce as scientific beings need to be cared for within a framework of ethics, hence the title of this chapter. I am borrowing an idea from Whitehead through his key interlocutor Isabelle Stengers who says that the explicit task of philosophy is that 'it should take care of our abstractions'. Stengers insists that we as human beings own up to our abstractions and not attempt to escape them, thereby investing in an empiricism and in science, in order to be true to their potentiality. Stengers says Whitehead 'endeavoured instead to counter-effectuate abstractions, pragmatically evaluating and modifying the kind of lure and constraint that abstractions provide' (2005: 164).

Care of the Abstract

Let us return to the plane of immanence to ask what it is to care for the abstraction which is always already operating at every singular point that makes up the plane. Singularities structure spaces of possibility. A singular point in a system articulates the tendency of that system to be in a steady-state or stable oscillation. Mathematically speaking, and if we take a curve as representative of a system, singularities are points of inflexion where the curve is poised in readiness to change direction or alter its behaviour, depending on its adjacencies. It is impossible to reach the singularity as it is pure potentiality, it can only be approached asymptotically. This implies that the singularity itself never becomes actual (DeLanda 2002: 13) but is always in the process of actualisation. Compositionally therefore, the plane as an abstract geometry is that which gives singularity its actuality: 'What we call virtual is not something that lacks reality but something that is engaged in a process of actualization following the plane that gives it its particular reality' (Deleuze 2001: 31).

But on closer inspection of the mathematics of the plane that is made up of multiple singularities, there can be a condition where the relations continue to exist when the terms in relation vanish. This abstractness of the non-relation relationalities of singularities on the plane is apprehended mathematically through infinitesimal calculus of the differential kind. In corollary, the mathematical sense can be affectually apprehended because the plane is a geometrical abstraction in itself. Duffy, in discussing Leibniz's idea of potential infinity, says:

> We can't grasp the actual infinite, or reach it via an indefinite intuitive process. It is only accessible for us via finite systems of symbols that approximate it. The differential calculus provides us with an 'artifice' to operate a well founded approximation of what happens [. . .] without ever actually reaching it. (2010: 139)

Mathematics as 'artifice' is an externalisation of the intensivity of the process of individualisation on the plane, and it is in mathematics as an abstract reality that the plane takes on its own reality, that returns to affect its continual genesis. As Deleuze says, 'The plane of immanence is itself actualised as an object and a subject to which it attributes itself' (2001: 31).

Symbolic externalisations of internal processes such as mathematics as abstract artifice are not pre-given, generic or universal, but can be seen as a type of what Stiegler calls 'image-object' that possesses a technicity and a history (Stiegler 2002: 147). As humans participating in immanent life – Deleuze's 'a life . . .'[3] of events and singularities actualised as subjects and objects that dissipate again into potentiality – we constantly encounter image-objects as abstractions constructed in science, media, computing, the visual and performing arts, architecture and so forth that persist as molar actualities on the plane of immanence. We can extrapolate to say that these image-objects are *given* to us; we *inherit* the mathematical as abstractions and make them our own in the construction of our mental images.

While it is difficult to fathom an image-object without a mental image, Stiegler's more remarkable argument is that there has never been a mental image which is not in some way the *return* of an image-object (Stiegler 2002: 148). So, while mental images and image-objects are phenomenologically imbricated, a temporal difference exists between the two images. Mental images are fleeting and their length of retention varies depending on individual circumstance and physiological capacities, whereas image-objects persist as material abstractions and irreducible materialities indexical to the development of technological devices. The interplay between mathematics and immanence has therefore a technicity and its own historicity. And this cannot be more clear on the plane of immanence, with its multiple curves with multiple singularities pleated as matter, each with its own sphere of influence. An individual, a body, an entity that is expressed in the process is only one of several tendencies and capacities on the plane, and its effectuation is due in large part to the history of the process. Another way to look at this is that the individual, body, entity is rendered intelligible only when a mathematical geometry with its own technics and history is 'projected' onto the pleats of the plane of immanence (Duffy 2010: 142).

If part of human individuation in immanent life is reliant upon the symbolic abstractions of mathematics and geometry whose technicity 'retain' the history, or memory, of their affectual force as external to the human being, and this force is projected or inherited by the human individual to influence internal mental and psychic images and expressions, then it becomes imperative to care for the regimes of attention that abstractions provide which influence the process of individuation. Abstractions can be read as a technical means by which social and psychic expressions are inherited through symbolic externalisations such as geometry and calculus as branches of mathematics.

Stiegler argues, through his concept of tertiary memory as the retention of primary sense perception and secondary experience and sensation of the remembered past, that the symbolic realm retains not only human experience but also the regimes of 'attention' (2010: 8). If regimes of attention are retained through technics of abstraction, the 'internalisation' of attention comes not as something lived but through the intergenerational inheritance of something that arrives from the outside. Think about the human attentional capacities shaped and provided by the abstract concept of the differential in infinitesimal calculus as a relation which persists after the actual entities of the relation have vanished, or the concept of imaginary or irrational numbers in mathematics – such as the square root of two ($\sqrt{2}$) or π as 3.14159 . . . – whose exact numerical value cannot be ascertained, nor can it be represented by regular numerical fractions as a ratio of two whole numbers. These mathematical abstractions shape human attention in retaining the technics by which whole generations are able to apprehend and remember the world as it is.

In Stiegler's framework, abstract mathematics would be part of the formation of nascent attention, a turning to the imagination. This realm of the imagination is real, but works on semblances as opposed to representation. Mathematics enables a thinking that *feels* (for) the type of grammar that produces partial images rather than complete objects. This attentiveness is corporeal and affectual, for it is only through the performance and re-performance of mathematics that the illusions of the partial objects it creates become real concrete instantiations. The partial or 'transitional objects' opened through mathematical play are forms of tertiary retention that can only appear in transitional spaces that 'form the basis of all systems of care and nurturance: a *transitional* space is first and foremost a system of caring' (Stiegler 2010: 15, emphasis in original). The care for the abstractions as constructed retentions, which create expectations at conjunctions of singularity is therefore paramount, as without them attention and therefore appearance or expression is impossible.

Conclusion

Performativity in digital architecture expressed as the Deleuzian plane of immanence conventionally moves from the abstraction of the actual plane to the molecular entities that lie beyond – pre-individuated or pre-articulated of the yet-to-become – in order to apprehend the formation of the architectural in all its inseparable variations. However, the chapter has argued, using mathematics and by reflecting on the conjunction between Simondon's transduction of information in individuation and Spinoza's ontologisation of epistemology in common notions, that abstractions extensive to the process of individuation on one hand work logically and metaphysically to describe ontogeneses, but on the other they are themselves ontogenetic as they participate in the process. That is, abstraction in epistemology is co-extensive with the ontology of individuation.

While the zone of subjectivation or individuation on the plane of immanence can be described as the pleats of matter on the plane, it has another dimension, that being the affectual or imaginary, governed by an attentional capacity. The realm of the imagination has a technics that arrives from topological mathematics and infinitesimal calculus. The infinitesimal in Leibniz's mathematics described by calculus is imagined and affectual, and is within a transitional and not purely geometrical space. If used to describe the plane of immanence, the transitional dimensions of mathematics are already within the subject, but only some are actualised at the conjunctions at points of singularity; the rest of the plane is vague and chaotic.

This provides a very different way to use digital architecture to help understand the world. Immanence in digital architecture is usually defined as a move away from the intentional creativity of the design individual, towards the automated vitality of relational entities. But if mathematics, conventionally seen as abstract and technical and therefore extensive to immanence, is shown to have an affectual and imaginative dimension that is folded back into the ontological condition of individuation, it reclaims a place for digital architecture to contribute to the perceptual experience of extensive continuity, with the vagueness of minute percepts, 'the haze of dust without object' out of which form emerges only to fall back into it (Parisi 2009: 367).

This potential is released in abstraction if the abstraction is cared for as regimes that influence attention. Stiegler's concern about the crisis in the battle for 'intelligence' in the light of the destruction of attention by psycho-technical regimes in the modern capitalist societies becomes significant in this argument about computational technologies in architecture. The capturing and formation of attention in the young by technical and media industries is not only a threat to the processes of what Stiegler calls human maturity, but to global social and cultural development. Only if we understand the ontology of the abstract as evolving social, mental and technological configurations that construct tertiary retention can the inherited internalizations in the processes of individuation – viz. education – be properly assessed (Stiegler 2010: 7).

This continuity established between potential (individuation) and empirical (abstraction) realms of digital architecture reclaims the role of abstraction. Abstractions as actual but singular acts in digital architecture are made without any exacting sense of unified truth, but rather with a generic one. That is, abstractions are local and temporally specific events that do not reify the truth, but act to strengthen the anticipation of coming truth, and thus increasing the fidelity and conviction to the act itself. As Alain Badiou says, abstraction acts by forcing new bits of knowledge into being, but without verifying this knowledge (2004: 65). This means that abstractions are therefore specific evental sites that may give rise to situation-transforming truth procedures that build conviction in and fidelity of future judgements in digital architecture.

Notes

1. As Deleuze says, 'A mode of an attribute and the idea of that mode are one and the same thing expressed in two ways, under two powers', those being the power of acting and the power of thinking. For accounts of Spinozist parallelisms, see Deleuze (1992: 113–17, 133) and Hardt (1993: 89).
2. Simondon continues by saying: 'The system harbours a certain incompatibility with itself, an incompatibility due to the impossibility of interaction between incommensurable terms of extremely disparate dimensions.' The system appears stable only because the speed of transformation is low, and in fact there is no absolute distinction between form and matter. Deleuze and Guattari call this the process of stratification (1987: 40).
3. Deleuze says, 'We will say of pure immanence that it is A LIFE, and nothing else. [. . .] A life is the immanence of immanence, absolute immanence: it is complete power, complete bliss' (2001: 27).

References

Agamben, G. (1998), *Homo Sacer: Sovereign Power and Bare Life*, trans. Daniel Heller-Roazen, Stanford, CA: Stanford University Press.
Badiou, A. (2004), *Infinite Thought: Truth and the Return of Philosophy*, trans. O. Feltham and J. Clements, London: Continuum.
Bennett, J. (2010), *Vibrant Matter: A Political Ecology of Things*, Durham, NC: Duke University Press.
Bryant, L. R. (2011), 'A Logic of Multiplicities: Deleuze, Immanence, and Onticology', *Analecta Hermeneutica*, 3, 1–20.
Canning, P. (2001), 'God is Of (Possibility)', *Parallax*, 7: 4, 66–88.
DeLanda, M. (2002), 'Deleuze and the Use of the Genetic Algorithm in Architecture', in N. Leach (ed.), *Designing for a Digital World*, London: Academy Press, pp. 117–18.
Deleuze, G. (1992), *Expressionism in Philosophy: Spinoza*, trans. M. Joughin, New York: Zone Books.
Deleuze, G. (2001), *Pure Immanence: Essays on a Life*, trans. A. Boyman, New York: Zone Books.
Deleuze, G. and F. Guattari (1987), *A Thousand Plateaus: Capitalism and Schizophrenia*, trans. B. Massumi, Minneapolis, MN: University of Minnesota Press, 1987.
Deleuze, G. and C. Parnet (1987), *Dialogues*, trans. H. Tomlinson and B. Habberjam, New York: Columbia University Press.
Duffy, S. (2004), 'Schizo-Math: The Logic of Different/ciation and the Philosophy of Difference', *Angelaki: Journal of the Theoretical Humanities*, 9: 3, 199–215.
Duffy, S. (2010), 'Deleuze, Leibniz and Projective Geometry in the Fold', *Angelaki: Journal of the Theoretical Humanities*, 15: 2, 129–47.

Hardt, M. (1993), *Gilles Deleuze: An Apprenticeship in Philosophy*, London: UCS Press.

Meillassoux, Q. (2008), *After Finitude: An Essay on the Necessity of Contingency*, New York: Continuum.

Parisi, L. (2009), 'Symbiotic Architecture: Prehending Digitality', *Theory Culture & Society*, 26: 2–3, 346–74.

Rawes, P. (2012), 'Spinoza's Geometric Ecologies', in S. Loo and A. Douglas (eds), *Technics, Memory and the Architecture of History, Interstices: Journal of Architecture and Related Arts* (Auckland), 13.

Simondon, G. (1992), 'The Genesis of the Individual', in J. Crary and S. Kwinter (eds), *Incorporations, Zone 6*, New York: Zone Books, pp. 297–319.

Spinoza, B. de (1996), *Ethics*, ed. and trans. E. Curley, Section II, London: Penguin Books.

Stengers, I. (2005), 'Deleuze and Guattari's Last Enigmatic Message', *Angelaki: Journal of the Theoretical Humanities*, 10: 2, 151–67.

Stiegler, B. (2002), 'The Discrete Image', in J. Derrida and B. Stiegler, *Echographies of Television*, Cambridge: Polity Press, pp. 147–8.

Stiegler, B. (2010), *Taking Care of Youth and the Generations*, trans. S. Barker, Stanford, CA: Stanford University Press.

Whitehead, A. N. (2004), *Concept of Nature*, New York: Prometheus Books.

Chapter 15

Making a Rhizome, or Architecture after Deleuze and Guattari

A conversation on the practice of atelier d'architecture autogérée

Anne Querrien, Constantin Petcou and Doina Petrescu

This conversation between two architects, Constantin Petcou and Doina Petrescu, founders of the *atelier d'architecture autogérée* (*aaa*) and a sociologist, friend and partner in their projects, Anne Querrien, is part of an ongoing discussion that commenced some years ago, soon after *aaa* was formed. This conversation, reframed and added to here for the purposes of *Deleuze and Architecture*, focuses on their current project *R-Urban*, which is located in Colombes, near Paris and which is read through one of Deleuze and Guattari's key concepts – 'the rhizome'.

Interstices, Rhizomes, Resilience

> *Constantin Petcou (CP)*: Since 2001, *aaa* has developed a collective practice encouraging local residents to participate in the reappropriation and collective management of space in the city. The aim was to create a network of self-managed projects and to appropriate and transform temporary, available and underused spaces. We have identified particular types of space – urban interstices, leftovers, wastelands and temporarily empty spaces – as offering the possibility of collective territories, and a new, specifically urban form of commons.[1] These are commons that need to be reclaimed and reinvented in fragments, through the reappropriation of small abandoned or unused spaces that, until now, have resisted development speculation. The management and use of these urban commons was also meant to allow the reinvention of other social, cultural, environmental and political commons. The starting point was the realisation of a temporary garden, made out of recycled materials on a derelict site located in the La Chapelle area in the north of Paris, in the 18th *arrondissement*, where Doina and I were living. This project, called *ECObox*, has been progressively extended into a platform for urban creative production, curated by the *aaa* members, residents and

external collaborators, catalysing activities in the whole neighbourhood. The platform, including the garden, has subsequently moved three times, taking different forms in different locations and involving new users. A number of new projects using *ECObox* as a model have emerged in the neighbourhood and in other parts of Paris. As a consequence of this project, we were invited in 2006 by the DPVI urban regeneration agency of the 20th *arrondissement* to initiate a project in the St Blaise area in a former passageway that was closed and unused for many years. The aim was to provoke civic appropriation and host emerging activities in the neighbourhood. The plot of this project, *Passage 56*, was only 200m², but we have used it in a way that could host most of the activities proposed by residents during public consultation, including gardening, cultural and leisure activities. We have built a small wooden building (with a green roof and powered by solar panels), dry compost toilets for public use, rainwater collectors, cultivation plots, seed catchers and a wild bird corridor. The project is very much centred on the idea of 'popular ecology', as it is meant to host and disseminate ecological practices in the neighbourhood. As in the case of *ECObox*, a number of similar projects emerged in the area, initiated by some of the *Passage 56* users.[2]

Doina Petrescu (DP): In fact, it is this idea that we took further in our last project *R-Urban*, where we want to address issues of resilience, not only at the scale of neighbourhood proximity but also at the scale of the city and of the region. *R-Urban* is a bottom-up strategy that explores the possibilities of enhancing the capacity of urban resilience by introducing a network of resident-run facilities to create complementarities between key fields of activity, such as the economy, habitat, urban agriculture, culture. It initiates locally closed ecological cycles that support the emergence of alternative models of living, specifically producing and consuming between the urban and the rural contexts. The strategy is centred on the active involvement of citizens in developing collaborative practices and creating solidarity networks from a local to a regional scale.

We are currently developing *R-Urban* in Colombes, a suburban town in the north-west of Paris, in partnership with the local municipality and a number of organisations, including and involving a diversity of local residents. The project is meant to gradually create a network around three pilot units, each with complementary urban functions, bringing together emerging citizen projects that follow the logic of resilience. These three units continue the principles we have developed in our first projects, acting as catalysts that stir up dynamics in the area, but we are much more strategic this time about the nature and extent of these dynamics, nurturing and diversifying them as much as possible so they can become a resilient network which expands to larger scales and involves as many residents as possible [see the project website <http://r-urban.net/>].

CP: To summarise our approach, we suggest that *aaa*'s practice is not based on a series of individual projects resulting from commissions and competitions (as is the case with most commercial practices in architecture); instead it is a strategic construction of a long-term approach that is gradually deployed as both a political and a professional inquiry starting with many hypotheses that are further tested, by experimenting with a number of social and spatial devices, agencies and projects.

As such, *ECObox* can be considered a first phase of exploring the hypothesis of collective self-management and trans-local networking that has been continued with *Passage 56* and is now developed at another scale in *R-Urban*. This is an experimental approach in permanent dialogue with theoretical analysis, or what Charles Sanders Pierce has defined as a combination of induction and deduction resulting in abduction, that is much closer to the way researchers or artists develop their own projects. We explore several hypotheses in relation to the same idea, to test it and push it further within different fields and using different tools: sociology, art, media activism, and by collaborating with different others: activists, students, inhabitants.

DP: This is one way of looking at our practice, in terms of Deleuze and Guattari's concept of the rhizome. Our practice functions like a rhizome of ideas, hypotheses and challenges, that grows gradually by connecting up many contributions and by following the opportunities of created or encountered productive contexts.

Anne Querrien (AQ): During the 1970s a lot of experiments took place around new practices and ways of working in different intellectual fields, but the social demand was for creativity and change, with an imperative to create whatever one could imagine rather than to explore with the local people the different dimensions of urban life. The collective agency of the profession was limited to the dialogue between clients, funders and designers, and input from ordinary people was delegated to sociologists and psychoanalysts, those who were supposed to know about the needs of the non-qualified. With such poor social agency, architecture at that time was nothing more than the final projection of the desires of the tiny social groups architects belonged to. In relation to Félix Guattari, some experimental work was conducted on collective institutions, linking architects, inhabitants and social workers, especially in kindergartens and in mental health institutions. The La Borde Clinic experience about which Félix Guattari has extensively written is one of the best known examples (Guattari 1974). These projects showed how difficult it is to do collective work on space, especially if the issue of living together is not at stake. People who conceive spaces for others and don't share time with them cannot imagine how the spaces will be used. They do not understand how architecture can be a sensitive machine reinventing space in relation to its deterritorialisation, which is the very condition of modernity. Architecture can escape the demand to build fortifications against those social phenomena we cannot avoid.

CP: The increasing part that private developers, motivated by profit, play in large-scale urban and architectural production means that urban space is conceived according to the logic of profit rather than principles of social necessity, well-being and local interest, which involve participation and cooperation and collective governance by residents. The current situation is that urban, public space is deemed to be outside the scope of democratic debate and as such becomes a very powerful device of subjectivation, as it is used as a 'social machine' that codifies subjects according to different social norms and values, thereby creating hierarchies and segregation.

As Deleuze and Guattari have remarked, capitalist logic manipulates the social field for exclusively financial interests: 'Capitalism is the only social machine that is constructed on the basis of decoded flows, substituting for intrinsic codes an axiomatic of abstract quantities in the form of money' (2004a: 153). Our work as architect-citizens is to recodify and reterritorialise the fragments of urban space that have escaped from this generalised control through design and along monetary flows. We make spaces accessible for appropriation by users employing collective modes of management. These are spaces that could further generate other initiatives, producing rhizomatic dynamics through the dissemination of new ways of living toward collective resubjectivation practices.

Making Common Infrastructure

AQ: Making accessible doesn't mean simply opening what is closed; here we remove ourselves from the binary thinking that opposes 'closed' and 'opened'. We prefer to approach things 'in the middle', as Deleuze and Guattari recommend in *Mille Plateaux* [*A Thousand Plateaus*]. Deleuze's work on difference and repetition suggests ways of escaping from binarisation, from the oppositions created by capital, and liberating a production of subjectivity that picks its matter from both sides of any binary. This matter from both sides is precisely what produces the rhizome and develops its interconnective activity.

DP: We also speak about the concept of the rhizome in terms of transmission, in terms of the appropriation and multiplication of our projects by others. This is not an ordinary way of networking. It is what we like to call a 'live' networking. Our approach to architecture is to construct the conditions of possibility for a rhizome of projects, it is about 'making a rhizome'. As Anne has pointed out in one of her previous texts, 'making a rhizome is about going towards the other, not as an enemy or a competitor with the idea of destruction, but in the perspective of an alliance and the construction of a temporary micro-territoriality soon to be shared with others, by the new offshoots of the rhizome' (Querrien 2008: 115).

CP: In the projects we initiate, our role is to start, sustain and expand the networks that emerge around actions, spatial devices, processes and affects, which at the same time permit personal and collective becomings. Through our work we participate in the identification of social-spatial entities in formation, which transform continually into new networks. We are, if you like, the 'gardeners of the rhizome', but we pass on this role, little by little, to other users who wish to become stakeholders. In this process our role as initiators and agents diminishes progressively until it fully disappears, while the capacity of the network to develop and reproduce itself grows. Others may play the role of 'gardeners' of the project. These networks of action and affects, which are mechanisms of spatial democratic construction, are necessarily rhizomatic, playing with proximity, multiplicity and temporalities that are at the same time short, long and sustainable.

The *ECObox* project, for example, has been moved and reinstalled several times by the users themselves, and the system of organisation and occupation has been reproduced by other independent initiatives, both civic and professional, in the same neighbourhood and elsewhere in other cities and even in other countries.[3] Some inhabitant-users of the project *Passage 56* have started to initiate similar projects, following the same model. We call this a rhizomatic transmission, where a project has the capacity to transmit all the information that is necessary to the reproduction of a project, which after transmission becomes itself a new source of information and transmission independent of the relation with the initial project. Despite the temporary existence of these projects in different locations, the accumulation of knowledge by experience is transmitted and reproduced in new projects which, even if new and singular, also take over the same model, using the same protocol and process.

DP: *Making a rhizome*, as an alternative approach to architecture, is a way of constructing the infrastructure of a common territory, the infrastructure of *commons*. In this *making a rhizome* of our projects, we have worked with those who were available and wanted to work in an invisible and underground alliance of 'little by little' propagation, those who knew how to take into account time and cyclical nature, who had the patience to wait for it to grow and develop, who had both the knowledge of transmission and were willing to undertake an apprenticeship. Ivan Ilitch talks about conviviality as an alternative to capitalist production: 'Conviviality is opposed to productivity [. . .] productivity is conjugated with "to have"; conviviality with "to be"' (1973: 43). A relational and cooperative practice, such as the one we have developed, has a different temporality and a different aim to those of a neo-liberal practice: rather than looking for the material value of profit, it creates the conditions for a liberating experience that changes both the space and the subjects.

CP: *Making a rhizome* is indeed a political project, but it is also an economic project: it is about how to assemble, or how to mutualise within rather modest means. How to act at a big scale by federating a plurality of small contributions? How to generate long-term dynamics with micro and temporary interventions?

AQ: Deleuze defines the rhizome as a multiplicity of offshoots that are tended in time, and in space, upfront, behind, beside. But there is also a way of making a rhizome by subtraction.

CP: Developing projects with very limited means, and enabling, through the new dynamics initiated by users, the emergence of new projects generated with little money, the *aaa*'s spatial approach is a multiplication by subtraction, a multiplication based on what is at hand. In the projects initiated by *aaa*, even the presence of an architectural object is not always a necessary condition. A minimal architectural presence allows for a better rhizomatic and self-managing dynamic. The management of our projects is also based on minimal means: the day-to-day maintenance of *Passage 56* doesn't cost anything, it is a space that is self-sufficient, that is managed voluntarily, and that uses nearly exclusively rainwater (90 per cent). Other projects that were inspired by *Passage 56* are also running in a similar way. As Deleuze and Guattari suggest, 'the multiple *must be made*, not by always adding a higher dimension, but rather in the simplest of ways, by dint of sobriety, with the number of dimensions one already has available – always $\{n - 1\}$ (the only way the 1 belongs to the multiple: always subtracted) . . . A system of this kind could be called a rhizome' (2004b: 7, italics in original).

The economy of the rhizome

AQ: This is also how to do a minimum *with a maximum of effect*. It is a question of how to achieve this, as compared with others who use many means to produce the same effect. The problem is how to build machines. A machine is first defined by an effect, which can be produced by some device, linking things together in ways that have never been experimented with or experienced before. Deleuze gives the example of Archimedes, who stated that he could 'lever' the earth if he had a long enough stick. This is the 'lever effect', which through a minimum means produces a maximum effect.

DP: A maximum of (qualitative) effects with a minimum of means – isn't that somehow contradictory?

AQ: This minimum requires lots of effort to be conceived, installed, maintained . . . This minimum is an architecture in itself . . . a concern to produce an effect by architecture with a minimum of means and *without guarantee*.

CP: In our projects we preserve the possibility for space to evolve with its users; our projects involve forms of minimal intervention, remaining in this way open, indeterminate, adaptable and transformable in time by new users. It is, as Henri Lefebvre said, the use that produces space (1991).

AQ: In this respect, these minimal means for a maximal effect produce interaction with others; the indeterminacy produces effects on users. By contrast, the state and other forms of administrative power need guarantees for everything we do. Although involving partnerships with public institutions, *R-Urban* does not give any guarantee of success. The *R-Urban* strategy experiments with social devices that are linked with material devices involving the locals so as to create agencies in which they become stakeholders. Although we start with some hypothesis, there is no guarantee in advance what will happen, no guarantee of success. The architectural project is situational, relational, it is developed along with the process, it has to be reshaped continually and maintain its experimental status.

DP: Isn't it contradictory to act in contexts in which one needs to advance hypotheses, for which one needs to negotiate support and funding, without giving a guarantee on the success of the project – for example, the guarantee of success and impact that the EU, or the City of Colombes, might want from *R-Urban*, a project which they support? This begs the question, how can one do experimental work in contexts that are highly regularised and constrained, projects which are not friendly to risk-taking? Here is the whole art – how to construct new territories, which are at the same time stable and uncertain . . . And also, to speak in Deleuze's language, how to construct war machines, even *soft* war machines?

AQ: This is a pragmatic question. Things need to be co-produced without explanation or request for approval. Most participatory practice in architecture is nothing but ideology, establishing instruments to control public opinion, of the kind: 'we explain the project to people and possibly change the project a bit so they agree with it'. For *aaa*, participation means to be involved on a project with inhabitants and do things together for a longer period of time. The originality of our work is exactly this involvement and installation of the practice on site, thus taking possession of a place together with inhabitants who are living close to the area, and to little by little transform a place with them, in order to invent new practices at the same time.

This is what the 'local' means: to be there. Those who participate in the 'rhizome making' of space need to be there and to give it time. To be there is to be able to connect with somebody you had not anticipated you would encounter, and to be able to create links between this person and others. This demands a minimum of social time, because to be able to give shape to social relations needs time. But nothing takes your whole time. On the contrary, each participant must be an intercessor among several processes and be able to influence them and be influenced by them.

CP: *aaa*'s projects are strongly embedded in the local, without being simply local projects, limited socially and geographically and locked in on themselves. Inside a local project, one should guarantee a non-local potentiality, one should leave space to some kind of 'outside' (Deleuze 2000). Following Deleuze and Guattari, I suggest that we need to adopt the 'wisdom of plants: even when they have roots, there is always an outside where they form a rhizome with something – with the wind, an animal, human beings' (Deleuze and Guattari 2004b: 12). *aaa*'s projects make a rhizome with other projects, with new actors, with future dynamics. At a certain moment, we have to accept that they do not belong to us any more, they are completely autonomous, but also responsible for their own future.

Transformative Participation

AQ: All this is made as it goes: networking with inhabitants, architects and artists . . . the constitution of a heterogeneous milieu, which couples creativity and the local and includes knowledge production, making things and attending unusual events. Nevertheless, the mediation by professionals between inhabitants and political power, the *advocacy planning*, has shown its limits: in France, at least, there is a general disappointment with participation . . . You are somehow proposing a new approach to participation, which does not pretend to 'mediate' but acts in the middle together with all actors (Querrien 2005).

DP: With *R-Urban* we proposed a bottom-up approach to ecological regeneration that commences at the level of everyday life, in which ecological principles extend beyond environmental aspects to include social, cultural and economic concerns. It is the aggregation of many individual and collective interventions that choose to function together within complementary metabolic networks.

Transformations have to take place at the micro-scale with each individual, each subjectivity, and this is how a real culture of resilience is constructed. As Rob Hopkins puts it, 'Resilience is not just an outer process: it is also an inner one, of becoming more flexible, robust and skilled' (2010). The culture of resilience includes processes of re-skilling, skills-sharing, building social networks, learning from others, learning from other experiences. These micro-social and micro-cultural practices are related to lifestyles and individual gestures; they prompt attention to details, to singularities, to the capacity of creativity and innovation that operates at the level of everyday life. *R-Urban* maps in detail this local capacity to invent and transform, but in parallel [also maps] the administrative constraints that block it, proposing ways of bypassing them through renewed policies and structures.

Deterritorialisation, Reterritorialisation

AQ: Our project is no longer about designing the territory, but about drawing ecological lines, about 'gardening' and 'building' the transition towards an ecological city. This means that it is no longer about trying to impose order over space, or about creating a hierarchy within living spaces, but about retrofitting in a way that dismantles hierarchies. In relation to a specific 'territory', it is about acting as a tangential force of deterritorialisation, offering residents and other civic actors an opportunity to stage their own forces of deterritorialisation and compose them as architecture. This architecture is no longer represented by specialised drawings, but offers tools and sites to enact the desires of residents and stakeholders.

It is a deterritorialisation *for* users, which inscribes their history in another history. In former participative experiments, such as the one in Roubaix, with the Almagare neighbourhood in the 1970s, for example, it appeared that a process conceived to lead only to the programme of a new neighbourhood with inhabitants was not enough, because the inhabitants of the new quarter were not completely the same as those who lived there before. There is a need for architectural work that is a continuous process, especially where inhabitants have been cast out from their traditional frameworks, as is the case in the suburbs of today.

For Deleuze, *reterritorialisation* is as important as *deterritorialisation*. This is completely ignored by architects for whom stones are the best guarantee of social conduct. I offer an example from thermodynamics: if molecules are heated for a certain time they will start to form new configurations. If you stop heating them, they will distribute themselves randomly. Architecture is a way of heating human molecules. Architecture must be a continuous process that keeps producing effects. In Roubaix, users have not continued this trajectory without new 'heating'. The principle there is the second law of thermodynamics: if one continues heating, the molecules continue to produce new configurations and agencies.

CP: The *aaa* team has a role to play here as catalyst. Particularly with respect to our approach, which is to transmit the role of catalyst to others. We stir up a catalytic dimension, which may already be lying dormant in each one of us as inhabitants of the city, but which is anaesthetised by our lifestyles, social conventions and not least by the current limitations and regulations imposed on urban space.

AQ: This can happen only if there is a reterritorialisation with a minimum of anchorage. Land-based labour, DIY ecological practices, all these make people venture forth from their places on a regular basis, just as within a gardening practice. This is in order to constitute a new existential territory, which is anchored in everyday life practices – a point of continuity between what we used to do and what we could potentially do.

CP: The spaces *aaa* have realised welcome everyday life and open it to heterogenesis, a constitutive heterogenesis within spaces, users, activities, across scales and temporalities, and which allows and reinforces heterogenetic becomings, generating new users and new networks. We use an approach that is a 'making rhizome' by following a principle of heterogeneity (Deleuze and Guattari 2004b: 7).

Desiring Machines

AQ: I think that when one speaks about architecture, the 'rhizome' and the 'machine' are confounded. The rhizome covers the social aspects, just like the desiring machine covers the psychic and the political aspects. *R-Urban* is also a desiring machine – and this machine will create relational aspects, a state of mind and a model for getting active and moving further.

DP: It is probably more of a machine than a project . . .

CP: It is also more than a machine, because it introduces capacities to recodify the social machine in a different way. Social codes are based on some concreteness. For instance, when we coined the term *R-Urban* at the beginning, it was to suggest the strategy of reintroducing experiences of rural life into the urban suburbs. We realised after a while that this idea was important, but not strong enough to ignite the true dynamics of the project. The term *R-Urban* also suggested the idea of recycling, reusing, resilience and restoring the urban, which could also mean regenerating the urban. We understand it in the sense of developing local activities in a different way, making them more concrete, more sustainable and more desirable.

The projects and the spaces developed by *aaa* with minimal means paradoxically allow for more social, cultural and subjective diversity. This is like in ecology where, as Clément noted, 'the poverty of a soil [in a pedological sense] is a gauge of diversity' (2004: 188). The minimal economy of means also implies a space which is not overdesigned and has provision for a diversity of agencies and reconfigurations; it guarantees the capacity to welcome newcomers into the project. From another point of view, this simplicity can more easily support new assemblages [*agencements*], as well as a necessary deterritorialisation of the process. We follow Guattari's conclusion where he speaks about existential assemblages [*agencements existentiels*]: 'a more gentle deterritorialisation, however, might enable the assemblages to evolve in a constructive, processual fashion' (Guattari 2000: 45). To describe it differently, these spaces express a strange familiarity [*unheimlich*]. They allow for a progressive transition from individual action to small group action, and then to collective and public action. Multiple processes of deterritorialisation and reterritorialisation are in place, composed of new users, new collective practices and new everyday life practices.

DP: We can always question this authority we give to ourselves: who are we to teach others how to make a rhizome? We are not the authors of the rhizome after all, but perhaps its gardeners, those who bring the tools and the seeds. At *ECObox* we provided the 'sofware', so to speak, the idea of civic reclaiming and of mobile installation. The current users of the *ECObox* projects, as well as those of the other projects that took inspiration from it, consider themselves the authors of their current projects. Our current project *R-Urban* takes this need into consideration and proposes a strategy that recomposes a series of existing and emergent projects organised in a network. This won't be possible without finding ways of weaving such projects and strategies into the whole context. This *mise en relation* is a form of shape-giving which uses tactics to create a configuration which didn't exist before. We are the catalysts of a construction, of an interaction . . .

AQ: Within a rhizome there are different viewpoints, the constitution of a plurality of viewpoints about a *commons*. In the same way that there is a principle of equality between these viewpoints, they can also become as many points of anchorage in the real as possible, many sources of vitality for ourselves and for others.

Striating the Smooth, a Collective Action

DP: In this way, we can say that our approach consists in some ways of 'striating the smooth' (Deleuze and Guattari 2004b). There is a real tension between these two modes of spatial distribution, which are involved in our projects. There is a tendency, on one hand, to work with the informal and with everyday life to give them structure, and, on the other, to create immediacy and direct contact, to create proximity within the overly controlled framework of the city, as well as fluidity and mobility without polarisation.

AQ: Deleuze and Guattari also speak about the *patchwork*, which refers to how American pioneer women used to stitch quilts together from small pieces of cloth, with equal creative investment in the aesthetic of each of the pieces, which when they are sewn together contribute to the aesthetic of the whole (Deleuze and Guattari 2004b). They fabricate big pieces through the assemblage of small fragments. The sewing places for women in distant villages were places of socialisation and sharing, which disappeared completely with the invention of individual sewing machines. In addition to speeding up the process the sewing machine isolates the sewer; she is now able to finish the patchwork quilt alone at home in just a day.

DP: So we try somehow to recreate such places of patchwork. Through our pilot projects we create collective activities that require the contribution of many, for instance civic gardening, recycling, etc.

CP: The logic of cooperation is close to a feminine logic of socialising, caring, reproducing, exchanging, sharing, offering solidarity, also the gift economy, which are all practices familiar to women (Petrescu 2007).

DP: In fact we have also realised the important role that women play in our projects. In the *making a rhizome* of our projects, we have worked with those who wanted to work in an invisible and underground alliance of 'little by little' propagation. As we have said, we worked with those who knew how to take into account time and cyclical nature, who had the patience to wait for it to grow and develop, who had both the knowledge of transmission and the will to pursue an apprenticeship. For the most part, those who did the work of the 'rhizome', who tended the active lines, the offshoots of the project, were women.

Rhizomatic Commons

AQ: Architecture after Deleuze produces rhizomes of different scales, building up a-centric networks that connect heterogeneous elements. This architecture is an active intervention enabling the interlinkage of networks and ways of living without 'centres'. Architectural objects blossom in between these networks, emerging from the mix of skills provided by architects, inhabitants, users, researchers, social workers.

It always starts at the periphery of a system: conditions at the periphery keep the lines of the rhizome moving, exploring its territorial expansion or intensification. Guattari and Deleuze's architecture does not come with a new site, with a model or with principles to demonstrate a new way to capture a local setting. It is rather an opening towards alterity that is built by new relations organised with the locals considered within all their strata, including residents of course, but also members of unions and organisations and owners of small firms. These newcomers to architectural projects are introduced to the collective work through workshops on common interests organised with artists and architects working elsewhere on some of the same topics. Junctions between groups always need to remain partial, to connect on an intense line and to avoid building rigid representations. These lines of intensity are becoming more numerous over time, they mix in with the rhizome and nurture architectural activity.

CP: The diversity of activities developed by *R-Urban* should allow not only a new assemblage and emerging agencies, but also a gradual disassembling of a system in crisis. To slowly escape from the generalised footprint of the neo-liberal economy, which has excluded all other forms of material and symbolic exchange, we must dismantle one by one our ties to the market system and leave the system to make change possible. We must undo, dis-assemble – *des-agencer*, as Deleuze and Guattari might say – and go beyond the neo-liberal logic in order to re-assemble new ethical, environmental and long-term ecological agencies (Deleuze and Guattari 2004b). This re-assemblage is a collective act based on the conviction of each participant.

The *R-Urban* strategy relies on 'off-market' elements that can potentially leave the system, for example interstitial spaces, community associations, marginalised or emerging practices, and can be integrated in new agencies and collective processes of re-assemblage.

DP: Antonio Negri calls this process a reappropriation of the *commons*. According to him, this is the contemporary revolutionary project: the capturing, diverting, appropriating, reclaiming of the commons as a constitutive process. It is at the same time a reappropriation, a re-assemblage and a reinvention (Negri and Ravel 2007). This undertaking needs new categories and institutions, new forms of management and governance, space and actors – an entire infrastructure that is both material and virtual (Negri et al. 2007).

R-Urban tries to create this new infrastructure, this re-assemblage of new forms of commons: from collective self-managed facilities to collective knowledge and skills, and forms of groups and networks. The facilities and uses proposed by *R-Urban* will be shared and disseminated on different scales, eventually constituting a network open to different users, including adaptable elements and processes based on open source knowledge. The resilient city is a city of sharing, empathy and cooperation; it is a rhizomatic *city of commons*.

Translated from the French by Doina Petrescu

Notes

For a selection of projects by Atelier d'Architectutre Autogérée see http://www.urbantactics.org/projects/projects.html

1. The 'commons' traditionally denoted common-pool resources – usually, forests, rivers, pastures, atmosphere – the management and use of which were shared by the members of a community. They were spaces that no one could own but everyone could use. The term has now been enlarged to include all resources (whether material or virtual) that are collectively shared by a population or a significant group.
2. See the project website: <http://56stblaiseactualites.wordpress.com/>.
3. Projects connected to *ECObox* have emerged in the last few years in the La Chapelle area (i.e. Canopy, Jardin d'Alice, Jardin Bois Dormoy, Shakirai).

Similarly, the users of *Passage 56* have initiated three more projects in the St Blaise neighbourhood: 53, 59, 61. New similarly based projects are now emerging in Paris suburbs (the 6B in St Denis, etc). Internationally, *ECObox* became the model for urban tactics and strategies in the Aulabierta project, Seville and for *ECObox Isola* in Milan.

References

Clément, G. (2004), *Manifeste du Tiers paysage*, Paris: Sujet/Objet.

Deleuze, G. (2000), *Foucault*, trans. S. Hand, Minneapolis, MN: University of Minnesota Press.

Deleuze, G. and F. Guattari (2004a), *Anti-Oedipus*, London: Continuum.

Deleuze, G. and F. Guattari (2004b), *A Thousand Plateaus: Capitalism and Schizophrenia*, London: Continuum.

Guattari, F. (1974), *Psychanalyse et transversalité*, Paris: Maspéro.

Guattari, F. (2000), *The Three Ecologies*, trans. I. Pindar and P. Sutton, London: Athlone.

Hopkins, R. (2010), 'Building Resilience: What Can Communities Do?', in R. Heinberg and D. Lerch (eds) (2010), *The Post Carbon Reader: Managing the 21st Century's Sustainability Crises*, Healdsburg, CA: Watershed Media, pp. 335–60.

Ilitch, I. (1973), *La Convivialité*, Paris: Seuil.

Lefebvre, H. (1991), *The Production of Space*, trans. N. Donaldson-Smith, Oxford: Basil Blackwell.

Negri, A. and J. Ravel (2007), 'Inventer le Commun des Hommes', *Multitudes*, 31, 7–23.

Negri, A., A. Querrien, C. Petcou and D. Petrescu (2007), 'Qu'est-ce qu'un espace biopolitique', *Multitudes*, 31, 80–98.

Petcou, C. and D. Petrescu (2005), 'Au Rez de Chaussée de la Ville', *Multitudes*, 20, 75–82

Petcou, C. and D. Petrescu (2007), 'Agir l'espace: Notes transversales, observations de terrain et questions concrètes pour chacun de nous', *Multitudes*, 31, 101–14.

Petrescu, D. (ed.) (2007), *Altering Practices*, London: Routledge.

Querrien, A. (2005), 'How Inhabitants Can Become Collective Users: France 1968–2000', in P. Blundell Jones, D. Petrescu and J. Hill (eds), *Architecture and Participation*, London: Spon Press, pp. 111–20.

Querrien, A. (2008), 'Les cartes et les ritournelles d'une panthère arc en ciel', *Multitudes*, 34, 111–25.

Querrien, A. (2009), 'Le Rhizom contre le desertification/The Rhizome Against Desertification', in D. Petrescu, C. Petcou and N. Awan (eds), *Trans Local Act: Cultural Practices Within and Across*, Paris: *aaa-peprav*, pp. 323–34.

Notes on Contributors

Andrew Ballantyne is Professor of Architecture at Newcastle University, UK. He has written widely on architecture and identity, and his books include *What Is Architecture?* (2002), *Architecture Theory* (2005), *Deleuze for Architects* (2007) and *Architecture in the Space of Flows* (2011). His *Architecture: A Very Short Introduction* (2003) has been translated into 20 languages, and is now available with more illustrations as *Architecture: Brief Insight* (2010). He has chaired the Society of Architectural Historians of Great Britain and his historical studies include *Architecture, Landscape and Liberty* (1997), *Architecture as Experience* (2005), *Paliochora on Kythera: Survey and Interpretation* (2008), *Rural and Urban: Architecture Between Two Cultures* (2004), *Tudoresque: In Search of the Ideal Home* (2011) and *Key Historic Buildings* (2011).

Simone Brott lectures in architecture at Queensland University of Technology in Brisbane. She completed a PhD on Architecture and Deleuze at the University of Melbourne and a Masters in the History, Theory and Criticism of Architecture and Urbanism at Yale School of Architecture. She is the author of *Architecture for a Free Subjectivity: Deleuze and Guattari at the Horizon of the Real* (Ashgate, 2011).

Karen Burns teaches in the architecture programme at the University of Melbourne. Her architectural theory and history essays have been published in the journals *Assemblage*, *AD*, *Transition* magazine and *Architectural Theory Review*, and her writings have been included in the following collections: *Desiring Practices*, *Post Colonial Spaces*, *Intimus* and *Collectives* (forthcoming).

Bernard Cache is an independent theorist, architect and industrial designer living in Paris with a workshop-based practice, Objectile. Cache founded Objectile together with his partner Patrick Beaucé in 1996 to conceive and manufacture non-standard architecture components. Cache researches the use of digital tools and computational techniques for architectural conception and production, termed 'non-standard architecture' by the Centre Pompidou exhibition of 2004. Cache has played an important alternative role by delving into history, philosophy and mathematics to uncover the relationship between today's computational and material technologies and the traditions of the past. He applies research into characters such as Plato, Euclid, Vitruvius and recently Dürer (among others) to inform today's production of architecture. His numerous publications include *Earth Moves: The Furnishing of Territories* (1995), *Fast-Wood* (2007) and *Projectile*s (2011).

Kim Dovey is Professor of Architecture and Urban Design at the University of Melbourne. He has published widely on social issues in architecture, urban design and planning – his books include *Framing Places* (2nd edn, 2008), *Fluid City* (2005) and *Becoming Places* (2010). He currently leads research projects on conceptions of place, urban intensification and informal settlements.

Cameron Duff is Monash Fellow in the Social Sciences and Health Research Unit (School of Psychology and Psychiatry) at Monash University, Melbourne. Duff's research explores the application of the philosophy of Gilles Deleuze to the study of health, illness and society. This work examines the links between the body, space, affect and relationality and their impact on the characteristic features of health and illness in specific research settings. Duff was awarded his PhD in Political Theory from the University of Queensland in 2002 for research assessing the implications of Michel Foucault and Gilles Deleuze's work for the development of a novel political and experiential ethics.

Hélène Frichot is Assistant Professor in Critical Studies of Architecture, School of Architecture and the Built Environment, KTH, Stockholm. While her first discipline is architecture, she also holds a PhD in philosophy from the University of Sydney. Hélène is co-curator (with Esther Anatolitis) of Architecture+Philosophy <http://architecture.testpattern.com.au>, a public lecture series and forum that commenced in 2005. Recent publications include: 'The Forgetting of the Ethics of Immanence' (*Architectural Theory Review*, 2012); 'Drawing, Thinking, Doing: From

Diagram Work to the Superfold' (*ACCESS*, 2011);'Following Hélène Cixous's Steps Towards a Writing Architecture' (*Architectural Theory Review*, 2010); 'On Finding Oneself Spinozist: Refuge, Beatitude and the Any-Space-Whatever', in Stivale, Holland and Smith (eds), *Gilles Deleuze: Image and Text* (2009).

Catharina Gabrielsson is Assistant Professor in urban theory at the School of Architecture KTH, Stockholm. She has published extensively on architecture, art and urban issues since the mid-1990s. Her practice spans from architecture to editing, translating and curating. Her doctoral thesis *Att göra skillnad* (published in 2006 as *To Make a Difference: Public Space as a Medium for Art, Architecture and Concepts of the Political*) explores the material, spatial and imaginary dimension of public space through a series of cross-readings between political philosophy, art and architecture. Her more recent research, mainly conducted in London and Istanbul, revolves around the concept of 'beginnings' in architecture, encompassing notions of initiation, originality, process and change set against architectural claims of authorship and permanence. This work is currently being compiled into a book, *Housework: Maintaining Architecture*. She has contributed to several research anthologies, such as *Field/Work* (2010) and *Curating Architecture and the City* (2009).

Christian Girard is an architect and theoretician practising in Paris. He received his doctorate in philosophy from the Université Paris I Sorbonne in 1983. Girard was Professeur d'Architecture at the École d'Architecture Paris-Villemin (1993–9) and served as chair from 1996 to 1998. He is a founding member of the École Nationale Supérieure d'Architecture Paris Malaquais, which opened in 2000, where he is Professor and Head of the Digital Knowledge Department. He holds an Habilitation à Diriger des Recherches from Université Paris 8, Philosophy Department (2012). He has lectured in France, the USA, Japan, Belgium and Brazil and serves on the editorial board of *Chimères*, founded by Deleuze and Guattari. His works and projects have been exhibited in Paris, Florence, Mexico, Seoul, Montreal, Berlin and Rotterdam. Both his practice projects and his critical writings have been published in Europe and worldwide (<http://www.theorytag.com>).

Mike Hale is a registered practising architect based in Sydney. He has worked on a wide range of projects, including the Sydney Olympic Tennis Centre complex, Stadium Australia, the MLC tower North

Sydney, as well as many smaller commercial and residential projects. Mike attended the Architectural Association in London after completing his BArch in Sydney, where he first encountered Deleuze's work while reading for his MA(Arch) in Architectural Histories and Theories. He later followed this with an MLitt (Phil) at Sydney University where Moira Gatens supervised his treatise on Deleuze and painting. Mike recently finished his PhD research under the supervision of Paul Patton in the School of History and Philosophy at the University of NSW, which focused on Deleuze's concept of the new, materiality, design and sensation.

Deborah Hauptmann is Director of the Delft School of Design (DSD) and Associate Professor of Architecture, TU Delft. Her research interests include philosophical notions of time and space in relation to architecture and urban theory, specifically developed through a close reading of Henri Bergson and Gilles Deleuze; the problematic of the virtual; the geo-poetics and socio-politics of the city; and issues pertaining to the limits and extensions of trans-disciplinary thinking. Hauptmann's most recent publication is *Cognitive Architecture – From Biopolitics to Noopolitics: Architecture and Mind in the Age of Communication and Information,* co-edited with W. Neidich (2010).

Marko Jobst is a Senior Lecturer in Architecture and the MSc Architectural Studies Programme Leader at Greenwich University, UK. He has an MArch and MSc, from the DIA Belgrade University and a PhD from the Bartlett School of Architecture, University College London. He also contributes to the Mikser Program for Cultural Exchange (Belgrade/ New York/London). Jobst has an interest in relating film, philosophy and experimental writing, and has written for *The Architects' Journal* about the relationship between architecture and film. He is currently writing a book about the London Underground and the philosophy of Gilles Deleuze.

Stephen Loo is Professor of Architecture at the School of Architecture and Design, University of Tasmania. He has published widely on the spatiality of language, affect and the biophilosophy of the contemporary subject, which includes ethico-aesthetic models for human action, posthumanist ethics and experimental digital thinking. Recent publications include 'The (Not So) Smooth Flow between Architecture and Life', in Andrew Ballantyne and Christopher Smith (eds), *Architecture in the Space of Flows* (2012), and 'De-signing Ethics: The Good, the

Bad and the Performative', in Oksana Zelenko (ed.), *Design and Ethics: Reflections in Practice* (2012). His current research project (with Dr Undine Sellbach) concerns the connections between ethics, psychoanalysis and the space of the entomological imagination, with forthcoming publications in *Angelaki* and *Parallax*. Stephen is a practising architect and founding partner of award winning architectural, design and interpretation practice Mulloway Studio.

Adrian Parr is an Associate Professor in the School of Architecture and Interior Design and the Department of Women's, Gender, and Sexuality Studies at the University of Cincinnati. She is the author of *The Wrath of Capital* (2012), *Hijacking Sustainability* (2010) and *Deleuze and Memorial Culture* (2008), and the editor with Michael Zaretsky of *New Directions in Sustainable Design* (2010) and *The Deleuze Dictionary* (2nd rev. edn, 2010).

Constantin Petcou is an architect, based in Paris, whose work focuses on the intersection between architecture, urbanism and semiotics. He coordinates several research projects and European networks (*Peprav, Rhyzom, R-Urban*), has published a number of articles and book chapters, and co-edited *Urban Act: A Handbook for Alternative Practice* (2007) and *Trans-Local-Act: Cultural Practices Within and Across* (2010). He is co-founder of *atelier d'architecture autogérée*, a collective platform which conducts explorations, actions and research concerning urban mutations and socio-political practices in the contemporary city. *aaa* has acquired an international reputation and has become an important reference for contemporary participative practices in architecture and cultural initiatives related to sustainability.

Doina Petrescu is Professor of Architecture and Design Activism at the University of Sheffield. She is the other co-founder of *atelier d'architecture autogérée*. Her research focuses on two main strands – gender and space within contemporary society and participation in architecture. She is the editor of *Altering Practices: Feminist Politics and Poetics of Space* (2007) and co-editor of *Architecture and Participation* (2005), *Urban Act* (2007), *Agency: Working with Uncertain Architectures* (2009) and *Trans-Local-Act* (2010).

Anne Querrien is sociologist, urbanist and part-time philosopher, who has taken early retirement and lives in Paris and Brittany; she is a member of *atelier d'architecture autogérée* and is on the editorial boards of *Multitudes* and *Chimères*. She collaborated in the 1970s with Félix Guattari at CERFI and the journal *Recherches*. She has published, among others, the book *L'École mutuelle: une pédagogie trop efficace?* (2005).

Andrej Radman is Assistant Professor of Architecture at the Delft School of Design, TU Delft. His research addresses the ecological approach to perception by psychologist James Jerome Gibson and his unwitting affiliation with Deleuze's radical anti-representationalism. Radman is also a practising architect and recipient of the Annual Award for Best Housing Architecture awarded by the Croatian Architects Association. He is a member of the Dutch National Committee on Deleuze Scholarship.

Chris L. Smith is an Associate Dean (Education) and Associate Professor in Architectural Design and Techné at the University of Sydney. Chris's research is concerned with the interdisciplinary nexus of philosophy, biology and architectural theory. He has published on the political philosophy of Gilles Deleuze and Félix Guattari, technologies of the body, and the influence of the eclipse of Darwinism on contemporary architectural theory. Presently Chris is concentrating upon the changing relation the discourses of philosophy, biology and architecture maintain with respect to notions of matter and materiality and the medicalisation of architecture.

Index